DATE DUE

ARCHAEOLOGY
of the
BRITISH
ISLES

ARCHAEOLOGY
of the
BRITISH
ISLES

With a gazetteer of sites in
England, Wales, Scotland and Ireland

Andrew Hayes

St. Martin's Press, New York

First published in the United States of America in 1993

Typeset in 11/12pt Garamond 3
by Graphicraft Typesetters Ltd, Hong Kong
and printed in Great Britain

ISBN 0-312-10205-4 (Cl)
      0-312-10248-8 (Pbk)

Library of Congress Cataloging-in-Publication Data

Hayes, Andrew.
   Archaeology of the British Isles : with a gazetteer of sites in
England, Wales, Scotland, and Ireland / Andrew Hayes.
      p.   cm.
   Includes index.
   ISBN 0-312-10205-4 — ISBN 0-312-10248-8 (pbk.)
   1. Excavations (Archaeology)—Great Britain. 2. Historic sites-
-Great Britain. 3. Great Britain—Antiquities. 4. Great Britain-
-Gazetteers. I. Title.
DA90.H35   1993
936.1—dc20   93-4856
                                                           CIP

Contents

LIST OF ILLUSTRATIONS

ACKNOWLEDGEMENTS

I would like to thank Mr P. Kemmis Betty of Batsford for commissioning this work, S. Vernon-Hunt for her editorial services, Nola Edwards for the line drawings, the staff of Midsomer Norton Public Library for assistance with inter-library loans, and the Bath Reference Library. For supplying photographs: Mrs C. Sunderland of Batsford, Mr H. Webster of Highlands and Islands Enterprise, Ms J. Stuart and Ms G. Boyle of the City of Bristol Museum and Art Gallery, Mrs Mhairi Handley, Ms Claire King and Ms Anne Woodward of the Royal Commission on Historical Monuments of England, Ms Sian Newton of the Welsh Tourist Board, Dr D. Wilson and Ms J. Darrell of Cambridge University Committee for Aerial Photography, Mrs A. Clemence of the Corinium Museum, and Mr Bill Marsden. Last, but not least, I should like to thank my family, friends and students for all the support and encouragement which alone made this book possible.

PREFACE

The writers on antiquity generally find more difficulty, in so handling the matter, as to render it agreeable to the reader, than in most other subjects. Tediousness in any thing is a fault, more so in this than in other sciences. 'Tis an offence, if either we spend such time in a too minute description of things, or enter upon formal and argumentative proofs, more than the nature of such accounts will well bear. Nevertheless the dignity of the knowledge of antiquities will always insure a sufficient regard for this very considerable branch of learning, as long as there is any taste or learning left in the World. *William Stukeley, Stonehenge.*

To condense the story of over a quarter of a million years of the human occupation of the British Isles is not a task to be entered into lightly. But I hope that my readers will not find me guilty of too many lapses from the high standards set by my eighteenth-century predecessor. For in the past generation British archaeology has been transformed by the application of new techniques, new theories and exciting new discoveries. The result is that an image of the past has begun to emerge that has called into question many basic assumptions about the lives and times of our ancestors. We are now better equipped than ever before to grasp how society, culture and landscape developed into their present form. This book aims to introduce these new insights to a wider audience. For the sake of convenience the familiar, traditional periods have been used, but readers should always be aware of the underlying sense of continuity that runs through all of these rather arbitrary divisions of time. Finally to tempt the armchair enthusiast out into the field I have supplied an extensive gazetteer of sites to visit in England, Wales, Scotland and Ireland.

A.R.M. Hayes
Midsomer Norton
June 1992

1 VENDETTA

'Archaeology', declared the late Sir Mortimer Wheeler, 'is not a science but a vendetta against the past.' It is a vendetta pursued with a single-minded determination worthy of any Corsican or Mafioso, using whatever tool comes to hand, from show-piece monuments to the slightest of traces visible only under a microscope. For it seems to be in the nature of mankind to be intensely curious about its origins. We all need to feel a sense of continuity with what has gone before and what will come after us. Pre-scientific societies sought to meet this need with legends that told how gods and heroes created and ordered their worlds. But the real roots of modern archaeology lie in the Renaissance, when the rediscovery of the vanished glories of Greece and Rome stimulated an explosion of intellectual curiosity that could no longer be satisfied by the pious myths of medieval times.

From the sixteenth century onwards scholars in the British Isles sought to discover the origins of their nations by exploring the visible monuments, while at the same time delving into those Classical and medieval texts that had survived. Their interests were all-embracing, ranging from the romantic relics of the recently defunct Gothic world to the mysterious megaliths that belonged

1 Age calls to age: a portrait bust of a Roman aristocrat from the villa at Lullingstone (Kent; 289). The type of find that inspired his spiritual descendant, the English country gentleman, to explore the past. (*Photo: RCHME.*)

to the remotest imaginable past. By the eighteenth century it was a mark of an educated man of taste and leisure, whether country parson or studious squire, to indulge in a little mild antiquarianism. While those who could afford it made the Grand Tour to examine the ruins of Classical antiquity, others just as eagerly explored the mansions, churches, castles, abbeys, Roman ruins and megaliths of the English countryside (1).

Antiquarians often formed small collections of coins, pottery and tools that farmers or workmen had discovered by accident during the course of their labours. To better fill their 'cabinets of curiosities' many began to dig in their own right, especially into the barrows where the richest pickings were to be found. Then, as the Industrial Revolution got underway, countless objects were uncovered as canals were dug, quarries opened, railroads constructed and towns extended. Spoils that enriched many a public museum and private collection, but had been divorced from their proper contexts, made little contribution to a better understanding of the past.

Archaeology comes of age

Unlikely as it may seem, the credit for transforming archaeology from a treasure hunt into a science belongs to a retired officer, General Pitt Rivers (1827–1901). For during the course of his military career he had become intrigued by the way in which slight improvements in weapons slowly accumulated to produce a both more advanced and also lethal model. A similar process of evolution, he reasoned, must have occurred in the development of every man-made object. As a tangible illustration of his theory he began a huge collection, now displayed in the Pitt Rivers Museum in Oxford, of artefacts from all ages and countries. But after he had the good fortune to inherit Cranborne Chase, a magnificent estate covering 11,700ha (29,000 acres) of prime Dorset land, the General went far beyond this typically Victorian passion for collecting.

Cranborne Chase would have offered a happy hunting ground to any antiquarian: it was littered with prehistoric earthworks, none of which had ever been explored. Pitt Rivers could not resist the opportunity presented to him to dig, but his methods were to be very different from those of his contemporaries, most of whom were little better than treasure hunters; for the General was interested not merely in enriching his collection, but rather in what the artefacts could tell him about the past. To him a fragment of coarse pottery could have a greater scientific value than any ornament of precious metal. As a consequence he turned his back on the fashionable spectator sport of barrow digging and started to excavate settlements and defences, previously neglected by his peers due to the relative scarcity of finds on these types of sites.

To his eternal credit Pitt Rivers realized that the context of each find had to be carefully recorded if much of the potential information that it might be made to yield was not to be lost to posterity. Each of his excavations began with an accurate survey of the site. When trenches were dug he paid careful attention to the different layers of soil, called strata, that were revealed; for each stratum often has its own distinctive colour, texture and finds. Some could be shown to be the direct result of human activity, the piling up of a bank for example. Others, such as the slow silting up of a ditch, were clearly of natural origin. The dates of strata could be estimated from the finds they contained. By recording the stratification of a site he was able to build up its story as he dug down from the upper, and hence youngest, strata down through the deeper, older strata. Rather than indulging in fruitless speculation about his finds the General preferred to let the evidence speak for itself. So that later generations should be able to see exactly what he had discovered he promptly published comprehensive accounts of his excavations featuring accurate plans, sections of the trenches showing the strata and a complete illustrated catalogue of all the finds. These are volumes that set standards that are still followed today.

Excavation techniques have been refined since the General's time, yet the basic principles remain much the same today. Before starting to dig, a site is accurately mapped with reference to a surveyor's datum point erected just outside its limits. Then the first trenches can be sunk. At one time it was common practice to dig a site in squares, leaving baulks of unexcavated earth to allow continuous reference to the stratigraphy of the site. But recently, open excavation has become more popular, opening up large areas in their entirety. Part of the reason for this is that baulks are often found to be in the wrong place, obscuring vital features, so that they are more often a hindrance than a help. Soil is removed, using a trowel, in layers called spits, some 5–10cm (2–4in) thick, and the positions of finds noted accurately with reference both to the metre squares a site is notionally divided up into and to the datum point. Each find is given a number and entered into the site register and catalogue, taking care to note accurately its position. Samples of the soil removed are also kept and sieved for small finds or subjected to scientific analysis. A complete record is kept throughout, using both detailed drawings and photographs. When an excavation is closed, however, the archaeologist's work is only just beginning. He or she then has to arrange for the storage, conservation and publication of finds, co-ordinating the work of many other specialists, such as biologists, chemists and geologists, who each have their own contribution to make to the complete understanding of any site.

Pitt Rivers was the last of the great gentleman amateurs. After the First World War a new breed of professionals took over the lead, steadily improving on his methods and insights to complete the transformation of archaeology into the science of today. But this does not mean that there is no place for the amateur in modern archaeology. Excavation is indeed a highly skilled activity and should never be attempted by the inexperienced. Neither should metal detectors be used anywhere near a site, for they cause irreparable damage by removing finds from their archaeological contexts. The enthusiast should rather join one of the local societies or museums that organize training excavations. Lists of other digs which accept volunteers, including complete novices, are published annually by the Council for British Archaeology.

Landscape with figures

Only a few of the hundreds of thousands of potential archaeological sites will ever be excavated. Consequently the mass of detail about specific sites needs to

2 A bird's-eye-view of a typical native settlement of the Roman period at Crosby Ravenscroft (Cumbria). *(Photo: copyright of the University of Cambridge Committee on Aerial Photography.)*

be placed in context, set against the wider picture of the landscape that influenced, and in its turn was moulded by, humans. To examine the settlement pattern and land use of an area, archaeologists often undertake a field survey. This is done by dividing the area to be studied into a grid, then walking each of the squares, or a sample either chosen at random or regularly spaced, recording any finds and other features of significance. Much useful information has been obtained by this method, but there is a limit to what can be detected at ground level. One major limitation is the fact that only the later periods tend to be well represented by surface finds, earlier artefacts being too deeply buried to be easily disturbed.

In the pioneering days of aviation, shortly after the First World War, it was noticed that many sites, invisible on the ground, stood out clearly from the air. Within a few years thousands of new sites were discovered, photographed and planned, revolutionizing our knowledge of the ancient landscape in the process. Archaeologists look for three main things on aerial photographs: shadow marks; soil marks; and crop marks. Early in the morning, or late in the afternoon, the long shadows cast by the sun can reveal the positions of banks and walls long since ploughed out or robbed down to their foundations (2). Disturbing the soil, by the digging and refilling of pits for example, may also leave distinctive soil marks, especially if the top soil differs from the subsoil. Crops are affected by underground features because their growth depends on the availability of

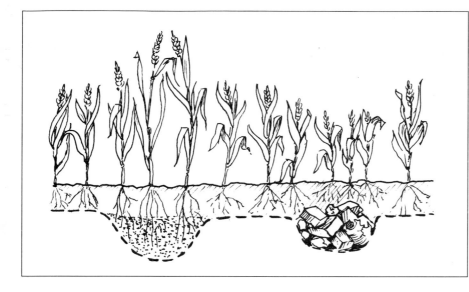

3 The origin of crop marks. Plants growing above a damp, filled-in ditch are much taller than those above a drystone wall. These differences are invisible at ground level but show up from the air.

water. Plants growing above a dry wall, for example, will have access to less moisture than those growing over a waterlogged, filled-in ditch (3). As a result they become relatively stunted and ripen less quickly – slight differences that are invisible on the ground but show up from the air as crop marks. The fact that more crop marks could be seen in limestone regions than on heavy clay soils, however, seriously misled a generation of archaeologists. They assumed that prehistoric farmers were incapable of working the heavier clay soils, which effectively limited settlement to the lighter soils of limestone regions. The clay covered lowlands were thought to have been left as dense forest until cleared by the pioneer Saxon settlers. In fact clay naturally retains more moisture, which makes crop marks unlikely to develop except under conditions of extreme drought.

Back at ground level the techniques known as remote sensing also allow the archaeologist to 'see' buried features. Resistivity surveying works by analysing the electrical conductivity of soil, based on the principle that damp soil conducts electricity better, and hence has less resistance to the flow of current, than dry soil. In practice this means that when electricity is passed through the soil between electrodes, water-retaining pits and ditches will show up as areas of low resistance and walls as ones of high resistance. The best results are obtained when the soil is dry enough to give good contrasts. Magnetic surveying works on quite a different principle and can be used to detect local variations in the earth's magnetic field caused by such man-made features as kilns, hearths, ovens and ditches. Soil-sounding radar is still in the experimental stages, but has recently been used with success at the royal barrow cemetery at Sutton Hoo (Suffolk); when the results are fed into a computer they can be used to generate three-dimensional slices through a site. Finally, metal detectors have been a mixed blessing to archaeologists. Used responsibly they can be a useful tool in surveys, allowing the excavator to pin-point artefacts or modern rubbish. Unfortunately they are also used by well organized gangs of looters who are destroying vital information about the past for personal gain. Although remote sensing has traditionally been used as an aid to the excavator in deciding which parts of a site to dig, it is increasingly being seen as an alternative to excavation. For some scholars argue that as excavation is destruction it is better to leave sites that are not threatened undisturbed.

Studying the remains of animals and plants provides the key to reconstructing the wider environmental contexts of sites. Soil samples are now routinely sieved and even quite small pieces of organic material can be extracted using a flotation tank. In the latter method paraffin, which will selectively coat organic material, is added to the sample, which is then mixed with detergent and water in the tank. Any organic material, such as leaves, twigs, seeds, small bones or insects, will float in the froth that is formed on the surface and can be easily collected for further study. Other treatments can be used to prepare samples for microscopic analysis.

Plant material tends to rot unless it is preserved under the waterlogged conditions which stop decay. Wet sites are therefore among the most informative of all archaeological digs in the amount of organic material they preserve. Unfortunately they are far from common. Plant material survives more frequently in a carbonized form: the remains of fires or the products of the preparation of strains of prehistoric cereals that had to be roasted to separate the grain from the chaff. Other seeds have survived as impressions on pottery.

Another avenue of scientific investigation is to look for phytoliths, microscopic particles of silica derived from plant cells, which often survive when organic material has been otherwise completely decomposed or burnt. Similarly much information about water-laid deposits can be obtained from diatoms, microscopic skeletons of silica found in certain types of algae. Possibly the most informative of all organic remains, however, are the microscopic grains of pollen which can survive for thousands of years buried in soil or in waterlogged deposits (4). Each plant species has its own very distinctive type of pollen, easily identified by a botanist. By determining the type and amount of pollen present an archaeologist can ascertain whether the site was set among forests, cultivated fields or pasture, and whether the climate was warmer, colder, drier or wetter than at present. By taking deep cores through wetlands the technique has allowed the many changes in climate from the end of the last Ice Age down to the present to be plotted.

Snail shells and insect remains can also provide much the same information as pollen, but have the added advantage that the living animals are often quicker than plants to respond to changes in the environment as their life cycles are shorter and they often inhabit very specific habitats. At Avebury

4 Pollen grains as seen under the microscope, typical of the kinds of evidence used by botanists to reconstruct past environments and climates.

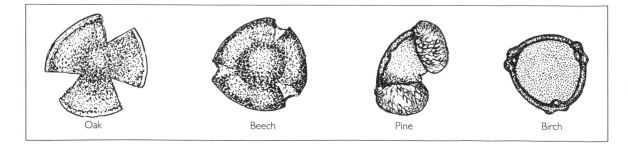

Oak   Beech   Pine   Birch

(Wiltshire), for example, the number and type of snails found in the strata under the henge's bank have revealed changes in its environment in the past ten thousand years, from tundra to woodland and finally to the familiar downland. The discovery of the remains of the Dutch Elm beetle in Neolithic deposits, to take a further example, strengthened the view that the rapid decline in the amount of elm pollen throughout Europe around five thousand years ago was not caused by a change in the climate or by human activity, but was a prehistoric forerunner of the modern epidemic of Dutch Elm disease. Other invertebrates, lacking in hard parts, are not so prominent in the archaeological record. But the eggs of worms have occasionally survived in waterlogged deposits to indicate the intestinal parasites our ancestors and their animals suffered from.

Bone survives well in the soil, except under acid conditions. Once archaeologists tended to discard the bones from an excavation, content with a simple identification from a zoologist. Now it is realized that bone analysis has some interesting insights to offer on past lifestyles. Changes in the physical characteristics of a species, for example, can illustrate the process of artificial selection in domestic stock. Differences in the age and sex of a species reflect details of farming practice and may show whether cattle, for example, are being raised mostly for meat or milk. Similarly samples of wild animals' bones can be used on earlier sites to make deductions about the contemporary climate, environment, hunting strategies and the season a site was occupied.

Digging up people

'Archaeology', the late Sir Mortimer Wheeler also said, 'ought to be about digging up people, not things.' Yet human bones were once almost totally neglected by archaeologists in favour of the grave goods buried with the dead. But modern studies of cemeteries, such as St Helen's-on-the-Walls in York, can provide a host of details about a population, such as life expectancy, infant mortality, the general state of health and nutrition, together with the incidence of accidents or acts of violence (see Chapter 10). One thing the first archaeologists were very interested in, however, was the question of race. During the nineteenth century there was an obsession with measuring skulls in an attempt to identify prehistoric races. Most of the conclusions reached, in retrospect, now seem as bogus as the craze for phrenology. But the study of the physical remains of the first Britons has yielded many interesting insights into the process by which we became human (see Chapter 2).

New technologies may in the near future allow archaeologists to investigate the relationships between individuals within a cemetery and to start looking at how populations have changed over centuries. Recently techniques have been developed that allow the trace amounts of DNA (the material of inheritance) present in bone to be cloned, repeatedly copying it until sufficient has been made to allow a chemical analysis to be carried out. The more closely related individuals are the more similarities there will be in their DNA.

One way in which the bare bones of the past can be fleshed out is through comparisons with modern peoples with a similar lifestyle. In the course of their

5 Whodunnit?
Forensic examination of
this skeleton from
Tormarton (Avon),
produced clear evidence
of foul play, the skull
wound and the tip of a
spearhead embedded in
the pelvis (arrowed).
*(Photo: courtesy of the
Archaeology Department,
City of Bristol Museum
and Art Gallery.)*

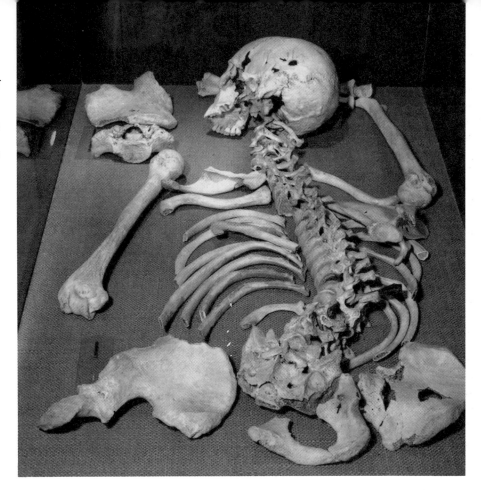

studies of humanity, anthropologists have shown how different ethnic and
social groups express themselves in distinctive ways. It is not even necessary
to go to the ends of the earth to observe this phenomenon, just consider how
dress, hairstyles, food, music and literature are used to define status in our own
society. Weapons, ornaments, tools, houses, shrines and graves, in other words
all the relics of a material culture which an archaeologist recovers, can be used
in a similar way to express an identity.

To V. Gordon Childe (1892–1957), archaeology was neither more nor less
than the past tense of anthropology. He drew on its theories to create the
concept of an archaeological 'culture', defined by groups of distinctive artefacts
that were repeatedly found associated together on sites of comparable age. Each
culture was thought to be the material expression of a separate people or social
group. Countless cultures were rapidly identified to account for the makers of
prehistoric artefacts. As the model was taken to extremes, invasions of new
peoples, analogous with the historical invasions of Normans, Saxons and
Romans, were postulated as having taken place to introduce each and every innovation in technology and the arts. This approach is highly misleading and right-
ly exposes archaeologists to the criticism that 'Prehistory is what no one knows
about people that never existed'. In the final analysis 'cultures' are a useful way
of classifying objects but no more than that; nothing can be known for certain
about the history and race of the people who made and used the artefacts.

Anthropology can, however, provide us with alternative models for the organization of society. Modern urbanized societies in the West are obviously very different from those of the past. But scattered throughout the world are communities with very different lifestyles, some of which may be similar to the way our ancestors organized themselves. That is not to say that these contemporary people are in any way 'primitive', their lives are every bit as rich, if not richer, than our own. For example, anthropologists are able to show the archaeologists that life among hunter-gatherers was anything but the nasty, brutish and short affair that had previously been assumed (see Chapter 2). They were also able to suggest what sort of society erected the great monuments of prehistoric Britain and speculate about what they might have signified (see Chapter 4). On a more general level, anthropology has many insights to offer into the ways traditional societies engage in trade, practise crafts, build their houses and monuments, farm, govern themselves, worship the gods and dispose of the dead.

The best way of understanding the past would be to experience it direct, but until a time-machine is invented the next best thing is to try to recreate it. This is the aim of experimental archaeology, whose practitioners learn by doing. For due to our modern lifestyles few of us have any knowledge or experience of the everyday activities of the past that left behind the evidence which archaeologists study. How many of us could make pottery, cast or forge metal, build a house from scratch or farm in the traditional manner? As a consequence there is an inbuilt ignorance of the very sources of information that archaeologists are called upon to interpret. Through trial and error the experimental archaeologists attempt to remedy this defect and learn to make the tools of the past and discover how they might have been used. Their efforts are inevitably handicapped, however, by not having access to the accumulated experience of generations. Even so, much has been discovered about ancient crafts, technology and farming by these studies that could never have been learnt in any other way (see Chapter 6).

A bridge between the cultures

Archaeology emerged from the Humanities in the 1960s and there was a determined attempt to redefine the subject as a science. 'New' archaeologists, inspired by the work of the American Lewis Binford, sought to discover the basic laws of human behaviour that find expression in the material culture of a people. Just like any other scientists they proposed theories, then tested them by collecting and mathematically analysing numerical data. Although many new insights have been gained by this approach, scientific laws, as generally applicable as those of physics or chemistry, have yet to be discovered. In retrospect, given the vagaries of human nature, it may have been too optimistic a quest. Yet even if archaeology has not become a science in the true sense of the term, as more and more techniques developed by scientists have been applied to the subject, archaeology has developed into a real bridge between the Arts and the Sciences, the two cultures.

Metal, pottery and stone artefacts are all now routinely analysed in order to determine the sources of their raw materials and the techniques of their manufacture. Under the scanning electron microscope the edges of flint tools, for example, can be seen to be marked with minute scratches and chips that are characteristic of what they were used for (see Chapter 2). Thin slices can be taken from stone tools or pottery, and examined in polarized light under the microscope. This clearly shows up the types and quantities of minerals present, enabling the sample to be matched with specimens from known sources (see Chapter 3). Sections cut from metal artefacts, chemically etched to bring out their crystalline structure, looked at under the microscope will also reveal information on the techniques used in their manufacture. Full chemical analysis can also be used to track down the source of the metal ore used by matching up the trace elements that are present.

Nowhere has the influence of the scientists been greater than on the techniques now used for dating. For the antiquarians British history began with Caesar's invasion of 54 BC. Any object that was neither Roman nor medieval could not be placed within their historical frame of reference. As a consequence they had no means of knowing whether they were older than the Christian era by a few years, centuries or even millennia. All that they could hope to do was to arrange their finds into a rough order of antiquity, for the older a stone axe or bronze weapon was, the more primitive in appearance it was thought to be. C. J. Thomsen (1788–1865), first Curator of the Danish National Museum, went one step further and reasoned that the knowledge and skill needed to make a stone tool was far less than that required to cast bronze or forge iron. He therefore proposed that prehistory be divided into three consecutive periods: the Stone Age, Bronze Age and Iron Age. But he remained unable to give them dates in calendar years. Only if objects could be linked with others found in the Middle East or Egypt, where the historical record extended back much further into time, could the age of an object be estimated with any degree of certainty.

Radiocarbon and other dating methods

The breakthrough came in 1950 with the announcement of a new scientific test, called radiocarbon, or C^{14}, dating, that had been pioneered by Dr Willard Libby in Chicago. By the application of this test any material derived from a once-living organism, such as wood, charcoal, bone, leather or cloth, could be accurately dated. The impact of C^{14} dating on archaeology has been so far reaching that it merits a short scientific digression.

All life is based on the element carbon. Most atoms of carbon have a central nucleus made up of 12 particles and it is therefore referred to as C^{12}, but an alternative, rarer form of the element also exists. This is known as C^{14}, because it has two extra particles in the nucleus. C^{14} differs from C^{12} in one other important respect, it is radioactive. Atoms of C^{14} break down by emitting radioactivity, becoming atoms of C^{12} in the process. Carbon occurs naturally in the atmosphere as the gas carbon dioxide. Most of the carbon contained within this gas is C^{12}. But a small amount consists of C^{14}, which is made by the action of cosmic rays from the sun on air. Carbon dioxide is taken up by plants, which

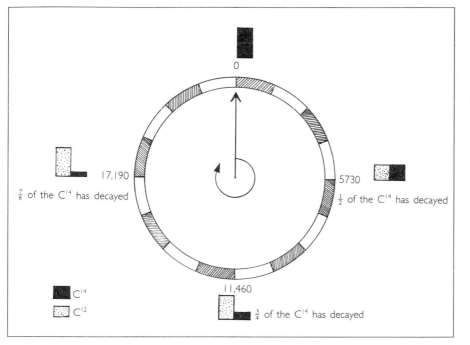

6 The 'radiocarbon' stop-clock, set ticking at the moment of death, used to date organic material. Fifteen minutes is equivalent to 5730 years.

use it to make food substances which are in turn consumed by animals. But living organisms lose carbon dioxide when they respire. The result is a constant recycling of carbon between the atmosphere and living things. While an organism is alive the C^{14} that is slowly decaying will be constantly replaced such that the overall amount present does not vary. But after death, C^{14} cannot be replaced and its level slowly declines. Consequently, the older a piece of organic material is the less C^{14} will be present. The rate of decay of C^{14} is not random. It is constant and unaffected by environmental factors. When 5730 years have elapsed only half of the original amount of C^{14} will remain, after 11,460 years only a quarter . . . and so on. It is as if a clock started ticking at the precise moment of death (6). So by determining the amount of C^{14} in a specimen its age can be estimated in calendar years for any piece of organic material up to an upper limit of *c*.48,000 years.

When results of C^{14} dating were first announced not all archaeologists felt able to accept the new technique and their doubts seemed to be justified when material from Egypt was analysed. For, to the intense disappointment of scientists and archaeologists alike, considerable deviations from the historically reliable dates were found. Even worse, the older an object was the greater was this margin of error. A sample of wood, for example, from the tomb of a pharaoh who lived in the third millennium BC was found to have a C^{14} date 600 years too young. Clearly if confidence was to be restored some method of compensating for these errors had to be found.

The solution was to come from an unlikely source – counting tree rings. As every schoolchild knows, the age of a tree can be calculated by counting the number of rings seen in a cross-section of its trunk and then dividing by two. The size of these annual growth rings is not constant, but varies from year to

7 Dendrochronology,
counting tree rings to
date timbers with
reference to a sequence
built up from living
specimens and
preserved material from
excavations.

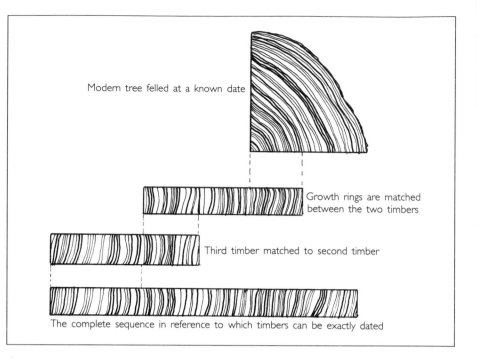

Modern tree felled at a known date

Growth rings are matched
between the two timbers

Third timber matched to second timber

The complete sequence in reference to which timbers can be exactly dated

year according to the weather. Starting with samples from trunks of living trees, then moving to beams from medieval buildings and finally to timbers from waterlogged archaeological sites, a sequence of tree rings has been gradually built up (7) that now extends back to *c.*5300 BC for the bog oaks of Northern Ireland. Timbers can now be readily dated by matching their annual growth rings to this sequence. As such, dendrochronology is useful as a dating technique in its own right, quite apart from the opportunity it affords to check independently the raw C^{14} dates.

Radiocarbon dates are now routinely corrected to take into account their inbuilt errors, which were possibly created by fluctuations in the amount of C^{14} present in the atmosphere. In order to tell whether a quoted date has been corrected, all archaeologists follow the same convention when giving dates. Uncorrected, or uncalibrated, C^{14} dates are written using lower case letters, 1250 bc for example, but corrected, or calibrated, dates are given capital letters, thus 1250 BC (8). Frequently dates are not expressed as a single year but in the following manner, 1250±100 BC, which is a way of taking into account the statistical uncertainties of the technique. In this case it means that although the likeliest date is 1250 BC, there is a two-thirds chance that it could be as early as 1350 BC, or as late as 1150 BC. Dates are also quoted as before the present, bp or BP, the zero year for 'the present' being fixed at 1950.

Since the development of C^{14} dating scientists have developed many other dating aids for the archaeologist. Some of the more useful can be applied to inorganic material. Thermoluminescence, for example, is used to date pottery. It works on the principle that pottery (and also such materials as burnt flint), contains small amounts of radioactive materials which decay at a steady rate, releasing radioactivity that displaces negatively charged particles, called elec-

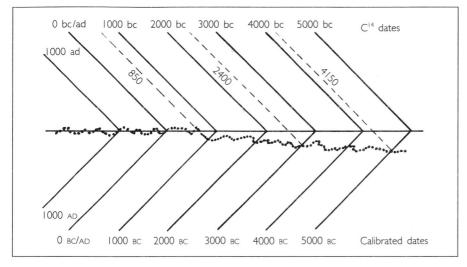

8 How tree rings are used to recalibrate C^{14} dates. Note how the errors increase with the age of the material. For instance a raw C^{14} date of 850 BC correpsonds to *c*. 1000 BC, but one of 2400 BC to 3000 BC.

trons, leaving them trapped within its crystal structure. When the sample is heated rapidly to over 500°C (932°F) the electrons are released, and as this happens they give off light, thermoluminescence. All the stored thermoluminescence in clay is released when it is fired, setting the clock back to zero. This means that the older a sample of pottery is the more thermoluminescence it will release on testing.

2 OUT OF AFRICA

Mankind evolved in Africa, somewhere along the line of the Great Rift Valley that stretches down the eastern side of that continent. Comparative studies of the DNA present within human and ape cells suggest that we diverged from a common ancestral stock between five and eight million years ago. The earliest known fossils of hominids, as scientists call these first human-like creatures, are only around four million years old. They were found in Ethiopia, Kenya and Tanzania and are referred to as 'Australopithecines', the 'Southern Apes'. Yet despite their name they are closer to ourselves than the apes; for although the creatures were small, about the size of a modern twelve year old, and had rather ape-like skulls they were already capable of walking upright like a human.

By two million years ago true humans had evolved, close enough to ourselves to be classified in our own genus. (Biologists give every organism a two-part name, the first represents its genus, the second its species. The genus indicates the group a given specimen belongs to, the species the exact type within that group. We are *Homo sapiens*, literally 'wise man'.) These early humans were nearer our own height, had larger, better developed brains than the Australopithecines and had discovered the use of both fire and stone tools, and how to co-operate effectively in the hunt.

It will never be known exactly when the first humans walked into Europe for they have left behind them little more than a few tools, bones from their meals and the ashes of their fires – slight traces that are easily overlooked or destroyed in the passage of time. Currently the earliest evidence for the human occupation of Europe is to be found at a few sites scattered along the Mediterranean fringe that date to between one and one-and-a-half million years of age. But it was only much later that the first settlers walked across the long-drowned land bridge from the continent of Europe into the British Isles.

The historical framework into which archaeologists tend to slot the first Britons was actually drawn up by geologists. Back in the nineteenth century they had realized that during the past million years the climate of the British Isles had been even more fickle that it is today; for in some of the strata excavated in caves and river terraces were bones of animals that prefer the cold, such as reindeer, musk ox and lemming. But in others there were the remains of hippos, hyaenas, lions and other tropical beasts. Piecing all this evidence together the geologists recognized four great Ice Ages, when glaciers, arctic tundra and cold grassland covered much of Britain (9). In between came milder interglacials when the climate was warmer than at present, although the presence of the ancestors of modern exotic animals should not be exaggerated and it is highly unlikely that the climate was anywhere near as balmy as that of the modern Serengeti. In reality an interglacial probably had an average temperature only a few degrees warmer than at present, but this was still warm enough to allow mixed deciduous forest to regenerate.

9 Palaeolithic Britain: major sites and extent of ice advances.

Quarrying at Westbury-sub-Mendip (Somerset), has unearthed what is currently the earliest evidence for humans in Britain. Here, workers have exposed part of a long filled-in cave system whose sediments could be dated to a warm phase, known as the Cromerian Interglacial, between 750,000 and 350,000 years ago. Mixed in with the bones of rhino, hippo, bison, horse, wolf, bear and deer were a few crude stone tools that may be as much as 450,000 years old. Unfortunately no human remains were discovered to show us what these first Britons might have looked like.

At present the discoveries at Westbury stand almost alone. Much of the slight evidence that once existed may have been destroyed long ago when the glaciers advanced during the Anglian Glacial, between 350,000 and 250,000 years ago. In the process the cold grasslands and tundra which replaced the woodlands were far less favourable to humans and from this period only a few sites, such as Kent's Cavern (Devon), can be identified. These seem to belong to a milder phase towards the end of the Glacial. Finally, during warmer conditions in the succeeding Hoxnian Interglacial, between *c.*250,000 and

200,000 years ago, evidence for the occupation of Britain at last becomes widespread and common.

Whatever the climatic conditions the first Britons had to put up with, their lives were moulded by the environment far more than we can possibly imagine, for they were hunter-gatherers, dependent for their livelihood on what could be obtained from the wild. In the past it was assumed that the lives of these people could only have been nasty, brutish and short. But recent studies of contemporary peoples with a similar lifestyle have demonstrated that their lives were in fact very rich and varied. In fact one anthropologist has even gone so far as to refer to them as the original 'affluent society'. San bushmen living in the Kalahari Desert of Botswana, for example, have ample time for leisure and socializing, spending an average of only 12 to 19 hours a week in the serious business of obtaining food; a working week that would be the envy of many of their supposedly more 'civilized' cousins!

The hunter-gatherer lifestyle has to be based on an intimate knowledge of the environment to maximize its food-bearing potential. There is a distinct division of labour. Women are occupied with pregnancy and childcaring for much of the time and so cannot join the men in the hunt. Instead they gather plants and other materials. Yet the nutritional significance of hunting should not be exaggerated. Studies in the field have shown that although meat provides a source of high-grade protein, most of the energy needed comes from plant foods that form the bulk of the diet. Hunting seems to be more important for its social significance, helping to foster the team spirit needed to bind the group together.

People such as the San and the Aborigines of Australia are nomadic, needing to change campsites as they exhaust the resources of their immediate area. But their wanderings are far from random. Each band or tribe has its own well-defined territory over which it roams, often in a seasonal pattern that maximizes the potential sources of available food. One consequence of this lifestyle

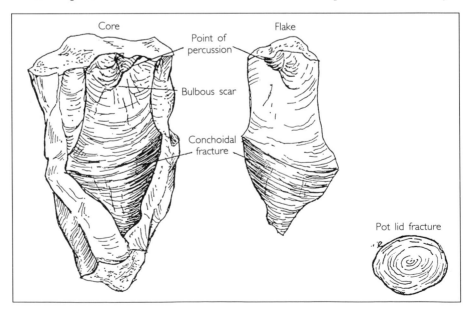

10 How to recognize flint tools. Look at the marks left by detaching a flake. At the point of impact is the bulb of percussion, near to it the bulbar scar, then a series of ripple marks that makes up the conchoidal fracture. Note how the same marks are to be seen, only in reverse, on the flake struck from this core. Compare with the natural 'pot lid' fracture caused by frost.

Core

Flake

Point of percussion

Bulbous scar

Conchoidal fracture

Pot lid fracture

is that such people tend to build small, rather flimsy, temporary huts at their campsite rather than invest labour in constructing large, permanent homes that would only be occupied for part of the year. The need to be able to carry all your goods also means that personal possessions tend to be kept to a minimum.

The basic building block of these societies is the band, a small group of between 25 and 50 people. This number seems to have evolved to minimize both social tensions within the group and its impact on the environment. To avoid a population explosion various methods of birth control are actively practised. The composition of a given band tends to be fluid, rather than rigidly fixed. While close relatives tend to stick together, both individuals and families often decide to transfer their allegiance to another group. Over and above their band identity these peoples often recognize the existence of a tribe: typically a group of between 200 and 800 people, who speak the same language or dialect and share most of the same customs. Social status within band and tribe is thought to be mainly egalitarian, but with some differences.

Man the toolmaker

As man is almost the only animal that regularly makes and uses tools it is appropriate that archaeologists classify the first Britons on the basis of the artefacts they made. Unfortunately, of all the many and varied objects fashioned from such perishable materials as wood, basketry and leather, only a single fire-hardened wooden spearhead has survived to place alongside the countless stone tools. This is why archaeologists refer to the entire period as the Palaeolithic, in plain English the 'Old Stone Age'. Individual tool types are conventionally grouped together into 'cultures', the three main cultural groups being used to subdivide the Palaeolithic into Lower, Middle and Upper phases.

To the uninitiated just how an expert distinguishes between a man-made tool and a natural piece of stone may seem mysterious, yet the signs are there if you know what to look for (10). When a flake is artificially removed from a flint nodule distinctive marks are left behind. On the fractured surface of the flake a 'cone of percussion' extends from the point of impact. This consists of a swelling, called the 'bulb of percussion', from which radiates a series of concentric ripples. The same marks, but in reverse, occur on the nodule from which the flake has been struck. This type of fracture, known as a 'conchoidal fracture', is different from most naturally produced fractures, such as the 'pot lid' pattern caused by frost. Flints worked by man are therefore usually easy to distinguish from natural artefacts which lack the distinctive conchoidal fracture.

Until recently attributing the exact uses to which tools were put was less easy, little more than a guessing game designed to tax the ingenuity of archaeologists. Fortunately, technology has now provided some solutions. As a tool is used minute scratches and chips form on its surface, patterns that are not random but distinctive enough when seen under a scanning electron microscope to 'fingerprint' the activities it has been used for. Six main groups of activities can be recognized: the working of bone, wood, hide, meat, antler and non-woody plants.

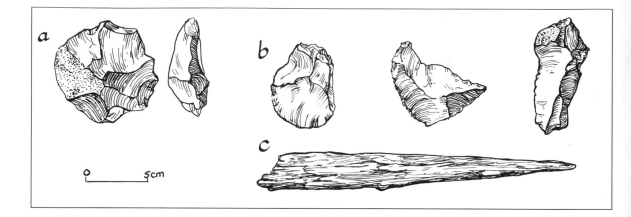

11 Tools of the Clactonian Culture from Clacton-on-Sea, Essex. *(After Leakey.)*
a choppers
b flakes
c fire-hardened yew spearhead

The earliest British Lower Palaeolithic culture currently recognized is the Clactonian, named after Clacton-on-Sea (Essex), where it was first identified. A characteristic product of this culture was the 'chopper', a rather crude implement that was manufactured by roughly chipping both sides of a flint nodule to produce a cutting edge. Only a few of the sharp flakes removed in the process were also used as tools in their own right (11). It dates to the last phase of the Anglian Glacial and the early phases of the Hoxnian Interglacial and is confined to the south-east corner of England.

The Clactonian was succeeded by the Acheulian Culture, named after the classic site of St Acheul in the Somme Valley. Its basic tool types were of ancient inspiration, first developed around $1\frac{1}{2}$ million years ago in East Africa (12). Typical of them is the 'handaxe', a term which, while convenient, is misleading, for handaxes were general, all-purpose tools that must have been used for a wide variety of functions, not merely the hewing of wood. In fact handaxes were so useful that the basic model remained in use, with improvements, for over three quarters of a million years throughout Africa, Europe and Asia.

Handaxes were made by striking anything between fifty and a hundred flakes from a core. For rough work one stone was used directly to strike another. More control could have been obtained over the size and shape of the flakes to be detached by using a wood or bone punch to direct the force of a blow. Batons of wood, bone or antler would have been used to finish off the tool. Careful studies of the debris left by flint-knapping at Caddington (Bedfordshire), showed that three men had been at work. One was an experienced and skilful craftsman, the second an apprentice who made many mistakes and the third at a level of competence somewhere between the other two. Few of the flakes removed were used as tools, most were simply discarded.

Over three thousand sites featuring handaxes have been reported, scattered all over Lowland England, below a line drawn from the Wash to the Bristol Channel. But only a few of these sites represent actual living places. Most handaxes are found in the naturally deposited alluvium of the gravel terraces which were laid down on the sides of valleys when rivers ran at a much higher level than today. Contrary to popular expectations the one place where few handaxes have been found are caves.

Where they exist caves would have been highly desirable residences, providing a ready-made shelter from the elements that was cool in summer and warm in winter. Occupation was, of course, confined to the cave mouth where some form of a crude windbreak was probably constructed to add to the natural facilities. Unfortunately over most of Britain, Palaeolithic people would have found few convenient caves and were forced to construct their own temporary shelters from branches, stones and skins. These open-air sites must once have been far more common than caves, but they are harder to find and more likely to be destroyed by erosion. One that helps redress the balance was discovered at Stoke Newington in Greater London. Here, excavation uncovered a working floor where handaxes were made, together with impressions in the mud of poles and a bed of ferns, all that remained of a shelter.

As the warm Hoxnian Interglacial gave way to the cooler conditions of the Wolstonian Glacial, between *c.*200,000 and 175,000 years ago, the temperate forest was once more replaced by open grassland. Sites belonging to this period are rare. It seems that faced with a reduced standard of living most of the inhabitants of Britain migrated back to Europe. Even when warmer conditions returned, with the Ipswichian Interglacial, between 175,000 and 70,000 years ago, there is little evidence to show that the population returned to anything approaching its former level. What is clear is that during the Wolstonian Glacial a major change had taken place in the techniques used to make stone tools. Clactonian and Acheulian tools had largely been cores left by removing flakes from a nodule. The new culture, known as the Levallois, after the site in the suburbs of Paris where it was first identified, made all of its tools from flakes, discarding the cores from which they had been struck.

Flakes have a major advantage over cores – their cutting edge is sharper and more even. They also allow far more efficient use of the material, giving more cutting edge per kilo of flint. Archaeologists who have experimented with flint-knapping have found that to obtain the best results the size and shape of a flake to be struck has to be determined by carefully preparing the top and sides of a core. Once this has been done, a thick flake, rather like a handaxe, could be removed by a single blow to the edge of the core. A flake could then be retouched by further chipping to make a variety of forms, which included a few handaxes but mostly consisted of new types. When the core had become too small to extract any further flakes it was simply discarded; these can be easily recognized as most are 'tortoise-shell' in shape – one side flat, the other domed.

12 Tools of the Acheulian Culture.
a handaxes
b flakes
(After Oakley and Roe.)

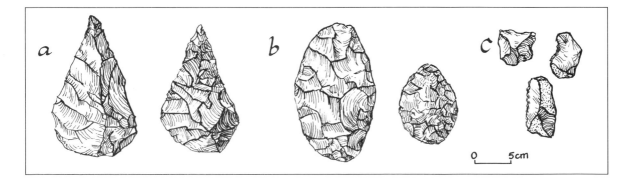

0   5cm

The missing link

The physical remains of the first Britons are far more elusive than the tools they made, for our earliest ancestors did not bury their dead, but simply abandoned their bodies without ceremony. Preservation of the bones depended on the slim chance that a body was rapidly covered shortly after death, protecting it from the elements and the attentions of scavengers. Throughout the nineteenth century antiquarians kept an eager watch on the gravel pits, both in England and on the Continent, that were such a rich source of handaxes. But each time the discovery of human bones was reported they were found, on closer examination, to be the remains from relatively recent burials that had been dug down into the ancient sediments. Then, in 1912, came the long awaited announcement that the 'missing link' had been found and what was more, he was an Englishman!

The story of this discovery, and of its ultimate unmasking as a fraud, is one of the most intriguing archaeological detective stories of all time. It began when Charles Dawson, a country solicitor and keen amateur antiquarian, noticed some interesting flints being used to mend a road. He succeeded in tracking down their source to a small gravel pit on Piltdown Common in Sussex, where workmen sold him part of a human skull. Dawson, assisted by Edward Woodward of the British Museum (Natural History), then excavated the spoil heaps belonging to the gravel pit, finding more fragments of the skull, a jaw bone, bones of extinct animals and stone tools of an extremely primitive type, older by far than the handaxes. When the skull fragments were pieced together Piltdown Man fitted everyone's expectations as to what the missing link should look like, by having a basically man-like skull, once occupied by a large brain, combined with a prominent ape-like jaw. In the absence of accurate scientific dating techniques archaeologists had to rely on the geologists to date Piltdown Man. From the sediments found at the site they estimated that he had lived between two and three million years ago.

As more hominid fossils were unearthed in Africa and elsewhere, Piltdown Man began to appear very much the odd man out and rumours began to circulate of fraud. To settle this controversy once and for all it was decided in 1949 to apply to the specimens a recently developed scientific test, fluorine analysis, to date them accurately. This technique is based on the principle that buried bones absorb the chemical fluorine from soil water, which means that the older a bone is the more fluorine it will have absorbed. To their surprise scientists found such a low level of fluorine in the Piltdown skull and jawbone, 0.1–0.4 per cent, that they could be no more than 50,000 years old. More accurate tests were carried out later, in 1953, which gave even lower values of 0.1 per cent for the skull and only 0.03 per cent for the jaw. To double check these results the amount of nitrogen in the bones was then measured. As the organic content of a bone decays after death this should slowly decrease. It followed that if the Piltdown material was millions of years old it ought to contain very little nitrogen. In fact tests showed high levels of nitrogen, 1.1 per cent in the skull and 3.9 per cent in the jawbone, not far short of the 4 per cent to be found in fresh bone. The conclusion was inescapable, the missing link was no more than a clever fake.

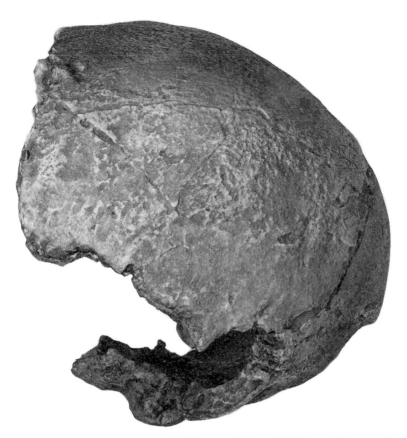

13 The Swanscombe Skull, remains of a young woman who lived and died *c.*325,000 years ago. *(Photo: courtesy of the British Museum (Natural History).)*

Once the truth was out it seemed all too obvious. Piltdown Man consisted of a human skull of fully modern type to which had been added the jawbone of a young orang-utan. The chin and the point where the jaw articulates with the skull, which would have revealed the fraud immediately, had been broken off by the forger. The entire specimen was then chemically stained to appear old. 'Whodunnit?' Well this is, and perhaps always will be, a mystery; whoever he was, he covered his tracks well. There is no lack of candidates, but not a shred of hard evidence against any of them. But while the exposure of Piltdown Man badly shook public confidence in archaeologists, the battery of scientific tests now available means that the success of such a fraud is unlikely ever to be repeated.

After Piltdown Man was dethroned the title of the 'first Briton' was awarded to the remains from Swanscombe (Kent). Here three bones, which fitted together to form the back of a skull (13), were discovered in Barnsfield Gravel Pit. Unlike the Piltdown find these bones, apart from their greater thickness, closely resembled those of a modern skull. At an estimated 1325cc the brain was well within the range of modern man. Unfortunately, as none of the facial bones survived we cannot reconstruct what it looked like, although from the general appearance it seems that 'Swanscombe Man' was actually a woman in her early twenties. A similar, but more complete, skull that was discovered in deposits of a comparable age at Steinheim, near Stuttgart (Germany), had prominent brow ridges and a receding forehead. Taken together all the evidence seems to imply that the remains belonged to an early, slightly primitive, representative of *Homo sapiens*, our own species.

Animal bones and snail shells found in the gravels allowed the world of the Swanscombe Woman to be reconstructed. They showed that she lived in a temperate, but cooling climate, towards the close of the Hoxnian Interglacial. As the position of the Barnsfield Pit demonstrated, the Thames, then a mere tributary of the Rhine, flowed 30m (100ft) above its present level. The broad flood plain of the river contained a variety of rich habitats that could be exploited by her people – marsh, forests and open grassland. Among them lived straight-tusked elephant, rhino, wild boar, fawn deer, roe deer, horse, bison and wild cattle.

Once Piltdown Man had been exposed as a hoax the Swanscombe skull was subjected to the same rigorous tests that had finally unmasked the fraud. But it passed them easily, having a fluorine content of 2 per cent, proving that it had lain in the gravels for a considerable period of time. Lately the skull has also been dated by Uranium/Thorium isotope analysis, a technique based on the same principles of radioactive decay as C^{14}, to *c.*326,000 bp (+99,000, −56,000 years).

Recent excavations have uncovered few remains of the first Britons to add to those from Swanscombe. Chief among these are the teeth, jaw fragments and a vertebra found during the excavations of Pontnewydd Cave (Clywd). These seem to belong to the same general type, but are really too fragmentary to be used to reach any firm conclusions. Thermoluminescence and Uranium/Thorium dating techniques place the remains between 225,000 and 200,000 years old. One interesting point is that the teeth have similar enlarged pulp cavities to those of the later Neanderthals who evolved in Europe from the early *Sapiens* population.

The long winter

Later Britons lived in a very different world to the Swanscombe Woman. For during the last great Ice Age, between *c.*70,000 and 8500 years ago, Britain was on the very fringes of the habitable earth, although the glaciers reached no further south than the Midlands. Directly south of the ice sheets was the tundra, where harsh winters and a short summer growing season combined to limit severely the amount of available food. Further south, the cold grasslands had more to offer, hosting herds of grazing animals.

Modern studies have shown that the idea of an Ice Age as one long, uninterrupted period of cold is a gross oversimplification. Within each of the traditional Ice Ages, phases of intense cold, called stadials, alternated with warmer interstadials when the climate was little different from that of today. For long stretches during the stadials, Britain may have been entirely abandoned, or at the most occupied only in the summer by hunters following herds on their seasonal migrations. During the warmer interstadials woodland spread over the land and bands of hunters settled down permanently. Even so the total population has been estimated at as little as 250.

During the first part of the last Ice Age, between *c.*70,000 and 35,000 years

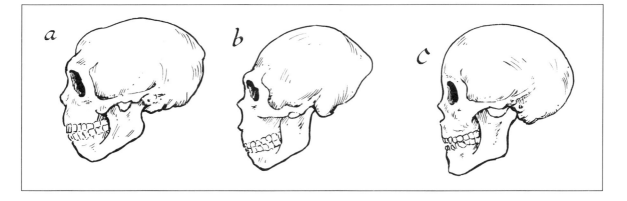

14 Skulls of early and
modern humans:
a early *Homo Sapiens*
b classic Neanderthal
c modern *Homo sapiens*

ago, Europe was occupied by a distinctive type of fossil human, the Neanderthals. They had thick skulls, featuring jutting ridges above the eyes and a sloping forehead, which suggested to the first archaeologists that they were dealing with a very primitive creature (14). The posthumous reputation of the Neanderthals suffered a further blow when the first complete skeleton was discovered at La Chapelle-aux-Saints in the Dordogne (France), which seemed to suggest that they could hardly walk upright.

Only recently, as new evidence has emerged, have Neanderthals been vindicated. To begin with the La Chapelle skeleton was discovered to be that of an elderly arthritic man and far from typical of a healthy adult. Other excavations have uncovered evidence that the 'sub-human' Neanderthals took care of injured and infirm individuals and buried their dead with some ritual. When the 'primitive' features of the skull were overlooked it was realized that the brains they once contained had an average capacity just as large, if not larger, than that of modern man. (A fact which anatomists think may be due to their larger body size rather than a sign of enhanced intelligence.) The conclusion now seems inescapable, the Neanderthals were sufficiently like ourselves to be regarded as a member of own species, if still relegated to a separate sub-species, *Homo sapiens neanderthalensis*. As one scientist has remarked, shaved and dressed and let loose in a modern city a Neanderthal man would be unlikely to cause comment. Whatever their biological status Neanderthals left few traces behind them in Britain. Of their physical remains there are only some teeth from Jersey. Even tools of the distinctive Mousterian culture are uncommon, largely confined to a few cave sites, such as those in the Somerset Mendips and the Creswell Crags (Derbyshire).

The days of the Neanderthals were numbered. By *c*.30,000 years ago they had been entirely replaced by a new strain of man, *Homo sapiens sapiens* – the 'wisest of the wise men', identical in almost every respect to ourselves. Some recent studies of the molecules in our cells have been used to suggest that modern European humans did not evolve *in situ* from Neanderthal stock, but originated in Africa between 200,000 and 100,000 years ago. To explain these drastic changes in the population of Europe some archaeologists have gone so far as to construct a melodramatic scenario of an Ice Age genocide in which the Neanderthals were actively exterminated by the more advanced newcomers, or driven into inhospitable regions where they rapidly became extinct. But recently

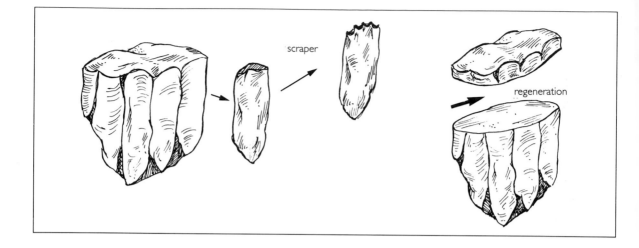

scraper

regeneration

15 Manufacture of blades. Note how the individual blades are detached after careful preparation of a core. They can then be retouched to form one of a great variety of tools

there has been growing belief that they may have made love, not war, until interbreeding resulted in their complete absorption. It is not impossible that we may all have a few Neanderthal genes.

Modern humans were, if anything, less well adapted physically to the prevailing cold conditions than the Neanderthals. Indeed most of the evidence for human occupation of Britain during the latter part of the last Ice Age comes from a warm spell between 26,000 and 20,000 years ago, together with the closing phases of the glaciation between 15,000 and 10,000 years ago when the climate began slowly to improve. Even so modern man figures rather more prominently in the archaeological record than the Neanderthals. It is likely that their more advanced material culture more than made up for their physical shortcomings.

The tools that Upper Palaeolithic humans made were based on blades (15), long flakes with straight sides that were struck from a carefully prepared core. The basic blade could then be chipped into a wide variety of shapes to form finished tools suitable to one of many different tasks (16). These cultures also made far more use of bone and antler. They were worked into such utilitarian objects as awls, needles and spearheads. Other objects cannot be so neatly pigeon-holed. They include the artefacts, common in France, known as 'bâtons de commandement' that have been found in the Cheddar Caves (Somerset) (see 17). What they were used for is open to question. As their name implies they were once thought to have been used as status symbols. More recent suggestions range from arrow straighteners to items of horse harness. Another bone from Gough's Cave was engraved with a meticulous tally. What it had been used to record is unknown; one suggestion is that the marks are related to the phases of the moon and were used to draw up some form of calendar. No matter how hardy these people were it is unlikely they would have survived without the ability to make warm clothing from furs like the modern Inuit (Eskimo). There is, of course, no direct evidence, but numerous flint scrapers, bone awls and needles have survived. Necklaces of fossil shells and animal teeth show that an embryonic 'fashion sense' was already in existence.

In France, Upper Palaeolithic hunters enjoyed a Golden Age, creating a rich

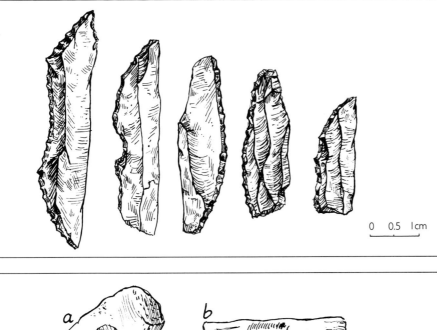

16 Upper Palaeolithic blade tools from Cheddar (Somerset).

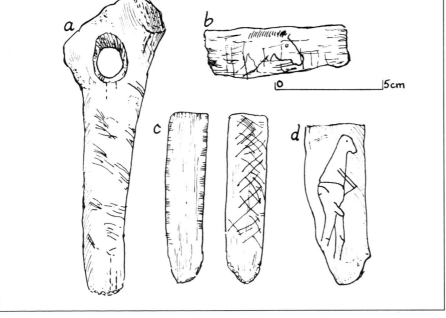

17 The earliest British art: decorated objects from Cresswell Crags and Cheddar Caves. *(After Megaw and Simpson.)*

cultural life for themselves that found expression in the earliest art of man. As befitted hunters, the cave paintings and carved bones that they created featured highly naturalistic animal designs; it has been suggested that these were used in rituals relating to hunting or totemism. By contrast Britain seems culturally impoverished. No cave paintings have ever been found. All that archaeologists have found to exhibit of the work of the earliest school of British artists are a few small engravings on bone, such as the horse's head and a pin man from rock shelters at the Creswell Crags (Derbyshire) (17).

The growth in human consciousness during this period is also illustrated by

18 Aveline's Hole (Somerset; 106), one of a group of Mendip caves occupied by Upper Palaeolithic hunter-gatherers. (*Photo: courtesy of the Archaeology Department, City of Bristol Museum and Art Gallery.*)

the earliest burial yet discovered in Britain. This, the 'Red Lady of Paviland', was found by Dean Buckland, one of the pioneers of modern geology, while exploring Goat's Cave in the Gower Peninsula, in 1823. 'She' lay in a shallow grave, liberally sprinkled with red ochre, the colour of life-giving blood. Close to the thighs were a few handfuls of sea-shells. Fragments of ivory rods, bracelets and a necklace of wolf and reindeer teeth also lay among the bones. Despite the presence of mammoth, woolly rhino, hyaena and cave bear in the cave, Buckland thought that the grave had been dug into these ancient deposits in Roman times. For, good clergyman that he was, he did not believe in the antiquity of humans. But as evidence from France mounted, the find was seen to be typical of Upper Palaeolithic burials and has now been dated by C^{14} to $c.16,510\pm340$ bc. Modern science has not only restored the true age, but also the true sex to the skeleton, for 'she' was actually a young man of 25.

Rather more gruesome were the finds recently made in Gough's Cave at Cheddar. Here, excavations in 1986–7 near the entrance of this tourist show cave uncovered the remains of two or three adults and a child. What was disturbing was that they were all deeply scored with cuts that were exactly the same as those on animal bones from the remains of their meals. Allegations of cannibalism were quick to surface but there is no hard evidence to support this theory. What was discovered may be the result of similar rituals to those practised by some contemporary tribes who remove the flesh from the bones not to eat but as part of their funerary rites.

3 BRAVE NEW WORLD

Twelve thousand years ago the great glaciers began their long, slow retreat north. As the Ice Age ended, the climate gradually improved and the look of the landscape was fundamentally altered. Botanists have been able to plot these changes by analysing pollen found preserved in waterlogged deposits. They have shown that the arctic tundra slowly gave way to woodland, as trees recolonized the land from their continental refuges. Initially these new forests were largely composed of pine and birch, but later, as Britain became warmer and wetter, deciduous trees such as oak, hazel and elm replaced them. For humans the consequence of these wide reaching changes was a complete reorientation of lifestyle. The great herds of horse, bison, reindeer and mammoth that had roamed the open tundra disappeared. In their place were forest species such as elk, red deer, wild cattle and pigs. Humans had but two choices – to follow the retreating herds north and try to maintain the old ways, or to grasp the opportunities offered by a Brave New World.

To survive required adaptability above all else. The potential supply of fresh meat was sharply reduced as woodland animals do not live together in large herds, but are found dispersed over a wide area. Yet to compensate, a warmer Britain now offered a greater range of food plants. Professor J. G. D. Clark has calculated that from an average oak and hazel forest the potential annual harvest could have been 1000 litres (222 pints) of acorns per tree, 0.5 tonne ($\frac{1}{2}$ ton) of hazel nuts per hectare and 50 tonnes (49 tons) of edible bracken roots per square kilometre (247 acres), to say nothing of numerous berries, fungi and other foods. Pollen analyses from several sites hint that humans may have not only passively exploited the forests, but learnt how to manage them actively to their own advantage, as trees found in forest clearings, such as hazel, ash and alder become more common in certain locations. Combined with numerous grains of charcoal this evidence of forest clearing suggests that just like the Native Americans, prehistoric hunters may have burnt the undergrowth to increase the amount of available fodder and hence the number of deer.

As the glaciers melted, sea level rose, flooding the broad, low-lying plain that linked Britain to Europe, creating the North Sea (19). The land bridge between Ulster and Scotland was also submerged. The melting ice fed many lakes, marshes and rivers which teemed with fish and wildfowl. To exploit this rich food source the first boats were made from hollowed-out tree trunks. Fish and shellfish of all kinds also flourished in the warm coastal waters. Great heaps of shells discarded by prehistoric hunter-gatherers, known as middens, still dot the coastline in many regions. In Lowland England most have been drowned by the rise in sea level; but in the north, the removal of the weight of the thick ice sheets caused the land to rise, lifting ancient shores and middens alike high above modern sea level. As a consequence middens are especially common along the west coast of Scotland, the Isles and the north-east coast of Ireland.

19 Mesolithic Britain.
The possible eighth-
millennium BC
coastline is indicated
by the 20 fathom
contour.

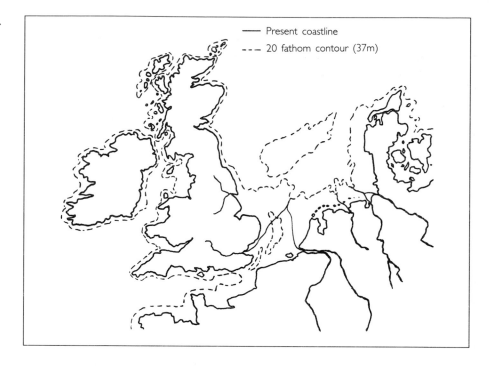

Present coastline
20 fathom contour (37m)

On the tiny Hebridean island of Oronsay a group of shell middens was
recently excavated by Dr Paul Mellars. These mounds, which lay just above the
ancient high-tide mark, consisted of layers of shells, interspersed with wind-
blown sand. Radiocarbon dates for the sites range from 6200 to 5400 bp,
calibrated to between c.5100 and 4350 BC. Species eaten on Oronsay included
limpets, periwinkles, dogwhelks, oysters, scallops, winkles, razors, cockles, crabs
and lobsters. But humans could not have lived on shellfish alone, for they are
not very nutritious; they hardly contain sufficient calories to compensate for the
energy expended in their gathering. Yet they are a perennial food source,
available all year round, that would have been a useful supplement to a more
varied diet. Numerous fish bones were also found in the middens and fish may
have been caught using shellfish as bait. Most of the animal bones belonged to
grey seals.

Characteristic of the tools used by these highly adaptable peoples were the
miniature flints that archaeologists call 'microliths', or 'small stones'. These
were made either by striking miniature flint nuclei to make tiny blades, or by
breaking up normal-sized blades. They would then have been mounted, using
resin, in wood or bone handles to form the cutting edges of finished tools. As
they are quite different from all previous tool types Professor Clark coined the
term 'Mesolithic', or 'Middle Stone Age', to describe the post-Glacial microlith-
using cultures. Another innovation of the period was the development of the
first true axes and adzes for woodworking. Mesolithic people also continued to
use a wide range of tools that would have been familiar to Upper Palaeolithic
hunters.

A warmer Mesolithic Britain was far more attractive to humans than ever
before. As a consequence, greater numbers of sites have been recorded than for

any previous period. In Scotland and Ireland they form the earliest reliable evidence for human occupation. But the Mesolithic peoples were still nomadic, with neither the time nor the inclination to erect more than temporary shelters when camp was made for a few days or weeks. Excavated sites usually consist of no more than a few hollows in the ground, post-holes, hearths, a scatter of animal bones, tools and flint-knapping debris. These probably represent the remains of wigwam type structures of brushwood or skin tents which were lived in for a few days or weeks until the resources of the surrounding area were exhausted.

Some of these camp sites are large enough to have accommodated a family, others show only the slight traces left by a couple of hunters where they paused overnight. A few more substantial houses have also been found. They may mark the sites of base camps, where several family groups came together at certain times of the year and which may have been occupied on a more or less permanent basis by the elderly and infants. One of the most interesting was on a bluff overlooking the river Bann at Mount Sandel (Co. Derry). Here a round-house, 6m (20ft) in diameter, with an internal hearth, has been uncovered and dated by C^{14} to *c*.7000 bc. Caves and rock shelters also continued to be periodically occupied in those areas where they were available.

Taken together the existing evidence suggests that Mesolithic Britain had a total population of around ten thousand. For most of the year this population was probably dispersed over their territories in small bands composed of two or three families. Only in times of plenty would bands have come together in larger numbers to socialize. Each band would have had their own recognizable territory through which they moved on an annual migratory round, exploiting its varied natural resources according to the seasons. From the distribution of base camps in southern England, on average *c*.10km (6 miles) apart, a typical territory may have been as large as 1000 sq.km (386 sq. miles).

Life on the land

To reconstruct the life of a people from a few hollows, post-holes, hearths and a scatter of tools and bones is no easy task. Fortunately at Star Carr, near Scarborough (North Yorkshire), excavations directed by Professor Clark uncovered enough organic material to allow an unusually complete picture of the life of these hunter-gatherers to be pieced together. The Mesolithic people had made their home on a low mound of gravel by the shore of a broad, shallow lake. Over the natural ground surface they had piled up brushwood, stone and clay to make an artificial platform covering 240sq.m (2583 sq.ft). Nothing resembling a shelter, however, was found on the platform. If one existed it may have been too flimsy to leave any traces. Alternatively the platform may have been a work site servicing a nearby living place.

From their base camp at Star Carr the people would have had access to a wide variety of habitats in the surrounding countryside. The waters of the lake, the reed swamps that surrounded it and the woods which covered the sides of the valley could all be intensely exploited by hunting, fishing, wildfowling and gathering. Analysis of pollen preserved in the waterlogged sediments showed that the site had once been surrounded by birch forests. Although this type of forest tends not to be rich in food plants, when combined with the resources of the lake a wide variety of edible plants was probably available. These included yellow water-lilies, nettles, reed rhizomes and goosefoot, to name but a few.

Among the animal bones the remains of 80 red deer, 33 roe deer, 11 elk, 9 oxen and 5 wild pigs were found during the excavation. Many of these bones had been smashed to extract the nutritious marrow. A single adult stag, the excavator estimated, might have yielded enough meat to feed a family of five for a month. A hint of the importance of the red deer in the lives of these people was given by the treatment of some skulls. Their frontlets, complete with antlers, had been cut away, hollowed out to reduce their weight, then pierced. Artefacts were thus created that may have been used in some cult ritual related to hunting, or even as part of the disguise adopted to stalk the living beasts. Fox, beaver, wolf, badger and pine marten may also have been hunted for their furs. Some have claimed that the wolf may have been a primitive type of domesticated dog used to help the hunters. Wildfowl and fish were also taken from the surrounding marshes using canoes, but only a single paddle survived.

The thousands of waste flakes and cores from flint-knapping that littered the platform showed that most of the tools the hunters and their families needed were made on site (20). They included types used for hunting, butchering, skinning and woodworking. Microliths were common. Antler was used to make points, and heads for hunting- and fish-spears, harpoons and mattocks to dig for roots. Tightly wound rolls of birch bark, found among the debris on the platform, may have been the source of resin to fix spearheads to their shafts and microliths into their handles. It is equally likely however, that they were intended as tinder, to be ignited during fire-lighting by sparks struck from pieces of iron pyrites found on site.

20 Mesolithic tools from Star Carr. *(After Clark.)*
a axe
b scrapers
c bone points
d microliths
e blades

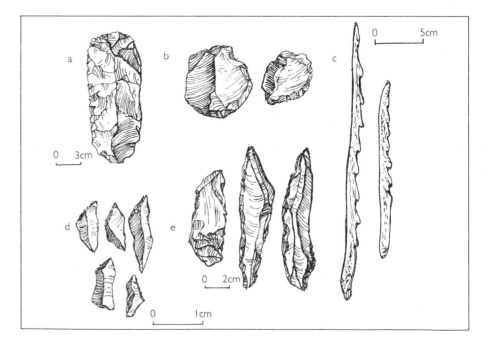

Taking into consideration the size of the site, food remains and the number of artefacts left behind, Clark estimated that around 25 people, four families, shared Star Carr. Spreads of occupation debris on the platform separated by mud implied that the site had been occupied on more than one occasion, the whole being dated by C^{14} to *c.*7500 bc. Antlers provided the clue to the season of occupation. Modern red deer shed their antlers in April, then promptly eat them. From May to September the new antlers are covered in 'velvet' and are too soft for tools. Stags with a full set of antlers could therefore only have been killed between October and April, which suggests a winter or spring occupation. In winter the deer congregate, dispersing to upland grazing areas in the summer. It is possible that Mesolithic humans came to Star Carr during winter to hunt, then followed the deer to their summer pastures; for on the surrounding high ground numerous small camp sites have been discovered.

While Mesolithic hunter-gatherers were engaged in intensively exploiting the woodlands, lakes and seashores of Europe, other communities in the Middle East were taking the first steps in the transition to an agricultural lifestyle. The wild sheep, goats, pigs and cattle in which that region abounded were domesticated, and wild cereals, the ancestors of modern wheat and barley, were brought into cultivation. Archaeologists refer to these first farmers as 'Neolithic', meaning 'New Stone', because of their characteristic polished stone axes. Farming was probably introduced into Europe from the thriving agricultural communities of what is now modern Turkey. By the late eighth and early seventh millennia BC, small farming villages were well established in the Balkans. From this bridgehead the idea of farming probably slowly spread out until by the sixth millennium BC farmers had reached the Channel and were poised to introduce a new way of life into the islands of Britain.

During the Mesolithic, the British Isles were mostly covered by the primeval deciduous woodland that botanists refer to as the 'wildwood', of which today's scattered forests are but a pale reflection. Before any crops could be planted, or animals grazed, the wildwood had to be cleared. The British Isles would never be the same again. Pollen samples illustrate the gradual impact of agriculture, and incidentally show that the Neolithic climate was drier and warmer by a few degrees than it is at present. The first slight traces of cereals are detected in the early fifth millennium BC – crops that appear to have been grown in small, temporary clearings, later reclaimed by the surrounding forest after the people moved on. By the middle of the fourth millennium, large-scale clearances had taken place over much of the British Isles. From this time onwards the proportion of tree pollen in samples falls dramatically and is balanced by a rise in pollen from cereals and the weeds of cultivated land, such as plantain (21). (In New England the spread of plantain after the clearances of the early settlers caused the Native Americans to name it 'White Man's Foot'.)

Experiments carried out in Denmark have shown that, using polished stone axes, one man could have cleared a hectare ($2\frac{1}{2}$ acres) of woodland for cultivation in about five weeks. After the land had been cleared the vegetation would probably have been set alight for the ash to act as a natural fertilizer. Once cleared, these small plots of land were probably prepared for planting by hand, using hoes or digging sticks. Later farmers used a primitive type of plough, similar to the ard of modern peasant farmers, which can score a furrow in the

21 A pollen profile illustrative of the effects of changing climate and human activity on vegetation. The impact of farming is clearly shown by the increased levels of grass, cereal and plaintain pollen.

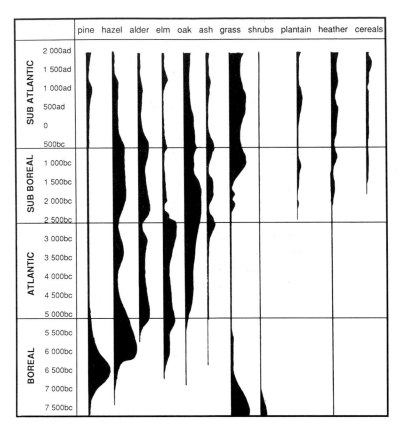

		pine	hazel	alder	elm	oak	ash	grass	shrubs	plantain	heather	cereals
SUB ATLANTIC	2 000ad											
	1 500ad											
	1 000ad											
	500ad											
	0											
	500bc											
SUB BOREAL	1 000bc											
	1 500bc											
	2 000bc											
	2 500bc											
ATLANTIC	3 000bc											
	3 500bc											
	4 000bc											
	4 500bc											
	5 000bc											
BOREAL	5 500bc											
	6 000bc											
	6 500bc											
	7 000bc											
	7 500bc											

22 The ard and true plough compared. Note how the modern plough has a coulter in front of the mould board that allows it to turn the sod. In contrast the ard can only score a furrow in the ground.

ground but is incapable of turning the sod (22). Marks left by the plough have occasionally been discovered under earthworks. The earliest yet known, dated to *c*.2810 bc, were found under a long barrow at South Street (Wiltshire) (23). Most of the cereals grown at this time belonged to primitive strains of wheat, called emmer and einkorn, with only a small amount of barley. Bones show that cattle, sheep, goats and pigs were all kept by the first farmers.

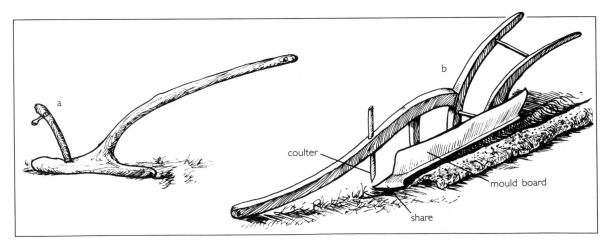

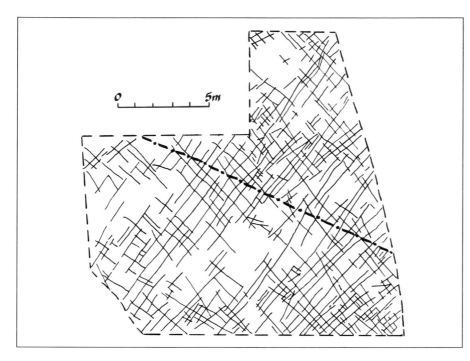

23 Ard marks preserved under the long barrow at South Street (Wiltshire), showing the characteristic cross-ploughing at right angles that was needed to break up the soil. *(After Evans.)*

In South America and South-East Asia tribes still practise a primitive form of agriculture, known as 'slash and burn', that was once thought to resemble Neolithic methods closely. This method involves the clearance of small plots of land from the dense tropical forests, felling the timber and setting it alight. For a few years the land is then extremely fertile, but as the nutrients are taken up by crops and not replaced the soil becomes exhausted. New land must then be cleared, the old is abandoned and the forest regenerates. New evidence emerging from the bogs of Ireland has shown that it is misleading to think that Neolithic agriculture was confined to such primitive, shifting cultivation, for between the valleys of the Behy and Glenulra, on the north coast of Co. Mayo (24), peat extraction has uncovered part of an extensive Neolithic field-system that must have been planned and laid out in a single act by a well-organized society. From the coast parallel walls, 1–200m (328–656ft) apart, run inland, connected at intervals by cross walls to form individual fields. A few ard marks were found during excavations but the fields may have been mainly used for grazing. While these walls would have been too low to keep in sheep or goats they would have been an effective deterrent to cattle. As the outer rings of a tree stump that had grown over one of the walls could be dated by C^{14} to *c*.2270 bc, these fields must have been laid out and in use before 3000 bc in calendar years.

It will never be known for certain what happened to the indigenous hunter-gatherers. Neolithic farmers were once cast in the role of American Pioneers: as they cleared more and more land to support a rapidly rising population they were thought to have massacred the Mesolithic hunters or pushed them into ever more marginal land, until their way of life was no longer viable and their culture became extinct. But only a small number of immigrants are likely to have made the crossing and Neolithic man enjoyed none of the overwhelming

24 The Neolithic field system emerging from the peat in Co. Mayo, laid out before 3000 BC to pasture cattle.

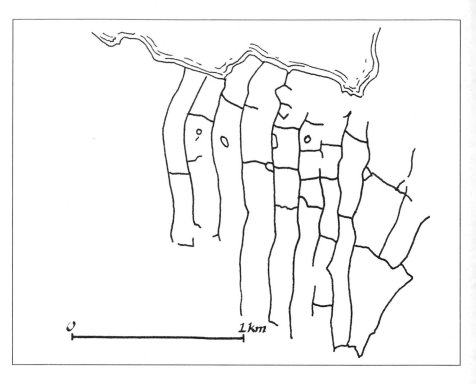

1km

technological advantages, such as firearms, of the Wild West. Instead, the highly adaptable hunter-gatherers may well have gradually adopted the new-fangled ways of their farming neighbours.

Hearth and home

Farmers are forced to settle down in one place to attend to their crops. This gives them an incentive to build more substantial and comfortable homes than those of nomadic hunter-gatherers. Even so the homes of the first farmers have generally left few traces for the archaeologist to discover, although enough has been found to suggest a settlement pattern that consisted more of farmsteads and small hamlets than one of nucleated villages.

One Neolithic house for which there is sufficient evidence to allow a reconstruction was excavated at Ballynagilly (Co. Tyrone). It was roughly square, 6 by 6.5m (20 by 21ft), about the same size as a traditional Irish peasant house. The two longer walls were built of planks set in trenches, the other walls were made up of posts. Until recently it was assumed that all houses of the early farmers were as humble. Then, in 1977, the remains of a large timber hall measuring 26 by 13m (85 by 43ft) were excavated at Balbridie (Deeside). From aerial photographs the excavator was confident that he was uncovering a hall belonging to the Dark Ages, but then sherds of unmistakable Neolithic pottery were discovered together with organic material that was dated to *c.*3500 bc. Rather than housing a Dark Age lord and his retinue, the Balbridie hall may have sheltered an extended family of the first farmers.

At Skara Brae in Orkney a lack of timber meant that the people were forced in c.3100 BC to build houses of stone (25). The result is a village consisting of eight small houses leading off an alley. Each house was made up of a single room, on average about 4 by 6m (13 by 20ft) entered through a low doorway. On either side of the door were stone boxes that, once filled with bracken and heather, had served as beds. That on the right-hand side was larger than on the left-hand side. Similar sleeping arrangements, the larger bed being used by the master of the house, the smaller by his spouse, were to be found on the crofts of the Hebrides into modern times. Above the beds stone shelves were provided to store personal possessions. Opposite the door a stone 'dresser' was usually found, one example still had a pot standing on its shelves. A hearth, outlined by stone slabs, lay in the centre of the floor. Other stone boxes lined with clay may have been used to keep limpets, as a stock of fresh bait.

The people of Skara Brae raised cattle, sheep and pigs, harvested cereals from their fields, fished and collected shellfish. Stranded whales were also eagerly

25 A Neolithic ideal home, complete with fitted furniture, at Skara Brae (Orkney; 396). *(Photo: courtesy of Highlands and Islands Enterprise.)*

26 Another Neolithic desirable residence, Knap of Howar (Orkney). *(Photo: courtesy of Highlands and Islands Enterprise.)*

exploited for their blubber, oil and bone. A small number of red deer bones shows that they occasionally supplemented their diet by hunting. Most of the tools that the villagers needed could be made from pebbles of flint, collected from their own beach, bone or antler. Any rubbish they generated was simply thrown out between the houses, which helped with insulation and eventually buried the houses up to their roof tops. All told the people of Skara Brae must have enjoyed a rich and varied life. Their houses were rebuilt on at least four occasions, until in *c.*2450 BC disaster struck, forcing them to flee, leaving most of their possessions behind them.

Old straight tracks

The paths used by the first farmers to link their settlements and fields are almost impossible to identify under normal circumstances. But peat extraction in the Somerset Levels often exposes timbers of ancient trackways that have been preserved through waterlogging. The Somerset Levels Project, under John and Bryony Coles, has shown that Neolithic communities laid down these tracks between 4000 and 2000 bc to link their settlements and open up the marsh for fishing, wildfowling and, in summer, rough grazing. During the warm, dry weather of the climatic optimum in the early Bronze Age they were no longer necessary. But construction was resumed when the climate became wetter in the late Bronze Age and Iron Age. Three main types of tracks have been discovered on the Levels (27). The simplest consist of hurdles pinned down on to piles of brushwood. Corduroy roads were made from split tree trunks and brushwood laid directly on to the surface of the bog and held in position by pegs driven into the peat. Plank tracks were made of planks of timber supported by pegs on an artificial raised bed of peat.

Studies of the materials used in track construction reveal that a relatively high level of organization was involved, for they are far more than a random accumulation of timber. Large quantities of long, thin rods, for example, were a product of the careful managing of coppiced woodland. Other components were prefabricated and brought to the construction site ready for assembly.

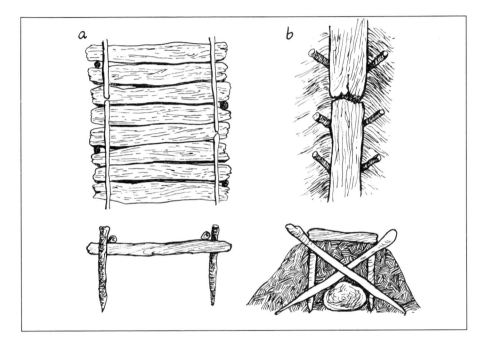

27 Tracks from the Somerset Levels:
a a 'corduroy' road, formed from split logs and brushwood pegged to the natural peat surface;
b a plank track, made by supporting dressed planks on a raised peat surface using pegs.

Most of the work involved would therefore have been taken up with felling, preparing and transporting the necessary timber. Tree-ring studies indicate that all the timber used in the Sweet Track was felled in the same year, in the winter of 3807 to 3806 BC, and this implies that each track was planned and built as a whole. Once the essential materials had been assembled it must have been a relatively easy task to put a track together. The excavators estimate that the Sweet Track, for example, which needed 6000 pegs, 2000 rails and 4000 planks could have been laid down in a single working day by as few as 12 adults. After completion, the tracks were regularly maintained.

Technology and tools

Many of the tools that were used during the Neolithic are little different to those of the Mesolithic, except for the polished stone axes, some of which were used to clear the forests for cultivation. A polished axe was made in two stages: first the basic shape was chipped out of a core, and then this roughout was polished smooth against a flat stone surface, probably using sand as an abrasive. A far more radical innovation than polishing stone was the discovery of pottery. All previous artefacts had been made from natural materials in their unaltered state. Now, for the first time, humans took a substance and deliberately changed it into something with entirely different properties. The development of this new technology was a sign of the times. Pottery is heavy, bulky and fragile, not a suitable material at all for nomadic hunter-gatherers who have to carry all their possessions from camp to camp. But settled farmers were able to make and accumulate bulky possessions.

Clay requires careful preparation before it is ready to be made into pots. First it has to be left to weather for a few years, then mixed with water, sieved to remove any debris, and allowed to settle. Next any air pockets must be removed by kneading as otherwise these would expand on firing and shatter the pot. Finally a tempering agent, such as sand, grit or shell, has to be added to reduce the potential shrinkage and warping that takes place during firing. As the potter's wheel had yet to be invented, Neolithic potters built up their vessels using coils of clay. Once finished a pot would be left to dry until it could be just marked by a finger nail; if too much moisture was left in a pot it would turn to steam on firing and destroy it. Purpose-built kilns have not been found on prehistoric sites in the British Isles, so the simple, but effective, technique of building a bonfire over the vessels, then firing it, must have been used.

Mining and marketing

Flint, the ideal material for toolmaking, has an uneven distribution, being common in some regions but rare in others. Initially flint was simply gathered for immediate use from wherever nodules outcropped on the surface. But it was not long before communities living near high-quality sources of flint organized themselves to mine and trade their surplus production with other, less well endowed regions. Mines have been discovered at several places in south and east England. At Grimes Graves (Norfolk) C^{14} dates showed that flint was mined from *c.*2800–1800 bc and continued in production during the early Bronze Age until the demand for flint dried up (28).

Miners used a standard Neolithic tool, the antler pick, to dig shafts down into the chalk to reach the best seams of flint. On average these shafts are between 5 and 12m (20 and 50ft) across at the surface, narrowing to about 3.65m (12ft) as they descend, and about 12m (39ft) deep (29). From the bottoms of many shafts, galleries, 1.5–0.6m (5–2ft) high, were dug to follow the seams of flint. No props were used to support the ceilings, which placed a limit on the size and length of the galleries. Instead the miners preferred to sink many shafts close together. It has been estimated that 20 men worked for 80–100 days to cut a shaft, followed by another 40 days to excavate the galleries. As little light penetrates underground they were provided with crude lamps made from hollowed out lumps of chalk in which a wick floated in oil. Access to the shaft bottoms was probably gained via ladders.

Each shaft seems to have been exploited only once, then filled in with

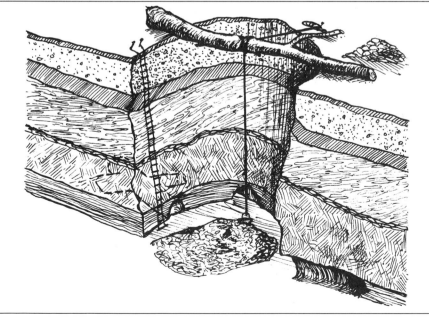

28 *(Above)* Mining
Neolithic-style,
galleries excavated for
flint extraction at the
bottom of a shaft at
Grimes Graves
(Norfolk; 203). *(Photo:
RCHME.)*

29 Reconstruction of a
flint mine at Grimes
Graves (Norfolk; 203).

rubble. Flint was knapped on the spot. Debris from this activity, consisting of waste flakes, cores, roughouts and broken tools covers a large area around the site. Flint was generally traded as axe roughouts from this site, not finished polished axes. A skilled man could have made one of these axe blanks in just under twenty minutes. Just who these ancient miners and flint-knappers were we can only speculate. Some have argued that the site was not controlled by a single tribe, but was neutral ground, open for exploitation by anyone who cared to make the journey to extract this essential raw material. Others point out that the expertise demonstrated by the miners would seem to imply that they were specialists, not casual labourers.

Good quality flint is largely absent from the north and west of the British Isles. In these regions polished stone axes were made instead, from fine-grained igneous rocks that could also be polished to take a sharp cutting edge. Geologists have been able to pin-point many of the centres of axe production by using a microscope to examine under polarized light thin slices cut from axes. This technique shows up clearly the different proportions of the various minerals in rocks and so enables the samples to be matched with those from known modern sites. The results have shown that 'axe factories' existed in Cornwall, the Lake District, northern Wales and Northern Ireland. The earliest, in Cornwall, were already in operation before 4000 BC. At most axe factories the raw material was readily available on the scree slopes covering the hillsides wherever a suitable rock outcropped. A piece of the right size had only to be picked up and roughed into shape before being ready for polishing. Only at Mynydd Rhiw (Clwyd), were shallow shafts driven into the hillside following the beds of a particularly prized outcrop of stone.

When maps of the find spots for these distinctive axes are plotted they can be seen to have been widely distributed throughout the British Isles. It is a trade that even seems to have had an international dimension, for axes made from an attractive green jadeite have been discovered right across Europe, from Britain to northern Italy. Although finely made, these specimens are rather too thin to be functional and were probably status symbols coveted by chieftains for the prestige they could bestow.

Analysis of the clay and tempering minerals used in Neolithic pottery have also shown that some vessels are found far from their places of origin. A style of pottery called Hembury Ware, for example, made from a type of clay that is only found at the Lizard Peninsula in Cornwall has been found at many of the early Neolithic ritual sites in southern England.

Distribution studies of Neolithic artefacts clearly show that some sort of trade was being carried out at a very early date. Anthropologists who have studied contemporary peoples with a lifestyle that must be similar to that of our Neolithic ancestors have shown that commerce as understood today is almost non-existent. Among such societies transactions, particularly those involving prestige goods, are not carried out with the intention of making a profit, but as a means of reinforcing social relationships within and between groups. Similar 'gift-exchange' networks may have existed in Neolithic Britain. It is surely no coincidence that many of these trade goods have been recovered from ritual sites.

4 MEGALITHS AND MOONSHINE

In the monuments they built to worship their gods and venerate their dead the first farmers have stamped their mark on the British Isles. But the hopes and fears, myths and legends, that motivated their construction have been irretrievably lost. Archaeologists can do no more than recover the material traces the rituals have left behind. Yet even this makes it quite clear that we are dealing with a very different world from fantasies of Druids, Extraterrestrials or Golden Age Sages that have been conjured up from the imaginations of the romantics. For the sake of convenience the monuments are often divided into 'Neolithic' and 'Bronze Age', but this obscures their underlying continuity. Fashions in monuments might wax and wane, but all were constructed and used by the same types of communities to fulfil similar religious, emotional and social needs.

Barrows

Neolithic communities of the third and fourth millennia BC tended to bury their dead communally under barrows. Archaeologists traditionally classify them into many different types. Among the most important are the long barrows of England and Wales – trapezoidal mounds in which burials were made within a stone or wood chamber at the broader, eastern end. The bare stones belonging to some of these chambers occasionally survive by themselves as dolmens or cromlechs long after the covering mound or cairn has been removed. There is also evidence that some of these monuments were intended to be freestanding, not buried beneath a mound at all. In Ireland and northern Scotland are found the passage graves: circular mounds with a single burial chamber at their heart reached by a long passage.

Most communities buried their dead, but only a few articulated skeletons have been found during the excavation of barrows. Instead there is commonly a jumble of bones marked with the distinctive signs of weathering. It seems that corpses were not placed immediately within barrows, but were first exposed to the elements until most of the flesh had decomposed. Only then were the bare bones interred. This custom is one that has continued to be practised by some tribal people right up to the present day. Some communities preferred to cremate their dead. The builders of the Irish passage graves, for example, placed the ashes of many individuals in large stone bowls in their burial chambers.

Corpses were probably exposed in mortuary enclosures, marked out by bank, ditch or palisade, inside which there was often a timber mortuary house. The remains of several examples have been discovered during excavations of earthen long barrows. At Foulmire Fen (Cambridgeshire) one took the form of a

30 Death in the Neolithic. The jumble of disarticulated human bones that filled the north chamber of a long barrow at Hazleton (Gloucestershire). *(Photo: courtesy of Allan Saville and the Corinium Museum.)*

rectangular chamber 7m (23ft) long, 1.5m (5ft) wide and 1.3m ($4\frac{1}{4}$ft) high, with walls of massive oak posts and a flat plank roof. It contained the remains of at least five individuals. Before the turf and chalk barrow was erected on the site the mortuary chamber was partially dismantled and burnt. Such timber structures may have been intended to have had a limited lifetime, maintained for a generation or two, before being sealed under a barrow. But the stone chambers were more permanent; with no rotting timber components requiring to be replaced, they may have remained in use for centuries.

As the exact conditions of the bones varies, from badly eroded to completely fresh and partially articulated, it has been suggested that they may have been gathered together at regular intervals, perhaps once a year, for a common ceremonial burial. Bones belonging to the same individual are occasionally found placed together, but more often they were all jumbled up with those of many others (30). What seems like disorder to us, however, may have had meaning for the Neolithic mind. For there are signs that bones were sorted out according to a plan, skulls placed in one area, long bones in another. Bones may also have been removed from the burial chambers for use in rituals elsewhere, which may account for the relative scarcity of skulls and long bones in some tombs. Barrows must have played a far more important role in the community than as simple mortuaries. To emphasize this point some were equipped with impressive facades and forecourts to act as a ceremonial focus. But exactly what went on there is impossible to tell from the traces of fires, pottery, animal and human bones that are discovered by excavation.

In the passage graves (31) the cremations are generally accompanied by ornaments of stone and bone, otherwise the dead were not buried with their personal possessions. Mixed in with the bones, however, are to be found sherds, tools and flint-knapping debris together with the bones of both domesticated and wild animals. Although seeming to resemble nothing more than a random accumulation of rubbish, everything must have been placed there with ritual intent. Large numbers of non-food animal bones, such as those of eagles, song-birds and dogs, found in certain Orkney tombs, have even led to the suggestion that a form of totemism may have been in force; the clans who built and used the tombs identifying with a particular species.

Just who merited burial in barrows we cannot tell. Many contain a small number of burials, which can only represent a tiny proportion of all the deaths occurring within the community that built them, presumably those of some elite group. What happened to those considered to be unworthy of barrow burial is uncertain. They may have been cremated, laid in unmarked graves or their bodies simply left unburied. Some tombs, however, contained the bones of hundreds of individuals and had clearly served as the communal burial vault of a small community over several centuries. In certain of these barrows high incidences of inherited defects proved that they were used by a closely related group of people.

The large numbers of bones recovered from some barrows gave archaeologists their first chance to analyse an ancient population. Dr Chesterman, for example, worked on the remains of 371 individuals from the tomb at Isbister in Orkney, excavated by John Hedges. He found that the age and sex ratios of this pre-historic population more closely resembled those of a Third World country than modern Britain. They were a young people, 75 per cent under the age of 20, with an average life expectancy at birth of 19 years 11 months. Only a few males lived on into their fifties and women, due to the hazards of childbirth, died much earlier than men. Infant mortality, however, at 49 deaths per 1000 live births was far lower than expected, a figure between 100 and 400 deaths per 1000 live births is common in areas without the benefit of modern medical care. This discrepancy may simply be due to the fact that an infant's bones are more fragile and therefore have less chance of preservation than those of an adult.

31 Bryn Celli Ddu (Gwynedd; 68), a rare Welsh example of a passage grave, a circular mound covering a megalithic chamber accessible via a short passage. (*Photo: courtesy of the Welsh Tourist Board.*)

The Isbister people were a little shorter than ourselves, the men being on average of 1.7m (5ft 7in), the women 1.61m (5ft 3½in). The bones show that they were no pampered elite class, but were used to hard physical labour from an early age. They suffered from many of our common ailments. Arthritis, especially of the spine, was extremely common. But their teeth, unlike our own, had few caries, instead decay was due to the grit in their stone-ground flour gradually wearing down their teeth until painful abcesses formed. There were relatively few cases of physical violence or accidental fractures among the bones.

During the later Neolithic, chambered tombs that had been in use for centuries were suddenly abandoned for no discernible reasons. At West Kennet (Wiltshire), for example, both the passage and the chambers leading off it were filled in up to the roof with clean chalk rubble, interspersed with layers of debris. At the same time the imposing facade was blocked with boulders. No new barrows were constructed to replace them, although those that existed often continued to be the focus for rituals long after the last ancestor had been laid to rest.

For god and profit?

On hills in southern England the first farmers laid out the causewayed camps, roughly circular enclosures surrounded by one or more concentric circuits of ditches and banks. Unlike the defences of Iron Age hillforts these earthworks do not form an unbroken line. Instead they are frequently interrupted by the causeways that have given them their name; some of these are wide enough to have formed useful entrances, others are so narrow that they can only be baulks left by the builders. When first discovered, archaeologists thought that causewayed camps had been used as cattle pounds. At the onset of winter, so this theory went, cattle were herded together, next year's breeding stock selected and the rest slaughtered. During this annual cull the herdsmen were thought to have bivouacked in the ditches. But analyses of the animal bones from these sites have failed to match the age and sex ratios predicted by this theory. Instead recent excavations have produced evidence that causewayed camps fulfilled a variety of social, economic, religious, funerary and defensive functions for early Neolithic communities.

At Hambledon Hill (Dorset), for example, Roger Mercer discovered that the centre of the hill had been enclosed with a single continuous bank inside a causewayed ditch. Offerings of both animal and human bone, flints and pottery had been placed on the ditch floor. These included complete human skulls deposited at irregular intervals and two flint cairns covering the remains of intact child burials. Initially the ditch was well maintained, being regularly cleared of silt, but later it was allowed to silt up and not even cleared when material from the bank collapsed into it. Even so, the ditch remained a ritual focus into which pits were dug to deposit more ash, pottery, human and animal bone.

The many disarticulated human bones found scattered through the ditches of causewayed camps were once taken as evidence for grisly cannibal feasts. In reality they were simply one of the places in which corpses were exposed. At Hambledon Hill, 60 per cent of the human remains were those of infants, while the remainder were split almost equally between adult males and females; figures that reflect the mortality rates of traditional farming communities far better than any samples from barrows. So it seems likely that while every corpse was exposed only the favoured few were later given full ritual burial in barrows.

Two long barrows were associated with Hambledon Hill. At both, the flanking ditches had received similar treatment to those of the camp, suggesting that their use was co-ordinated. On the south-east spur of the hilltop there was also a second, smaller Neolithic site, the Stepleton Enclosure. Its ditch deposits were very different from those of the main site. They contained little human bone and no complete skulls. Instead there was domestic debris from flint-knapping and antler-working, together with animal bones from the best quality joints of meat; evidence that led Mercer to suggest that a specialist group of undertakers may have lived at this site.

Within the main enclosure only the bases of deep pits had survived plough-ing and erosion. Among the contents of the fill were sherds of pottery, flints, antlers and polished stone axes, deposited in a manner that suggests a ritual assemblage rather than a random accumulation of rubbish. Analysis of both pottery and axes shows that many had originated far from the site. These in-cluded sherds of Hembury Ware, from the Lizard Peninsula in Cornwall, to-gether with axes from factories located in Cornwall, South Wales and the Lake District. There were even two specimens of imported jadeite. These finds have suggested to some that causewayed camps may have been meeting places where people gathered to celebrate calendrical feasts and rites of passage, possibly tied up with gift-exchanges – assemblies that fulfilled much the same mix of social, economic and ritual functions as a medieval fair.

Many, but not all, causewayed camps were clearly located to take advantage of natural strongpoints; it should therefore come as no surprise that while their earthworks are never as formidable as those of Iron Age hillforts they occasion-ally fulfilled defensive roles. At Hambledon Hill the original simple earthworks were supplemented in *c.*3500 BC by three concentric ramparts, 2500m (8200ft) long, on the southern slope of the hill, where it was most vulnerable to attack. The outer one was a simple bank of dumped rubble dug from an interrupted quarry ditch, but the inner two were timber framed. That there was a very real need for defence is shown by the fact that the camp was violently destroyed in *c.*3300 BC. The rampart had been deliberately fired, and among the burnt chalk rubble was the complete skeleton of a young man, who had been carrying a child when he was struck down by the flint arrowhead that still lay in his ribcage.

Sacred circles

During the latter half of the fourth millennium BC causewayed camps went out of use. Many of their functions were taken over by a new type of ritual site, the henge (32). Although the name derives from the 'hanging' stones of

32 Sacred circles, the henges at Knowlton (Dorset; 260), where millennia of pagan worship were later exorcised by building a Norman church. (*Photo: RCHME.*)

Stonehenge, most consist of no more than a circular bank and ditch interrupted by one or two simple gap entrances and relatively few enclose stone circles. As the ditch was generally located inside the bank, it is unlikely to have had a defensive function. The largest and most impressive henges were constructed on the chalk downlands of Wessex.

At Durrington Walls (Wiltshire), little remains above ground of the earthworks surrounding a 10ha (25acre) enclosure. Rescue excavations by Geoffrey Wainwright in advance of road building showed that the ditch was once 12.5m (41ft) wide, narrowing to 5.6m ($18\frac{1}{2}$ft) at the flat bottom, 5.5m (18ft) down. Between 18 and 21m (60 and 70ft) outside the ditch were the eroded remains of a bank, 33m (110ft) in diameter. The one entrance that was discovered took the form of a simple causeway without a gate to control access. Charcoal from

under the bank gave a C^{14} date of 2630±70 BC for the monument. An estimated 900,000 man hours would have been needed to construct Durrington.

Within the limited area excavated, parts of two circular timber structures were discovered. The better preserved example was located 27m (90ft) north-west of the entrance. Only half was excavated, the rest was left untouched as it did not lie within the area threatened with destruction. From the way the individual post-holes intersected, four distinct phases of construction could be recognized. In the early phases there were four concentric rings of posts, with an overall diameter of 23m (75ft), this arrangement was later enlarged to 38m (125ft) with the addition of a fifth ring of posts.

At Durrington, and other such sites, the post-holes of these circular structures often increase in size and depth towards the centre, which suggests that they were intended to take increasingly taller and thicker posts. At 1.8m (6ft) across and 2.1m (7ft) deep, those of the inner ring could easily have held posts up to 9m (30ft) tall. Although some prefer to think of these circular structures as timber versions of stone circles, others interpret them as quite sophisticated

34 A reconstruction, based on excavated remains from Durrington Walls (Wiltshire), of one of the large circular timber buildings commonly discovered during excavations within the earthworks of henges. (*After Wainwright.*)

34 A reconstruction, based on excavated remains from Durrington Walls (Wiltshire), of one of the large circular timber buildings commonly discovered during excavations within the earthworks of henges. (*After Wainwright.*)

buildings, the rings of posts supporting a sloping thatched roof (34). To build just one of these great 'round-houses' would have consumed the timber from 3.6ha (9 acres) of forest. As commonly reconstructed they are reminiscent of the ceremonial centres built by the Cherokee Indians in the eighteenth century AD to serve as the focus of their religious and social lives and where great feasts were held. Only a few finds were made within the Durrington 'round-house', but from outside came masses of broken pottery, flints, animal bones and charcoal, which could be the remains from similar feasting.

Henges ceased to be constructed, while continuing to be venerated, in the late fourth millennium BC. Many of their social and religious functions then seem to have been taken over by the stone circles which were erected throughout the Neolithic and the Bronze Age down to the late second millennium BC (35). One of the most controversial contributions to the study of stone circles and other megalithic monuments in recent years came not from a professional archaeologist, but from an engineer, the late Professor Alexander Thom. His statistical analysis of the results of a survey of over 150 stone circles throughout the British Isles implied that they had been laid out using multiples of a standard unit of length, a 'megalithic yard' of 0.829m ($2\frac{3}{4}$ft). But sceptics have found that there are marked variations in the 'megalithic yard' between different regions. They point out that while a standard of length may well have existed it may have been based, as were those of many pre-scientific societies, on measurements derived from the human body. The old English yard, for example, was once defined as the distance from the nose to the tips of the fingers of the outstretched arm of an adult male.

Many 'circles' are truly circular, but a significant number are not. Until recently this was attributed to incompetence on the part of the prehistoric surveyors. Yet when the industrious Professor Thom analysed these curious shapes he found that from a geometrical point of view they are actually quite complex. Some of the strange circular forms seem to have been attempts to lay out a circle using values of 2 or 3 for Pi (the ratio of the diameter of a circle to its circumference) instead of the actual value 3.14 . . .). Egg-shaped ellipses seem to have been laid out using right-angled triangles and Pythagoras' theorem a thousand years and more before the Greek mathematician had even been born. Critics, however, point out that these effects could have been obtained empirically, using stakes and ropes on the ground, without any theoretical knowledge of the principles involved. Just why their makers, who were perfectly capable of laying out circular circles, should have chosen these curious forms remains a mystery (36).

Another result of Thom's work is the realization that the astronomical alignments of Stonehenge are not the exception, but the rule. For many, if not all, of the circles and standing stones of the British Isles seem to incorporate astronomical alignments into their design. This should hardly have come as a surprise, however; long before the first stone circles were laid out there were

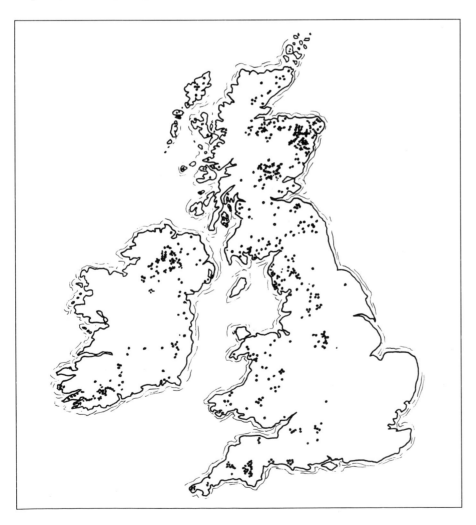

35 Distribution of stone circles. *(After Burl.)*

36 An exercise in ingenuity, how one of the curiously shaped stone circles may have been laid out using nothing more than a rope and pegs.

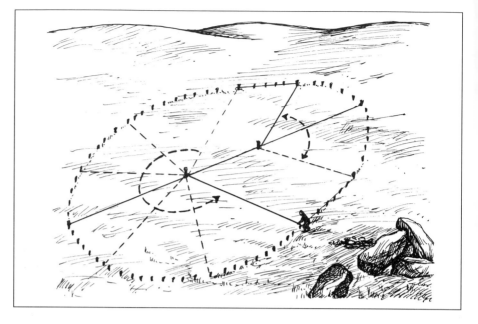

barrows whose plans were carefully designed to incorporate astronomical alignments, some of them quite sophisticated. The passage grave at Newgrange (Co. Meath) for example, was designed so that at dawn on the midwinter solstice the sun's rays shone through the space over the lintel, down the entrance passage and illuminated the burial chamber.

Anthropologists who have studied traditional farming societies at a similar level of development to Neolithic Britain have pointed out that they often use observations of the sun and moon to regulate the calendar that tells them the correct times to plant and harvest their crops. Thom believed that the first farmers had made accurate observations, particularly of the moon, that went beyond simple yearly and monthly cycles. He thought the monuments revealed that they were aware of quite complex celestial events that would only have revealed themselves over generations. Neither a telescope nor any other piece of complex apparatus would have been required, it simply needed a place to stand where the horizon could be clearly seen and a method of marking the position of the heavenly body being studied. Some scholars even went so far as to speculate that an elite class of astronomer priests once existed, handing down their wisdom through the ages by word of mouth. But this seems unnecessary; modern tribal communities base their calendars on astronomical observations without any scientific understanding of what is involved. Before the dawn of science the astronomical events that herald the seasons may have seemed like cause and effect, needing to be marked with religious ritual. In the final analysis, while most archaeologists now accept the importance of astronomical orientations of the prehistoric monuments they are careful not take them out of the context of their own time into the present.

Stonehenge stands out from all the other henges and circles of the British Isles. But the monument as seen today is the culmination of several phases of construction that spanned the Neolithic and the Early Bronze Age from *c.*3000

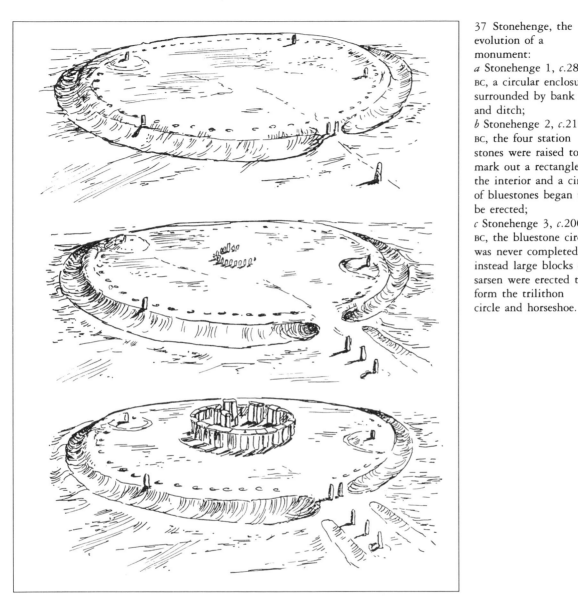

37 Stonehenge, the evolution of a monument:
a Stonehenge 1, *c*.2800 BC, a circular enclosure surrounded by bank and ditch;
b Stonehenge 2, *c*.2100 BC, the four station stones were raised to mark out a rectangle in the interior and a circle of bluestones began to be erected;
c Stonehenge 3, *c*.2000 BC, the bluestone circle was never completed, instead large blocks of sarsen were erected to form the trilithon circle and horseshoe.

to 1100 BC (37). The first Stonehenge was a circular earthwork enclosure, a typical Neolithic henge. Outside the single causeway entrance, the Heel Stone was erected. Inside the bank was a series of 56 shallow pits known as the Aubrey Holes. These had been dug, almost immediately refilled, then at a later date partially reopened to bury a mixture of earth, charcoal, ash, bones and flints. Human cremations were also inserted into some of the Aubrey Holes, the bank and the ditch. At the centre of the enclosure the ground was too disturbed by later activity to tell if it had ever been occupied by a ceremonial timber round-house.

Towards the end of the third millennium, *c*.2100 BC, two parallel banks and ditches were laid out from the entrance to form a short avenue and the four station stones were placed on the perimeter marking out a rectangle. A stone circle also began to be erected within the existing earthworks of the henge. Its stones belonged to a type of rock, known as 'bluestone', quite different from any that occurs naturally in the region of Stonehenge. Geologists eventually tracked down its source to the Presceli mountains (Dyfed), 386km (240 miles) north-west of the monument. At first archaeologists assumed that the bluestones had been taken down to the sea, lashed to canoes for the journey across the Bristol Channel and down the rivers of Wessex, before being dragged the final miles to Stonehenge overland; an epic journey which it now seems may never have taken place, for recent research suggests that the bluestones may have been transported to Salisbury Plain by glaciers. However the bluestones reached their final destination there was clearly a change of plan before the first stone circle was ever completed, and the megaliths that had been erected were removed, their sockets filled in with clean chalk rubble.

Stonehenge was transformed from a rather ordinary henge monument to something spectacular and unique in *c*.2000 BC. A circle of 25 sarsen trilithons (two uprights linked by a capstone) and a horseshoe of five trilithons were erected in the centre of the monument. Sarsens are blocks of natural sandstone that occur on the Marlborough Downs 32km (20 miles), from Stonehenge. Unlike most other megaliths these stones were not left in their natural rough state but were carefully dressed until they were quite smooth. First shallow, vertical grooves were made down the stones then the intervening ridges were removed using hammers of harder stone; a process that sounds rather crude but one that was nevertheless carried out with a high degree of skill. For the stones only appear to be straight, in reality they have a swelling in the middle designed to compensate for the distortions of perspective – an early application of the same technique that Greek architects were later to use on the Parthenon. As is only to be expected, the builders of Stonehenge seem to have been more familiar with working in wood than in stone. The lintels are secured to each other with tongue-and-groove joints and to the uprights with mortice-and-tenon joints, types familiar to any carpenter. Bluestones were also used *c*.1540 BC to form a circle and a horseshoe within the trilithons. Finally, in *c*.1100 BC the existing avenue was extended until it reached the river Avon, a total distance of 2.5km (1½ miles).

Astronomical alignments were significant throughout the history of Stonehenge. From its foundation, the monument had been orientated towards the midsummer sunrise. The four station stones erected in phase 2 marked out a rectangle, the short sides of which point towards the midsummer sunrise and the midwinter sunset, and whose long sides mark the maximum and minimum positions of the moon. The latter implies that the builders were aware of the 18.61 year lunar cycle. Further alignments have also been found for the trilithons.

Secret symbols

Barrows, causewayed camps, henges and stone circles form an impressive testimony to the architectural ability of the first farmers. Of their public art rather less has survived. The earliest work is represented by slabs lining the passage graves of Ireland that are carved with complex geometric designs. This may in turn have inspired the 'cup-and-ring' marks that are found carved into rock faces or the slabs of cist graves. From Cornwall to Orkney, Yorkshire to County Kerry, the same motifs were used over and over again throughout the second millennium BC. In addition to the eponymous cups and rings they include spirals, axes, hands and feet.

Over the past century numerous theories have been put forward to explain these curious marks. They have been interpreted as maps, star charts, secret signs left by metal prospectors to inform their fellow initiates, family trees, gaming boards, the inevitable fertility symbols and tattooist's pattern books to name but a few. Thom sought to relate their geometry to that of the stone circles and suggested that they were actually measured out in a 'megalithic inch'. Each theory in turn when placed against the facts has been found wanting. But whatever their intent, the simple point that the same designs are found so widely distributed would seem to imply that there was a considerable degree of cultural homogeneity over much of Britain.

The monument builders

Archaeologists once doubted that the supposedly primitive prehistoric societies of the British Isles could have conceived and constructed megalithic monuments unaided. Instead they looked for, and found, their origins in the East, among the tombs of Bronze Age Greece that resemble the passage graves. For decades conventional wisdom held that the necessary 'know-how' had been passed on along the trade routes through the Mediterranean and so on up the Atlantic coast. Initially C^{14} dates seemed to support this theory, but recalibration has now conclusively demonstrated that the megaliths of Western Europe are actually much older than their supposed Greek prototypes and must therefore be of native inspiration. Another of the once commonly held myths about the megaliths was that they resulted from some missionary cult, sailing the Atlantic seaboard spreading the good news in the manner of the Celtic saints of the Dark Ages. Some of the resemblance between British, Irish and Continental megaliths may simply be coincidental, the result of their being built by very similar communities to meet the same needs, using almost identical building techniques. Others, however, may genuinely derive from limited overseas contacts.

Anthropologists working among peoples at a similar cultural level to Neolithic Britain have shown that small agricultural communities are quite capable of erecting impressive monuments, megaliths not excepted. Any labour beyond the capacity of the village can be mobilized through co-operation with neighbouring settlements. An average barrow is estimated to have required around 5000 man hours, no more than a few months' work for the men of a family group. Causewayed camps and henges, however, required labour on a larger scale. To construct the camp at Hambledon Hill, for example, Mercer estimated that 50 men would have to put in a ten hour day for 90 days. An average henge would have needed a million man-hours', a year's, work for 300 people, and Stonehenge would have required even greater efforts, many millions of man-hours. Labour on this scale supposes the existence of a powerful organizing authority working on the small family and clan groups. It is possible that Neolithic society was what anthropologists classify as a 'chiefdom' society, in which individuals are ranked according to their descent from common ancestors. At its head is an hereditary chief who has the power to command agricultural surpluses and labour from his tribe of between five and twenty thousand members. Part of this bounty can be used to construct and maintain a ritual focus for the tribe in addition to a residential complex for the chief and his retainers.

Recent distribution studies carried out on the megaliths have suggested that Neolithic tribes may have used their ritual monuments as 'title deeds' to mark out their territories. On the Orkney island of Rousay (38), for example, there are 13 well-preserved megalithic tombs. Given the not unreasonable assumption that all were roughly contemporary and that the population density was similar to that of the recent past, a computer analysis suggests that each tomb was the focus for a plot of land supporting between 20 and 50 people. On the richer downlands of Wessex, by way of contrast, the monuments fall into five main groups, clusters of long barrows around major henges and causewayed camps which may mark out larger territories, on average 1000 sq.km (386 sq.miles) in extent. It has been suggested that the construction of larger ritual centres marks the transition from a society of small, loosely linked groups, into one organized into chiefdoms with the paramount chief having his ritual centre at Stonehenge. The total population of Britain has been variously estimated from tens of thousands to half a million.

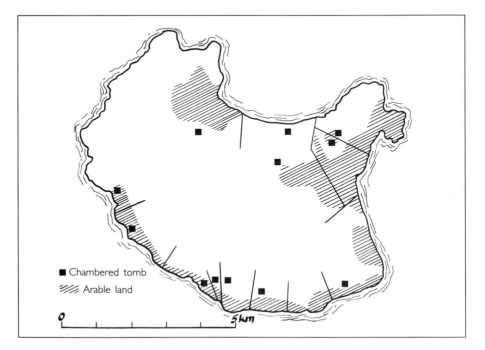

38 Hypothetical prehistoric 'territories' on the island of Rousay, Orkney. *(After Renfrew.)*

■ Chambered tomb

▨ Arable land

0   5 km

5 THE ROUNDHEADS

The custom of dividing prehistory into a Stone Age, Bronze Age and Iron Age grew up for the convenience of museum curators and archaeologists. But although in the nineteenth century the discovery of metal was seen as a significant milestone on the march of progress, in reality the 'Stone Age' world of the later Neolithic monument builders was not radically altered by the new technology. A decisive break with the past did not occur until the latter half of the second millennium BC, well into the so-called Bronze Age. Only then were traditions of ritual and burial that had evolved over countless generations given up and sites that had been venerated for hundreds, or even thousands of years, abandoned for ever.

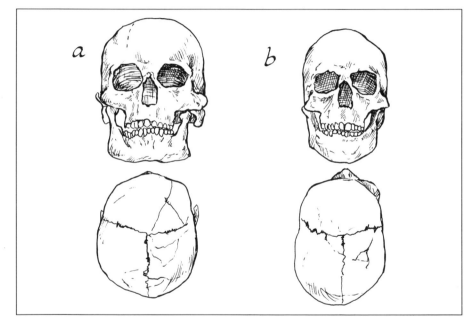

39 Round heads and long heads:
a the broad skull typical of burials in round barrows;
b the long skull typically found in long barrows.

To the nineteenth-century antiquarians nothing was as delightful as messing about in barrows. Yet even the most unobservant dilettante could not help but notice that there was a marked difference between long barrows and round barrows. For while the former covered mass graves, the latter held individual burials often accompanied by rich grave goods, including metal objects. The human remains also seemed to belong to a completely different physical type. Skulls from long barrows tended to be long and thin whereas those from round barrows were generally broader and round (39). 'Long skulls in long barrows, round skulls in round barrows' became an oft-repeated catch-phrase among antiquarians. Many of the 'roundheads' were buried with a distinctive type of pottery vessel, which was immediately seen as a sign of ethnic identity and, because of its shape, archaeologists came to write about a 'Beaker People'. The beakers may have been used to consume some new type of drink. Analysis of one specimen from Ashgrove (Fife) for example, revealed traces of mead. As evidence accumulated it seemed that the beakers, together with metalworking and individual burial, made up a culture widely distributed throughout Western and Central Europe.

It seemed only logical to the early archaeologists that the 'Beaker Culture' had been introduced by an invasion similar to those of the Romans, Saxons and Normans. Armed with their superior bronze weapons the 'Beaker People' were supposed to have swept across flint-using Neolithic Europe crushing all resistance in their path. Indeed the lack of evidence for Beaker settlements was taken to imply that they were a highly mobile tribe of nomadic pastoralists who were compelled to keep shifting from one temporary campsite to the next in search of fresh grazing. Some, less bloodthirsty commentators, however, envisaged that the 'Beaker Culture' had been spread by wandering smiths or traders prospecting for new sources of metal ores.

Archaeologists now recognize that it is both misleading and simplistic to conjure up a series of unending invasions to explain each and every observable change in the archaeological record. In reality, invasions are only one of a host of factors that can change the material culture of a society. Many of the European features observed in British prehistoric cultures are just as likely to have been acquired in the course of trade, immigration of specialist craftsmen or from small numbers of refugees, as from hostile mass migrations. Cultural ideas can even spread quite independently of population movements, by trade or technological exchanges for religious or ideological reasons. Even changes in the physical characteristics of a population are not always indicative of an infusion of new blood. The environment, especially diet, has an important role to play.

The present consensus of opinion holds that aspects of 'Beaker Culture' were adopted and adapted by indigenous societies and blended with their own cultural traditions in a process that extended from the late third to the early second millennium BC. At the same time metal was introduced and the status of individuals in society was redefined – powerful chieftains felt the need to demonstrate their rank through the possession of metal artefacts and other prestige goods. As part of this differentiation of status within society, individual burial beneath round barrows replaced collective burial in long barrows. Indeed one explanation of the change in burial practice is that the rank of the living was believed to be perpetuated in the afterlife. This rank may well have been inherited, for although most of the rich burials are of adult males there are smaller numbers of female and infant burials singled out for special treatment who possibly exercised power in their own right or else were its heirs. How the remains of commoners were disposed of is unclear; exposure, cremation or burial in unmarked graves are all possibilities.

The high-status individual, honoured by burial in a barrow, was placed in a pit dug into the ground surface near the centre of the mound (40). Both inhumation and cremation were practised. Initially the former was most in favour, the body laid on its side in the foetal position. In east Yorkshire waterlogged conditions have preserved massive oak coffins hollowed out of tree

trunks and crudely carved in the form of boats. Elsewhere the body was often laid to rest in a small box-like structure of stone slabs known as a cist. Toggles, pins and buttons, together with cloth impressions on metal artefacts, imply that the corpse was probably buried fully clothed or shrouded. When cremation grew in popularity to become the established rite, the ashes were placed within a pottery urn, or wrapped in cloth, leather or some other perishable material. In addition to these primary burials secondary interments were commonly made within the barrow. Whether these were family members or servants, whether they had all died at the same time or were less important corpses, stored elsewhere to accompany their lord, we cannot tell. What is clear is that even when the barrow had been constructed, secondary burials continued to be made in its sides, in some cases for generations.

40 An aerial view of the barrows at Winterbourne Stoke (Wiltshire; 329), an important cemetery near Stonehenge where the leading members of the communities that raised the ritual monuments of Wessex were interred over two thousand years. *(Photo: RCHME.)*

In their haste to reach the rich grave goods that accompanied primary burials, the early antiquarians often missed vital evidence which showed that the erection of a barrow was only the last stage in the funeral rites. At Pond Cairn (Glamorgan) the funerary rituals began with the cremation of a child, whose bones were washed before being placed in a pit, which was then filled up with stones and sealed with clay. Rough stone paving was laid over the site, an adult was cremated and the ashes deposited within an urn, covered by a stone slab, then placed on the paving. A hole was next dug in front of the urn and filled with hot charcoal and sealed with clay. A small mound of stone and turf was then heaped up over the urn. Following this, a ring of stones 18.6m (61ft) across, 4.8m (16ft) thick and 1.5m (5ft) high was constructed around the central mound. The bare earth between the two was found to be trampled solid, as if people had danced round and round the mound. Ash was scattered over the surface of the mound and the bare ground. Finally a small hole was dug in which a fire was kindled to receive an offering of grain. Just what these rituals meant to the people who so carefully carried them out we have no means of knowing.

Relatively few barrows were constructed during the latter half of the second millennium and the early first millennium BC. Instead the dominant funerary rite was cremation, with the ashes placed in flat cemeteries. Some barrows, however, continued to be used for large numbers of secondary burials. Apart from the basic urn (41), which was not always present, few other grave goods

41 A group of cinerary urns belonging to secondary burials placed in a round barrow at Deverel (Wiltshire), in the late second millennium BC. *(Photo: courtesy of the Archaeology Department, City of Bristol Museum and Art Gallery.)*

accompanied the dead. Not only does this make burials of the period difficult to identify, but it has also led to the suggestion that the established ruling elites had been overthrown. This theory is probably exaggerated; a likelier explanation is that people were simply using new fashions to express their status that did not require funerary ostentation.

Life on the land

The results of modern studies mean that it is no longer valid to think of prehistoric Britain as having been sparsely occupied by scattered settlements farming small-scale clearances in the forests. All the evidence points to a densely settled landscape that was intensively farmed and a social system controlled by an elite with the power to divide up the land and levy the necessary labour to build the boundaries.

A glance at any Ordnance Survey map will show that over many a British hillside the remains of prehistoric field systems, known as 'Celtic fields', are to be seen; or at least they were until their faint traces were obliterated by deep ploughing. A typical 'Celtic field' was square or rectangular in shape, with an area between 0.2ha ($\frac{1}{2}$ acre) and 0.6ha ($1\frac{1}{2}$ acres). Recent studies have shown that although some of these fields were indeed worked by the Celtic peoples of Iron Age and Roman Britain, many were laid out long before the Celts ever reached the shores of Britain.

Field boundaries have been preserved by fortunate chance. As first laid out they were marked with low stone walls, probably piled up from stones cleared from the land, ditches or fences. Repeated ploughing then caused soil to move down the hillside and accumulate against the lower boundary (42). In time a low bank, called a positive lynchet, was formed. The removal of soil below the boundary created a corresponding negative lynchet. Lynchets vary in height from a few centimetres to a few metres. Sometimes they are to be found only at the top and bottom of a field, but if a field was laid out against the contours of a slope, lynchets would form on all four sides.

Field-systems are difficult to date, for only a few artefacts are found associated with them. Sherds of pottery, deriving from the midden material that was spread on the fields as fertilizer, are occasionally found within the soil layers. At the best their age can be estimated from their relationships with neighbouring

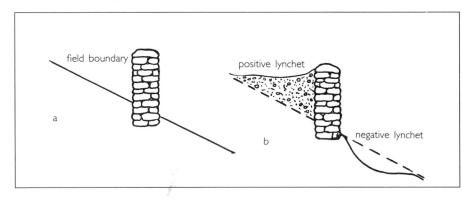

42 Formation of lynchets:
a stones cleared from a field are used to build a simple drystone wall; *b* erosion moves soil down the slope, forming a positive lynchet against the wall and leaving a corresponding negative lynchet below the wall.

43 The Dartmoor Reaves, long, linear boundaries laid out by communities using rough stone walls and banks in the second millennium BC to stake their claim to the land.

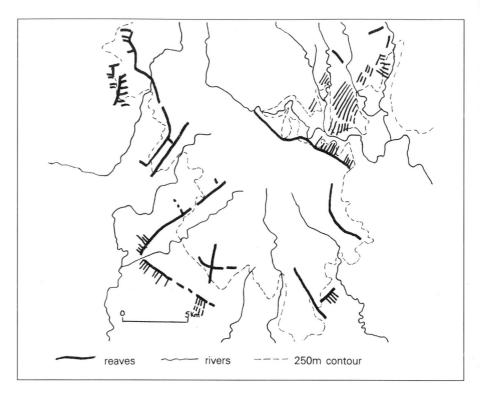

reaves   rivers   250m contour

44 (*Opposite*) An aerial view of typical Dartmoor reaves, a landscape 'fossilized' in the late second millennium BC when climatic change caused the abandonment of highland fields and pasture. (*Photo: RCHME.*)

settlements and monuments. As evidence has been collected it has become clear that by the early Bronze Age, *c.*2000 BC, extensive field-systems existed over much of the British Isles. Some seem to have grown up gradually, new fields being added as and when the need arose, but the overall pattern of others suggests that they were planned and laid out as a single act at the prompting of some higher authority.

A very different pattern of land use is to be found marked out by a system of low walls, known as reaves, across Dartmoor (43). Since 1975 they have been intensely studied in a co-ordinated approach that combines fieldwork, aerial photography and excavation. Individual sections of reaves were constructed using many different techniques, including ditches, earth banks and fences, in addition to the more usual drystone walls. The latter themselves vary from rough heaps of stones to accomplished walls (44). Each system of reaves, however, appears to have been planned and laid out at one time. Possibly small groups worked in their own ways, but to a common plan, to enclose their share of the land. Ten major reave systems have been identified, each covering a territory of between 200 and 3000ha (494 and 7400 acres). Together they interlock in a manner that suggests there was close co-operation between neighbouring communities. The high moor, above the 350–400m (1148–1312ft) contour, may have been left as common land, for no subdivisions were laid out beyond this line.

Reaves are no easier than the Celtic fields to date although they are obviously earlier than the bog deposits that began to form over them in the late second millennium BC. In places they follow earlier boundaries laid out with cairns and

stone rows, but elsewhere seem to ignore them. Reaves have now been found outside Dartmoor and are known to have been a common way of marking out land during the second millennium BC. What is also clear from pollen samples taken from both above and below reaves is that land use was unaffected by their construction, remaining rough grazing. Impressions of animal tracks preserved on buried surfaces show that herds of sheep and cattle were kept, together with a few horses similar to the modern ponies.

Elsewhere over much of southern England there appears to have been a radical reorganization of land use around the middle of the second millennium BC. This involved laying out long, linear banks and ditches, often without reference to the earlier field-systems. They are commonly known as 'ranch boundaries' because they were once thought to have divided the land up into large blocks of pasture land. On the Berkshire Downs, for example, Dartmoor style reaves gave way to a chequer board of 'Celtic fields' over which were later imposed the ranch boundaries. Once, such changes were thought to be a symptom of the deterioration in climate experienced in late Bronze Age Britain which led to a greater emphasis on pastoralism. Now it is recognized that this is an oversimplification. Within the 'ranches' there were also fairly large field-systems. It is probably better to think of these boundaries as controlling access to the land rather than for defining land use. As such, any changes in marking out the land are likely to reflect social development.

One of the prime reasons for the preservation of Bronze Age landscapes such as Dartmoor is the fact that in the late first millennium BC large areas of land were abandoned due to the formation of heath and bog. This was formerly attributed to the deterioration of the climate as in the late first millennium BC the Neolithic climatic optimum, when the weather was warmer and drier than at present, came to an end. Instead, possibly influenced by the eruption of Mount Hekla in Iceland in c.1159 BC, colder and wetter conditions prevailed. But prehistoric farming methods themselves may also have made a contribution to the change, for forest clearance can have serious environmental side effects, as many parts of the developing world are discovering to their cost. Deforestation can lead rapidly to soil erosion, leaching of minerals and soil acidification. Some of these problems may have been experienced in prehistoric Britain, contributing to the highland clearances. But whatever the reasons the end result was the same, large areas of previously viable pasture and arable land in the highlands were abandoned and never farmed again.

Hearth and home

Over much of lowland Britain there are few traces of Bronze Age settlements to set against the many barrows; a fact that has provoked more than one frustrated archaeologist to remark that 'Bronze Age Man died but never lived!'. But the remains of Bronze Age settlements are not as rare as that suggests, it is just a question of looking in the right place. The secret is to go to the bleak moors of the western highlands and islands where the deterioration of the climate in the late Bronze Age caused entire settlements to be abandoned. Elsewhere they have been largely obliterated by millennia of intensive farming.

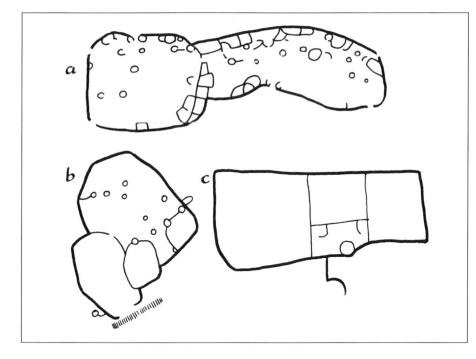

45 Settlement types on Dartmoor:
a the 'village' at Riders Rings;
b the pound at Legis Tor;
c the farmstead at Rippon Tor.

Concentrated on the west and south slopes of Dartmoor, for example, are settlement types, known as 'pounds' and 'enclosed villages', thought to have been occupied by pastoralists (45). Pounds were surrounded by a high stone wall, intended to prevent both the animals from getting out and raids by neighbouring settlements or wild animals. Inside were anything between 5 and 35 houses scattered over the enclosure. Animals would be herded back to the pounds at night and confined in the 'stock pens' built on to the sides of the enclosure wall. 'Villages' were made up of larger groups of houses than pounds, typically between 20 and 30, linked with low stone walls forming irregular enclosures. Few traces of fields are seen near pounds or villages, but on the eastern fringes of the moor, with the best soil and climate, farmers lived in isolated farmsteads made up of a few houses together with their associated fields (46).

The Bronze Age 'ideal home' on Dartmoor was the round-house, on average 3–8m (10–25ft) in diameter. The walls, up to 1.5m (5ft) thick, were made of small stones and earth faced with larger stone slabs. Entrances, some with exterior porches to exclude draughts, faced away from the prevailing north and north-west winds. The interiors formed single rooms, 4–5m (13–16ft) in diameter, the floors were partially sunken below the ground level. A conical roof of turf, thatch or heather was supported by a central post and in the larger houses with the aid of an additional ring of posts (47). Although some houses are larger than others none really stand out as belonging to high-status individuals. Prestige was obviously expressed in ways different to today.

Unfortunately Bronze Age households were too tidy and little has been left behind in their homes. When excavated, nothing but a few sherds, flints, querns and the like are found; only a few indications of how the internal space was used have survived. As the upper part of the floor area is more than usually

46 Bronze Age Dartmoor, the settlements abandoned late in the second millennium with the deterioration of the climate.

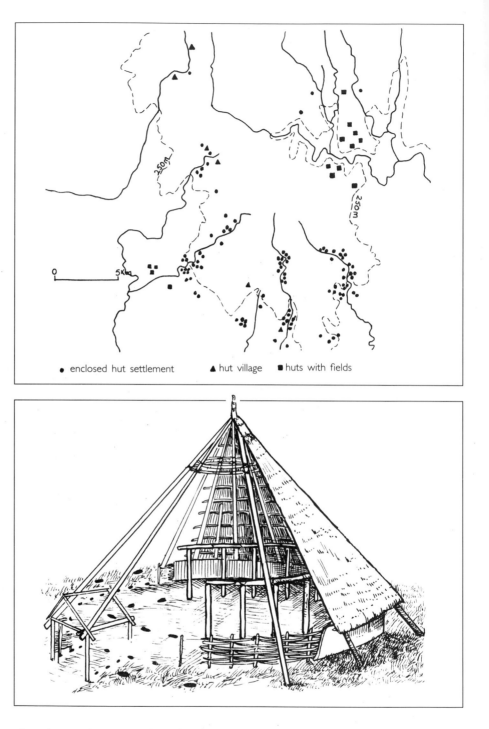

● enclosed hut settlement ▲ hut village ■ huts with fields

47 The Iron Age ideal home, a reconstruction of a round-house based on excavated remains at Pimperne (Dorset).

clean it may have served as the sleeping area. In the sunken part was the stone hearth, and by the sides of this were pits, some containing pottery vessels, that were used to cook the food using hot ashes or stones. Charcoal from these fires allowed the houses to be dated *c*.1300–1000 BC.

Round-houses similar to those on Dartmoor have a wide distribution throughout the British Isles, but they were not the only type of house in use. Recently the well-preserved remains of a very different type of structure, possibly a ceremonial structure rather than a home, have been excavated from the waterlogged deposits of Flag Fen, near Peterborough, which dates to the late Bronze Age. It was rectangular, measuring 6 by 6.5m (19½–21ft), with low walls, estimated at 60–70cm (23–27in) high and 0.5m (1½ft) thick. They had been constructed in lathe style, from narrow strips of wood laid on to sleeper beams and attached to the supporting posts by pegs. The eaves of the roof came down low, nearly to the ground, where they were supported by lines of posts. Two further lines of posts divided the interior into a nave and two aisles. The floor was formed of planks and woodchips, covered with sand or gravel.

An insight into prehistoric cuisine has come from the excavation of a different class of monuments, the 'burnt mounds'. These are to be found scattered over a large part of the British Isles, especially in Ireland, western Scotland and the Isles. Many of these mounds are horseshoe shaped and arranged around a central paved area in which there are traces of a wooden trough. When excavated they are found to contain thousands of heat-crazed stones, known as pot-boilers after their function. Many of these sites date to the second millennium BC, but others are later. Indeed travellers of the seventeenth century AD in Ireland described similar structures as being still in use.

Intrepid archaeologists have conducted culinary experiments to see just how prehistoric gourmets might have fared. They found that it took an average of half an hour to boil a trough of water using red hot stones straight from a fire. To keep it simmering, fresh stones had to be added every few minutes. If the magic formula of allowing 20 minutes of cooking for each 20lbs of meat plus an extra 20 minutes is followed a 10lb (4.5kg) leg of mutton could be cooked to a turn in three hours and forty minutes. So it is curious that animal bones are lacking from the general areas of these sites. Perhaps they were 'takeaways', or else used for baths or even to do the laundry!

Tools and technology

The 'Three Ages' model of the past is possibly most misleading when the early 'Bronze Age' is examined. In reality the introduction of metal did not revolutionize society and the majority of tools continued to be made of stone in the traditional manner. For a thousand years and more most 'Bronze Age' people lived and died without owning a single piece of metal. At first this precious commodity was reserved for the status symbols of an elite and there was none to spare to make tools and weapons for the common man. Only in the later second and early first millennia BC did the 'Bronze Age' really live up to its name. Metal was then more readily available and could be used for a wider variety of objects, including such mundane items as hammers, sickles, saws and chisels.

The first metal to be exploited by man was copper. In some regions this occurs as the pure metal, known as 'native copper', but more usually it is only to be found chemically combined with other elements as an ore. To take a natural product – the ore – and then extract an entirely different substance – the metal – was a radical innovation in human technology. With the sole exception of pottery man had previously only used materials in their natural states. Where ores outcrop on the surface they are easily detectable as green or purple minerals in the surrounding rock. But these surface deposits would have rapidly become exhausted, forcing prospectors to sink mines to follow the veins underground.

On the slopes of Mount Gabriel (Co. Cork) is a group of 25 shallow shafts belonging to a prehistoric copper mine that could be dated by C^{14} to *c*.1500 BC. Each shaft has a small entrance, about 1m ($3\frac{1}{4}$ft) high, from which a narrow passage slopes down to a small chamber, 5m ($16\frac{1}{2}$ft) wide and 1.6m (5ft) or less high. The ore had been extracted by the simple, but effective, means of lighting fires against the rock face, then dousing the red hot stone with cold water. As it suddenly cooled the rock would fracture and could then be easily hammered apart into convenient lumps, using the large pebbles that littered the floors of the shafts. The ore was then sorted from waste rock outside the shaft.

Once extracted ores must be heated with charcoal to at least 700°C (1292°F) to obtain copper. Carbon in the charcoal then chemically reacts with the minerals to release the free metal. As this is much heavier it sinks below the slag and can be easily separated. No elaborate equipment is needed for this process, good results can be obtained with no more than a small pit lined with charcoal and a pair of bellows.

Pure copper can be beaten when cold into simple objects, but in the process it becomes too brittle to be really useful. This is a problem that can be overcome by heating the metal above its melting point, 1083°C (1982°F), then pouring the molten metal into moulds of the required shape. Yet pure copper is not so easy to cast because air bubbles tend to form in the molten metal that spoil the finished casting. Alloying copper with tin or arsenic to form bronze removes this difficulty and also has the advantage of producing a much harder end product with a sharper cutting edge. It is hardly surprising, therefore, that bronze quickly replaced copper. Fortunately pebbles of heavy tin could be extracted by panning river gravels in Cornwall and other mineral rich areas.

Many Bronze Age moulds, both of stone and terracotta, have been discovered which were used to cast copper or bronze; the earliest consist of a single piece of stone carved with the negative image of the finished product. As a result all the early castings have one flat surface on the side that was left exposed to the air. Smiths later learnt how to make two-piece moulds, leaving small air holes to allow gases, that would otherwise form bubbles in the metal, to escape. Clay cores might also be inserted into these moulds to produce socketed tools. More elaborate, decorative castings were made by the lost-wax process. This involves making a model of the finished object in wax, which is then covered in clay. On heating the wax escapes, leaving a hollow terracotta mould into which metal can then be poured.

With a little practice any Palaeolithic hunter or Neolithic farmer could have made all the tools he needed from materials that were readily available. But with the discovery of metal, the technology involved in the manufacture of tools became more complex, requiring a degree of knowledge and experience increasingly beyond the ability of everyman to master. The inevitable result was the rise of specialists. At first they would mainly have worked for the elite, but as bronze became commoner in the late second millennium most settlements may have had their own smiths working on a part-time basis in between tending their fields. Most ordinary objects would have been well within the capability of these village craftsmen, but more technically advanced artefacts were probably the work of itinerant master craftsmen supported by aristocratic patronage.

Trading places

Metal users are dependent on scarce raw materials, for the ores of copper and tin have a limited distribution. This meant that those living in areas unendowed with ores had a new impetus to engage in trade. Even when broken, bronze tools remain valuable, and many collections of scrap metal, collected for melting down by some travelling tinker, have been found buried for future recovery near some prominent local landmark (48). Other hoards consist of high-quality finished objects, the stock of some merchant or possibly a personal store of wealth. Apart from metals, the growing differentiation of society also seems to have generated a small-scale trade in other high-status luxury goods, such as amber and jet.

Dazzled by the gold found in some round barrows in the Wessex region, archaeologists once thought that the chieftains of this region dominated the prehistoric trade routes, acting as middle-men in a metal trade that stretched

48 Any old bronze? Part of a hoard of tools and scrap metal from King's Weston (Avon). (*Photo: courtesy of the Archaeology Department, City of Bristol Museum and Art Gallery.*)

from Ireland to Greece. As a result of this trade the merchants and craftsmen of Mycenaean Greece were thought to have exerted a powerful civilizing influence on our barbarous ancestors. Certain objects, such as gold mounted discs and necklaces of amber, which can be matched with others found in Greece, seemed to provide evidence for these wider contacts. There were also small numbers of beads made from blue-green faience, a type of primitive glass developed by the ancient Egyptians and widely used throughout the Aegean and the Middle East. Chemical analysis and typological studies of this material have reached different conclusions. Some experts think that they are indigenous, others that they are exports from Central Europe. In either case their importance has been greatly exaggerated. At the most, they can only represent a few, isolated contacts that could not have greatly changed British cultures.

Even discounting the wilder fancies of an earlier generation of archaeologists, the manner in which the fashions of metal objects, and the technologies used to make them, evolved shows that Britain was often closely in touch with developments across the Channel. Chemical analysis has also been able to pinpoint the place of origin of some artefacts to Irish and Central European sources of ores. Recently, the wrecks of two ocean-going trading ships have been discovered off the south coast of England at Dover and Salcombe in Devon. The 95 artefacts recovered from the Dover wreck included European types of daggers, rapiers and axes that were in use in *c*.1100 BC. Not much is known about the structure of these wrecks but at North Ferriby (Humberside) the remains of three boats, dated to *c*.1500–750 bc, have come to light. All had a flat keel plank, formed from two overlapping pieces of wood, rather than a true keel, and were at least 12m (40ft) long. No metal was used in their construction, instead the planks that made up their sides were sewn together with yew saplings threaded through holes bored in the wood and the seams were then caulked with moss. Scholars are divided on whether the North Ferriby boats were sea-going or merely intended for river traffic.

A recent rescue excavation on the site of the bridge that takes the M25 across the Thames at Runnymede discovered that part of the river bank had been strengthened with vertical oak posts backed with a brushwood ramp, forming a simple wharf. Quantities of metalworking debris were found associated with these remains, both by the river bank and at the other site examined 400m (1600ft) inland. Although only a small area could be uncovered, Runnymede may well have been an important manufacturing and distribution centre during the eighth and ninth centuries BC that drew on the Thames Valley as its hinterland and engaged in cross-Channel trade.

Defence of the realm

Until recently, Bronze Age cultures, unlike their Iron Age successors, were not thought to have constructed defences. New discoveries, however, have shown that there never was a 'Golden Age' of peace and prosperity when humans were innocent and conflict unknown. Thousands of years before the introduction of iron, societies felt the need to defend themselves. It is now clear that well before 1000 BC a variety of defences had evolved to meet this need and late in the second millennium social unrest may have been rising as the climate deteriorated, putting pressure on the available farmland.

Excavations on the sites of some typical Iron Age hillforts in southern England have shown that their active life began late in the second millennium BC. On the Berkshire Downs at Ram's Hill, for example, three late Bronze Age phases, dating from *c.*1100 bc onwards, were discovered beneath the later hillfort. The earliest defences consisted of a flat-bottomed ditch and a low rubble bank. By themselves these would not have been a substantial deterrent and they were later strengthened with a double palisade. Within the 1ha ($2\frac{1}{2}$ acre) enclosure the excavators found only a few pits, post-holes and round huts, not enough to suggest that a large permanent settlement existed. Indeed, the remains have been interpreted as a cattle corral, the defences intended both to stop animals from straying and to make rustling more difficult.

Away from the hillforts there is another group of defended enclosures. At Springfield Lyons (Essex), for example, a ditch 1.5m (4.9ft) deep and a bank crowned with a palisade surrounded an enclosure 65m (213ft) in diameter that contained three buildings. At Flag Fen the well-preserved Bronze Age structure stood surrounded by a palisade on an artificial island in a shallow lake.

6 MEN OF IRON

Archaeologists all agree that by the Iron Age the British Isles were largely inhabited by Celtic peoples. But just when and where they arrived and whether this settlement took the form of a mass migration or merely a political takeover by a small elite, remains a matter of controversy. Traditionally Celts are identified with the makers of metalwork decorated in the Halstatt and La Tène styles that were widely distributed in Britain and on the Continent from the sixth century BC onwards. But in reality the only certain way to identify a Celt is from his speech.

Celtic languages form a branch of the Indo-European family, which includes almost all the European, Iranian and north Indian tongues. Two subdivisions of this branch are recognized, 'P' Celtic and 'Q' Celtic. The difference is that 'Q' Celtic languages have retained the original 'q' sound of the common ancestral tongue, which 'P' Celtic has transformed into 'p'. Modern Welsh and Breton are 'P' Celtic, Irish and Scots Gaelic are 'Q' Celtic, as can be seen from the following examples:

Irish	mac	ceathair	ceunn	cluv
Welsh	map	pedwar	pen	pluv
English	son	four	head	feather

Unfortunately as Iron Age cultures were orally based we will never be able to do more than speculate as to when Celtic languages were first introduced into the British Isles.

Life on the land

Earlier generations of archaeologists thought of the Iron Age as a radical break with the past, associated with the mass migrations of the first Celts. But in reality everyday life continued much as before. Iron using communities simply developed from indigenous late Bronze Age societies under the influence of new traditions introduced from the continent of Europe. The settlement pattern was little altered, though there seems to have been a rise in population for settlements are found closer together than ever, a mere kilometre apart in some regions. A typical farmstead consisted of three or four round-houses, together with their associated outbuildings, all enclosed within a bank, palisade and ditch.

For town dwellers of the late twentieth century AD it is difficult to imagine what the lifestyle of these self-sufficient farmers may have been like. Even excavation can only reveal the outlines of their fields, the bones of their animals, the carbonized remains of their crops and the post-holes of their settlements. But recently the work of Dr Peter Reynolds at the Little Butser Experimental

Farm has allowed a greater insight into the lives of our ancestors. One of his first projects was to reconstruct an Iron Age 'ideal home' based on excavated evidence uncovered at Maiden Castle (Dorset). This evidence consisted of an area of crushed chalk 6m (19½ft) in diameter, over which fragments of daub were scattered, surrounded by a ring of shallow post-holes, with a single post-hole in the floor's centre. As the post-holes were close together Reynolds reasoned that they had supported stakes around which withies were woven to make a kind of giant basket which was then given a liberal plastering of daub – a mixture of clay, straw, animal hair and chalk. He found that a thatched roof could be easily raised over these walls on a conical timber framework which did not even need the additional support of a central post. The result was a relatively comfortable house, strong enough to withstand gale-force winds and with the minimum of maintenence well able to stand up to the fickle British weather.

Little Butser has also provided many insights into prehistoric farming. One interesting investigation was carried out on the use of the pits that are such common features of any excavated Iron Age site. The experiments proved that grain could have been stored in the ground for years without deterioration. Once the pit is sealed the level of carbon dioxide gas, produced as grain respires, builds up to such an extent that it inhibits germination and decay, forcing the grain to become dormant. Spoilage of the contents will then only occur if there is such heavy rainfall that water seeps into the pit. On average a pit could have held enough grain to support a family of six for a year. But, as Reynolds has pointed out, not all pits were necessarily used for cereal storage. Others could just as easily have been used to make silage, prepare flax, store clay or hold water.

Another common feature of sites of this period are groups of four post-holes that are commonly interpreted as granaries. In many traditional societies, granaries are raised above the ground on stilts so that the air can circulate under their floors. This prevents grain from becoming damp while at the same time keeping out rodents. But this is only one solution to the problem of what these groups of post-holes were used for; other suggestions include byres, barns, workshops and chicken houses.

Iron Age farmers used a form of the ard, rather than the true plough, which can turn the sod in addition to scoring a furrow. Formerly it was thought that this simpler kind of plough would only have been effective on thin limestone soils. But experiments at Little Butser have shown that a wooden share fitted with an iron shoe could be almost as effective on the heavy clay soils as a true plough. The crops they grew were better adapted to the cold, wet climate of Britain than those previously grown. From the late Bronze Age onwards emmer wheat was replaced by a new strain of winter wheat called spelt, and naked barley by hardier hulled barley. Modern farmers have found that these cereals contain twice the protein of most contemporary strains and are able to give much higher yields than previously thought.

As the climate continued to deteriorate, becoming colder and wetter, pastoralism assumed a greater importance over arable farming, especially in the highland zone. 'Ranch boundaries', long linear earthworks, were laid out over the landscape to mark out grazing territories. Associated with them are rectangular ditched enclosures and the circular 'banjo' enclosures which may have been used as corrals to manage stock. Enclosed pastures were also laid out, surrounded with low banks and attached to hillforts, where the animals were brought in to bear their young or to take shelter at night.

Iron Age cattle were of the short-horn type, the modern representatives of which are tough animals able to graze on rough pasture and survive the rigours of winter. Analysis of bone samples shows that, apart from young bulls surplus to breeding requirements, most animals were old or diseased when killed which implies that they were primarily kept as a source of milk. It is also quite likely that cattle were the main way that the wealth of an individual and tribe was reckoned. The bones of sheep belong to a type similar to the modern Soay strain and have a similar age and sex profile to those of cattle. Most sheep were therefore killed long after their meat would have been past its best, implying that the animals were kept for wool; a view that is confirmed by the large numbers of spindlewhorls and loomweights discovered in settlements. Horse bones, however, illustrate a completely different pattern. Few, if any young animals, are present, only adult males. One suggestion is that they may have formed semi-wild herds like those on Dartmoor. Chickens were introduced into Britain late in the first millennium BC.

Hearth and home

At Glastonbury (Somerset) waterlogging has preserved much of the rich and varied organic material that has vanished from most other sites. The result is a unique glimpse of life in a small community, some 100 strong, on the eve of the Roman Conquest. The village was laid out by the lakeside on an artificial platform between 0.3 and 1.2m (1 and 4ft) thick and measuring 122 by 91m (400 by 298ft). It was made up of layers of brushwood, tree trunks, logs, rushes, bracken and peat all mixed together with clay and stone rubble. A palisade, made up of two or three lines of stakes bound together with coarse wattle-work, almost completely surrounded the village. Only a single gap entrance was left where the two causeways approached the village.

Within the palisade the positions of houses were marked by 80 low mounds, 4.5–12m (14.75–39ft) in diameter and 15–60cm (6–23in) high, formed as new floors of clay and timber were periodically laid over the old subsiding foundations; not all were contemporary. The majority of the huts had hearths of baked clay in the centre of their floors. Some had wooden floorboards. Around the perimeter of the floor, posts were driven vertically into the clay 15–38cm (6–15in) apart, wattles were then woven around them and plastered with daub. Charred beams and reeds, the remains of house fires, demonstrated that the roofs had been thatched, over a timber framework. Not all of these huts were intended for domestic occupation, some served as workshops and stores. Indeed Dr David Clarke thought that he could recognize a basic module, consisting of a pair of large houses associated with masculine pursuits facing a smaller round-house across a courtyard that had been used by women. One of these modules at the centre of the settlement was larger than the others and was flanked by two relatively small and poor modules. These he suggested were the residences of the village chief and his immediate dependants.

The people probably farmed the higher ground adjacent to the marshes that surrounded their village. From the carbonized remains of their food we know that they grew two-row and six-row barley, wheat and a small variety of bean. A curious type of unbaked cake was also found that had been made from whole, unground grain kneaded together with a sticky substance, probably honey. Bones of domesticated cattle, sheep, pigs, chickens and horses were common. Little game was hunted but wildfowl were taken with sling-shots in the marshes, and lead net weights show that the surrounding waters were fished.

The villagers practised numerous crafts. In their huts were primitive furnaces for casting bronze and smelting iron, crucibles and nozzles from bellows. All their tools were made from iron, but bronze was used for jewellery, needles and other small or ornamental objects. Smaller amounts of tin, lead and possibly glass were also worked. Large numbers of spindlewhorls and loomweights demonstrate the importance of weaving. Bone and antler were carved into numerous objects such as needles, dice, cheekpieces and bridle bits. Iron tools from the site included many intended for woodworking, such as billhooks, saws, gouges, chisels, adzes and files. The wooden objects from the site, such as stave buckets, lathe-turned bowls and wheels, show that these tools were used with a high degree of skill. The fine pottery, decorated with curvilinear designs, typical of the site, was made at centres on the nearby Mendip Hills. Evidence for wider exchange networks was provided by the Kimmeridge shale from Dorset that was carved on site into armlets, and a small amount of amber originating on the east coast.

The mortal remains of the people themselves were rather more elusive. Nine intact infant burials were found under floors or between huts, but no adults. Near the entrance of the settlement a group of skulls was discovered that may be linked to the documented Celtic veneration of the head. One skull was that of a young woman that had clearly been cut from her corpse then mounted on a stake. Isolated human bones were also found scattered all over the settlement, which caused the excavator to suggest that the life of the settlement had ended in a massacre. But it is more likely that it indicates that the villagers exposed their dead.

Technology and tools

The excavation of Iron Age sites of all types has revealed the importance of many and varied crafts, among the most important were pottery, metalwork and weaving. Some were carried out on a purely domestic scale, geared to the needs of the household alone. Others were the livelihood of specialized craftsmen who catered to the small, but lucrative, trade in luxuries.

In reality the 'metal' age only began with the exploitation of iron, for it has two great advantages over copper and bronze. Firstly, the necessary ores are far more widely distributed, which meant that tools made from the new metal were cheaper; and secondly, iron tools are more efficient. Iron can be extracted from its commonest ore, the oxide, by heating the crushed mineral with charcoal to 800–1000°C (1472–1832°F). This produces a black, spongy material, known as bloom, which is a mixture of metal and slag. But in contrast to

49 Weaving, an Iron Age cottage industry. Yarn was spun using a spindle, then woven into cloth on an upright loom. Finds of spindlewhorls and loomweights are common on sites of the period.

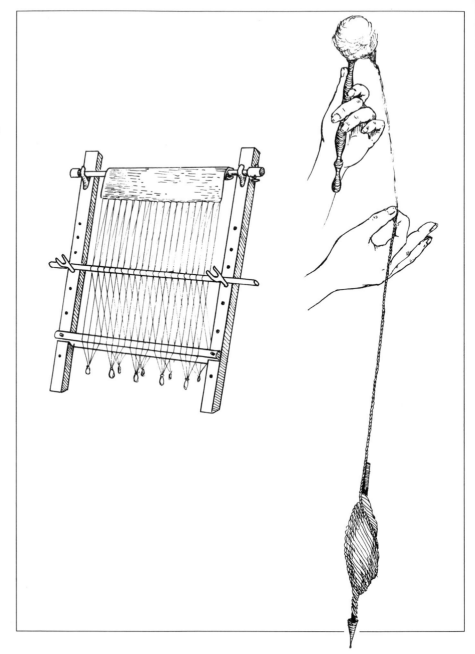

copper and tin, iron has a high melting point that was beyond the capabilities of prehistoric smiths to achieve. As a consequence iron tools could not be made by casting from the molten metal. Only by forging, hammering the hot bloom to drive off the slag, could an iron tool be shaped. The quantities of slag and other ironworking debris are such common finds on settlement sites that production must have been organized on a domestic scale.

Bronze was relegated to decorative metalwork such as cauldrons, bowls, scabbards, horse harness and fibulae (safety-pin brooches). Many of these artefacts, however, are richly decorated in the 'Celtic' style of art, otherwise known as La Tène, that was introduced into Britain in the fourth century BC. They were clearly luxury goods created for consumption by a wealthy aristocracy by skilled specialist craftsmen.

Although only a small amount of Iron Age cloth has survived the number of spindlewhorls and loomweights found during the excavation of sites seems to imply that every community spun their own yarn and wove homespun clothes (49). The techniques used were probably similar to those used by some peasant communities in Europe today. To make yarn a mass of raw wool is placed on a distaff, its fibres are then teased out of the bundle, twisted and passed through the central hole of a spindlewhorl – a simple aid whose weight adds the necessary tension as the threads are spun and twisted together. The spun yarn is then used to weave cloth on a vertical loom. This consists of two upright posts that support a horizontal beam from which the vertical warp threads hang down. These are kept taut by tying loomweights to their ends and a shed rod is used to separate odd and even warp threads. A heddle rod is then used to move the odd numbered warp threads back and forth to allow the horizontal weft threads to be passed through them. Periodically weaving 'combs' or 'swords' are used to compress the weft threads to give a tighter weave.

Trading places

The many centres of craft production must have been linked to form local and regional networks of exchange. International links during the period were also intensified as gradually Britain was drawn into contact with the economies of the more advanced Mediterranean world, although tangible evidence for this trade, in the form of artefacts, is rare until the first century BC. The most important Iron Age industrial and trading site yet known was excavated by Professor Barry Cunliffe at Hengistbury Head, near Bournemouth. Finds showed that during the first century BC the site was involved in a variety of local craft industries. Ornaments were made from Kimmeridge shale, iron was forged, copper (which analysis showed to have originated in Cornwall) refined and alloyed with tin to make bronze.

As a trading centre Hengistbury Head had the advantage of a natural harbour and access to its hinterland via the rivers Stour and Avon. British coins and pottery showed that this trade was mostly with the south-west rather than the tribes of the south-east. The site also seems to have served as an entrepôt for international trade, where foreign luxuries were imported and distributed, since a small, but significant, proportion of the sherds recovered belonged to Breton and Norman wares; and 25 coins minted by tribes of these regions were also discovered. Gaulish traders may also have acted as middlemen for Mediterranean produce, as more of the distinctive sherds belonging to amphorae have been found at Hengistbury than at any other site of the period. These elegant all-purpose packing jars of the Classical world were used to transport such commodities as wine, nuts, raisins and fish sauce.

Foreign trade appears to have been disrupted at Hengistbury in the mid-first century BC and never re-established, although the craft industries and domestic

50 An example of the earliest British coinage. (The horse is the survivor of the four horse chariot on the reverse of the Greek coin that originally inspired Celtic issues.) *(Photo: courtesy of the Archaeology Department, City of Bristol Museum and Art Gallery.)*

trade continued unhindered. Cunliffe has suggested that this was due to the Roman conquest of Gaul which resulted in the destruction of the Breton fleets. Finds of 'Gallo-Belgic' wares, made under Roman influence in Gaul, and the glossy red Arretine ware and glass vessels from northern Italy on settlement and burial sites, show that when the luxury import trade was resumed it was reorientated towards the south-east of England.

Prehistoric trade was limited by its reliance on barter, although Caesar records that iron ingots, possibly to be identified with the 'currency bars' discovered by archaeologists, were used as a medium of exchange. During the first century BC the idea of coinage was introduced into Britain from the Celtic tribes of north-west France (50). These coins were only issued by the tribes of southern and eastern England; outside this area coinage remained unknown until after the Roman Conquest. At first only gold pieces were minted, the value of which would have been far too high for most everyday transactions. Instead they may have been used for tribute, dowries, to pay mercenaries and for luxury imports. From the early first century AD lower value denominations of silver and bronze were also minted, which may represent the first stirrings of a monetary economy.

Defence of the realm

The Iron Age landscape was essentially a defended landscape, dominated by hillforts. A rising population coupled with a deteriorating climate, soil erosion, nutrient depletion and bog formation put increased pressure on what arable land remained. In response societies organized themselves to keep possession of their lands. Early archaeologists tended to concentrate on the defences of hillforts at the expense of their interiors. Recent excavations, most notably those of Professor Barry Cunliffe at Danebury (Hampshire), have helped redress the

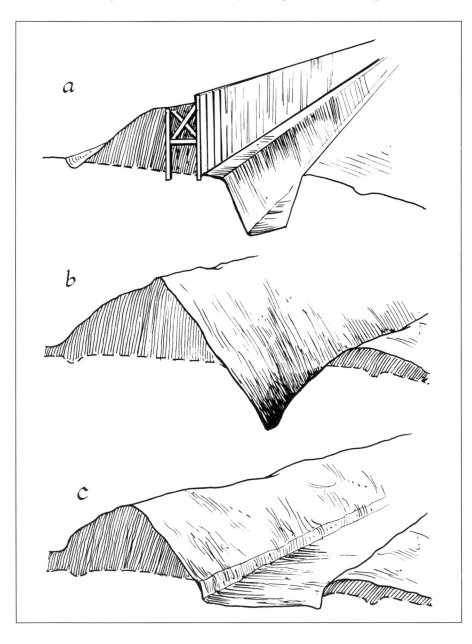

51 Excavation of hillfort ramparts demonstrates how they were rebuilt to take advantage of new developments in military technology. The three commonest types are, in chronological order: *a* a timber-framed box rampart; *b* the glacis, with a continuous slope from the ditch to the crest of the bank; *c* the Fécamp rampart, featuring a broad, rectangular ditch in front of the bank.

balance and shown that quite apart from their defensive functions some hillforts in southern England served Iron Age communities in many other capacities. As centres for administration, trade, craft, industry and religion many came to fulfil much the same role in the lives of the people as would later be assumed by the towns of Roman Britain.

At Danebury the earliest defences, laid out in the mid-sixth century BC, consisted of a single rampart interrupted in two places by gates and fronted by a V-shaped ditch. This rampart consisted of two rows of upright timber posts joined together by planks to form a wooden box, which was filled with earth and rubble dug from the ditch (51). During the early phases of occupation Professor Cunliffe found that most of the site, to the north of the track joining the two gates, seemed to have been used for communal storage of grain, at first in four-post granaries, later in pits. After they had been emptied many grain pits received offerings of pottery, iron tools, carbonized grain and animal bones. Some pits contained human remains, either complete articulated skeletons or more fragmentary remains that had been buried after much of the flesh had decayed. As no marks of violence could be detected on the bones, Cunliffe suggested that they had been deposited as part of a funerary ritual involving excarnation. To the south of the track typical round-houses were interspersed with more pits and granaries. These, he thought, were separate households, each with their own individual stores. Other houses were to be found in the shelter of the ramparts (52). Metalworking and weaving were important craft industries for the people of Danebury. They also traded for salt and the Kimmeridge shale that was used to make bracelets.

In the early fourth century BC the defences were remodelled into a glacis, a high bank of earth and rubble, which may have been crowned with a rough drystone wall. The new rampart had two main advantages over the old. Firstly,

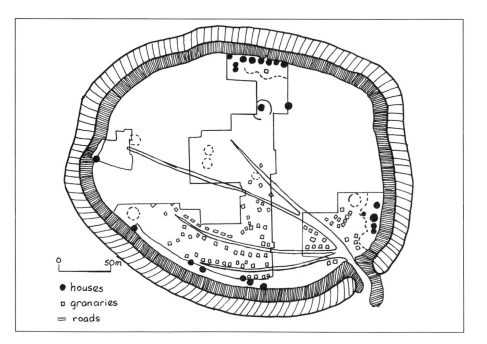

52 Plan of the hillfort interior at Danebury (Hampshire; 135) *c.*550 BC, based on recent excavations. (*After Cunliffe.*)

0   50m

● houses
□ granaries
= roads

as the slope was continuous from the bottom of the ditch to the crest of the bank the defenders would have been at a greater height than the attackers. Secondly, it overcame the problem of built in obsolescence which all timber-framed ramparts suffered from as their timbers rotted and had to be replaced. In the second or first century BC two further earthworks were added to Danebury outside the main enclosure. As neither was substantial enough to have fulfilled a defensive role they probably marked out enclosures for animals. Late in the first century BC the main V-shaped ditch was also redug to form a broad, flat bottom. Similar alterations took place at many other hillforts in southern England and northern France. Some archaeologists have speculated that this innovation was first developed across the Channel in response to the ease with which Roman legionaries stormed conventional hillforts.

At the same time as the defences were remodelled the interior was also replanned. Four- and six-post granaries were laid out in rows across the south of the site. Houses were built in the quarry ditches along the ramparts, especially on the north and east. Storage pits are found scattered over the site in clumps. During the later phase of occupation the land in the centre of the fort, which would have appeared to be on the horizon as seen from the east gate, was levelled to provide a firm foundation for four rectangular buildings that may have been shrines.

In spite of their often impressive defences (53), hillforts are more likely to have been designed for temporary refuge than to withstand a lengthy siege. Lack of water, for example, would have been a major problem as most contain no wells or springs within their ramparts. Contemporary accounts of Celtic warfare imply that it was more likely to take the form of raids for cattle and other booty than all-out wars of conquest. If a fort could not be taken by surprise the raiders probably contented themselves with pillaging the surrounding countryside, rather than settling down for a long siege. Yet at some sites there is definite evidence for enemy action.

The most vulnerable points of any hillfort were its gates. Two entrances pierced the earthworks of Danebury, one to the east and the other to the south-west. From simple openings set in an entrance passage, the defences of the gates became increasingly elaborate. In its final form, the eastern gate at Danebury was surrounded with flanking earthworks that would have enabled the defenders to control every approach route. Despite all these precautions Danebury came to a violent end around 100 BC. Excavations showed that the east gate was burnt down and in a nearby pit the remains of 21 mutilated corpses were found, they had been roughly thrown in without any grave goods and left to rot before the pit gradually silted up. The settlement within the ramparts was abandoned – tools were found still on the floors of some of the houses. After the sack, Danebury never sheltered more than a single farmstead.

Over much of Britain, hillforts remained in use up to and beyond the Roman Conquest. But in the south-east many were abandoned at about the same time as Danebury and replaced by systems of earthworks that archaeologists call *oppida* (sing. *oppidum*). These consist of linear banks and ditches that enclose large areas of land, possibly intended to restrict the mobility of cattle rustlers (54). Formerly they were considered to have been introduced by an invasion of the Belgae, a tribe from north-west France, in the first century BC, but they

could simply represent a natural development from the indigenous system of ranch boundaries. Although the term *oppidum* was used by Classical writers to refer to large, semi-urban communities, the area within these British enclosures was not heavily built up. Instead, there are commonly several small dispersed focuses of settlement. Some *oppida* replaced the abandoned hillforts as centres for trade, industry and ritual as shown by the large quantities of imported pottery and glass from northern Italy and Gaul that have been excavated at certain sites; others were the homes of tribal mints.

Religion and ritual

Archaeology can do no more than uncover the bare bones of Iron Age religion, although Classical writers allow them to be fleshed out a little. The pagan Celts, we are told, built no grand temples but worshipped their gods at sacred groves, springs and rivers. Indeed many of the finest examples of metalwork of the late Bronze Age and Iron Age have been recovered from a watery context or in pits, shafts and wells. One of the most spectacular of all these finds was made at Llyn Cerrig Bach on Anglesey (Gwynedd), during peat extraction at what had once been a small lake. Among the many votive offerings recovered were the bones of pigs, oxen, sheep, goats, horses and dogs, pottery and fine metalwork. The latter included items of horse harness, chariot trappings, swords, spears, ceremonial horns, cauldrons and slave chains that on stylistic grounds could be dated to between the second century BC and the first century AD. But the site had been too disturbed for archaeologists to tell if the collection had accumulated gradually or had been thrown in together in a single act.

53 Maiden Castle (Dorset; 296), tribal centre of the Durotriges, which assumed its present impressive form, after successive phases of enlargement, in the first century BC. In AD 43 the Romans under the future Emperor Vespasian, stormed through the east gate, where archaeologists discovered the possible casualties in mass graves, after which the site was deserted in favour of a new town founded on the site of modern Dorchester. *(Photo: RCHME)*

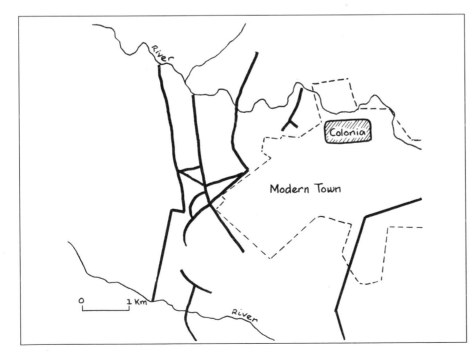

54 The *oppidum* at Colchester (Essex; 121), one of the main tribal centres of the Catuvellaunii from the later first century BC up to the Roman Conquest. It is typical of the linear earthworks, containing dispersed settlement, that replaced hillforts over much of south-east England. *(After Hawkes.)*

Only a few temples have been discovered to set against the veneration paid
to natural features. Simple square, rectangular or round buildings interpreted as
shrines have been found during excavations of hillforts at Maiden Castle (Dorset),
Cadbury (Somerset) and Danebury. Others are found associated with villages or
are sited in their own sacred enclosures. One of the most interesting once stood
next to a small village in the fourth century BC, now the site of Heathrow Airport
(55). It took the form of a small rectangular building surrounded by a colonnade that seems to anticipate the later Celtic temples of Roman Britain.

Archaeologists have also been unable to throw much light on the antics of
the Druids. What little is known has mostly been culled from Classical sources.
Caesar, for example, observed that Druids were highly influential in Gaulish
society, wielding considerable political and social influence in addition to their
religious functions. These included the practice of divination by observing the
flight of birds and the entrails of sacrifices. If the question posed was very
important a man might even be stabbed in the back, and the convulsions of
his death agony and the way his blood spilled on the ground were carefully
watched for omens. Criminals were also used for human sacrifice, placed in a
giant wicker man, together with all different kinds of animals, the whole then
set alight. But we are told very little about what the Druids actually believed
in, their gods are simply dismissed as barbarous versions of the familiar figures
of the Classical pantheon.

In 1984 evidence for what may have been one of the more gruesome Druidic
rites was discovered at the Lindow Moss (Cheshire) where peat-cutting exposed
a human body with multiple injuries. The unfortunate Lindow Man (56) had
been struck on the head with a blunt instrument, then garrotted and finally
had his throat slit before his naked corpse was thrown into a bog. It is likely
that he was the victim of a sacrificial rite or a judicial execution rather than a
frenzied prehistoric psychopath. Tacitus, writing about northern Germanic tribes
in the first century AD, records that human sacrifices were placed in bogs, not
only for religious reasons but also as a punishment for adultery and cowardice.
Radiocarbon tests on the body and the peat in which it lay gave no clear

results and at first the general consensus favoured a date in the fourth century BC, but recently new evidence has suggested that the body may have been deposited as late as the first century AD.

Relatively few Iron Age burials have been discovered to set against the potential population of the large number of hillforts and settlements. In their lighter moments archaeologists have been known to remark that whereas Bronze Age people died but did not live, Iron Age people lived but did not die! Most of the population may have been exposed or cremated and the ashes scattered over the fields and rivers without leaving a trace. High-status individuals initially continued to be treated as in the late Bronze Age – they were cremated and their ashes buried, occasionally as secondary interments in existing barrows.

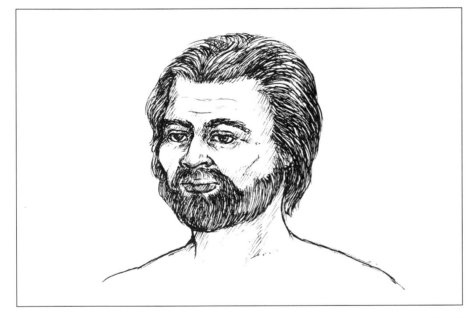

56 The face of the past, the features of Lindow Man reconstructed using the latest forensic techniques.

Later, inhumation gained in popularity, the body being laid out in a foetal position under a low mound, cairn or in a stone cist. A few of these graves contained rich grave goods: weapons for the men and jewellery for the women.

Two groups of burials are particularly interesting as revealing cultural influences from continental Europe. On Humberside large cemeteries have been discovered containing up to two hundred low circular mounds surrounded by rectangular ditches. Beneath these mounds the dead were accompanied by the dismantled remains of carts, together with the harness-fittings of horses and a joint of meat (57). As these graves closely resemble others across the Channel in the Seine-Marne region of France they are widely thought to be those of an alien aristocracy who invaded Britain in the fourth century BC.

In the south-east of England another group of cemeteries contained cremations in urns that had been turned on the potter's wheel. These cemeteries contained a few burial enclosures surrounded by a rectangular ditch. Each contained a central grave equipped with rich offerings of metalwork and pottery, including Gaulish imports. Surrounding the primary burial were subsidiary cremations with few or no grave goods. The grave goods allowed these burials

57 A chariot burial excavated at the cemetery of Garton Slack in Humberside (the scale measures 2m). One of hundreds made under small circular barrows within square ditched enclosures that show similarities with cemeteries in the Seine-Marne region of France. (*Photo: courtesy of Bill Marsden, copyright J.M. Dent.*)

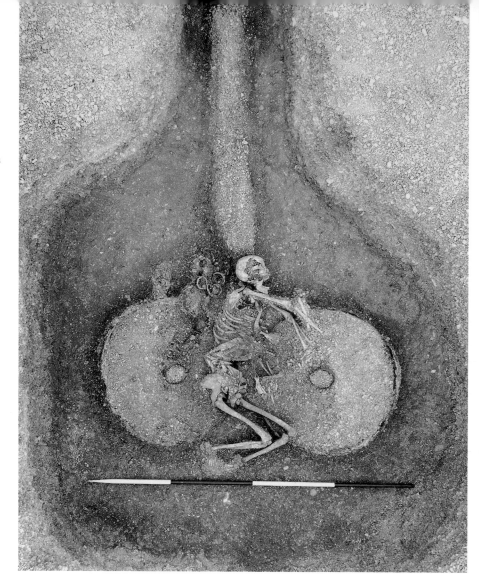

to be dated to between 50 BC and AD 50. They are similar to others in northern France, which has led to the identification of the people who were buried in them with the Belgae, a tribe from the areas of modern Belgium and north-west France, that Caesar mentions had settled in England.

7 THE ROMANS IN BRITAIN

Prehistoric Britain slowly evolved at its own pace, occasionally assimilating ideas, and the people that brought them, from across the Channel. Then in AD 43 the Romans invaded and set about forcibly converting the Celtic kingdoms into a province of their multinational state. The tangible remains of the Conquest have occasionally been encountered during the excavation of hillforts. The plan seems to have been first to soften the forts up with a bombardment of iron catapult bolts, before the gates were fired and stormed. After the battle was over the defences were slighted to make sure that they could never be manned again. Walls were tumbled down, banks pushed into ditches, timbers of revetments pulled up and gates fired, before the survivors were allowed to bury their dead; though sometimes forts were built inside the old defences.

All of lowland England was quickly occupied and after the initial gains had been consolidated the frontier zone was established along the line of the Fosse Way, the road that the legionaries built from Exeter to Lincoln. The province was then gradually extended to the west and north. Finally Agricola, governor AD 78–86, set about taking the Conquest to its logical conclusion by occupying Scotland. But although he easily defeated the northern tribesmen, a change of priorities by the central government led to his recall and the abandonment of much of the land he had won for Rome. His successors then had to make the arbitrary decision as to where to draw the line of the northern frontier.

At first this frontier was fixed at the shortest point, the Forth–Clyde line. South of this notional line the Scottish Lowlands were garrisoned by a series of forts. During the reign of the Emperor Trajan, AD 98–117, these forts were in turn abandoned and a further withdrawal took place, to the Tyne–Solway line. The new frontier was then marked with yet another episode of fort construction and refurbishment. Finally, shortly after the visit of the Emperor Hadrian to Britain in AD 122, the famous wall was constructed from Newcastle to Bowness-on-the-Solway, a distance of 80 Roman miles (73 modern miles or 117km).

Hadrian's Wall (58) was not designed as a fighting platform, nor as a second-century equivalent of the late unlamented Berlin Wall. Instead it controlled access to the province by restricting the mobility of the tribes, while leaving the Romans every opportunity to strike across. It was c.6.7m (22ft) high and the earlier parts of the wall were 3m (10ft) thick but this was later reduced to 2.25m (7ft). Part of the wall was erected firstly in turf, but this had been replaced by stone by c.AD 136. In front of the wall, except for the stretch above the steep crags, was a ditch 8.2m (27ft) wide and 2.7m (9ft) deep.

Attached to the wall at intervals of a Roman mile were the milecastles, small forts designed to hold thirty men. Between each pair of milecastles were two turrets, home to between eight and twelve men. Every 4 or 5 Roman miles there was a larger fort (59) in which up to a thousand men were based. These

58 The original
North-West Frontier, a
reconstruction of
Hadrian's Wall (206),
showing a milecastle in
the foreground and a
turret in the
background.

were built on a regular grid plan, initially in turf and timber, later in stone
once it became clear that they were to be permanent. At the heart of each fort
was the headquarters building (*principia*), the Commanding Officer's house
(*praetorium*), granaries and administrative buildings. Most of the interior, however, was filled up with L-shaped barrack blocks, each intended to hold
80 men. Immediately to the south of the wall was a broad, flat-bottomed ditch,
with a low bank on either side, known as the *vallum*. This may have been
intended to mark the boundary of a restricted military or customs zone, chan-
nelling all traffic across the frontier through the forts where it could be more
easily controlled and monitored.

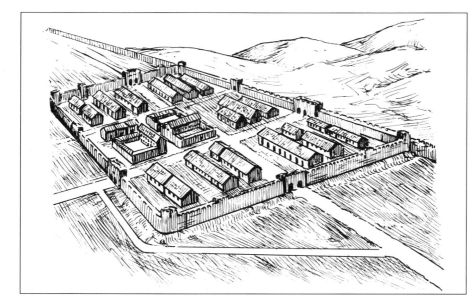

59 A fort on Hadrian's Wall. The garrison commander and his staff were based in the larger, central buildings, his men in the long barracks blocks. (See, for instance, 45; 93; 110; 124; 223; 401 and 443.)

Not long after the death of Hadrian, in AD 138, his system of frontier defences was largely abandoned and the frontier was shifted once more to the old Forth–Clyde line. The motive for the move is unclear, but there are hints that it may have been provoked by unrest amongst the northern tribes. The new frontier was marked by the Antonine Wall, named after the next emperor, Antoninus Pius. It ran for 40 Roman miles ($36\frac{1}{2}$ modern miles or 58.5km), from Bridgness on the Forth to Old Kilpatrick on the Clyde. Unlike Hadrian's Wall it was built of turf, on a stone foundation. Otherwise the defensive arrangements were similar to those of the older frontier line, with a ditch, milecastles, auxiliary forts, beacon platforms and a military road. In the mid-second century the Antonine Wall was in turn abandoned. From that time onwards only a few outposts continued to be garrisoned in the Scottish Lowlands, and the frontier was shifted back to Hadrian's Wall where it remained until the end of the Roman occupation of Britain.

The troops that garrisoned Roman Britain formed a professional volunteer standing army some 50,000 strong (60). They were divided into legions and auxiliary units. The legions were the elite troops, made up of Roman citizens; after the Conquest they were located well away from the main trouble spots, at Caerleon (Gwent), York and Chester. The more expendable auxiliaries who garrisoned the frontier forts were recruited from non-citizens, many of whom fought under their own officers and with the weapons of their ancestors. Units from Spain, Belgium and even Croatia are recorded as serving in Britain. Auxiliaries recruited in the province of Britain itself tended to be posted overseas as a matter of policy. Apart from its military duties the army was a major force in the Romanization process. For in peacetime it was a source of skilled men and muscle that could be called upon to advise on or execute public works beyond the competence of most civilians. On a more basic level the men formed a substantial market for food, manufactured goods and services. All this, of course, had to be paid for out of taxes.

City slickers

When the Romans took stock of their latest acquisition they found that they had conquered a land without that essential ingredient of Mediterranean civilization, the town. Once the fighting was over it was among their first priorities to found the towns through which the new province would be administered (61). On the site of the *oppidum* of the Catuvellauni, modern Colchester, a legionary base was converted into a Roman colony (a self-governing city inhabited by Roman citizens) and settled with veterans a mere five years after the invasion. As symbols of the new order towns were singled out for attack during the Boudican Revolt of AD 60, an event which left a thick destruction layer of carbonized material regularly encountered by archaeologists digging at Colchester, St Albans and London.

As the area under direct Roman control spread outwards and the military frontier advanced north, the garrisons of lowland England were withdrawn and a measure of self-government was handed back to the former indigenous ruling class who were encouraged to found towns, known as *civitas* capitals, to administer their homelands. Other towns grew up spontaneously in response to market forces, outside the gates of forts, around strategic road junctions and river crossings, or near to the sources of raw materials. By the end of the first century urban life had become well established in the wealthier south and east of the province. These towns fulfilled similar roles to their modern successors that often occupy the same sites – namely, as centres of administration, trade, manufacture, entertainment and religion.

Officially sponsored towns were laid out, often with help from army engineers, on a regular grid pattern in the best Roman style. Grand public buildings

60 *(Opposite)* The mark of conquest, earthworks of a Roman auxiliary fort hastily thrown up inside the ramparts of a hillfort at Hod Hill, (Dorset; 219), shortly after it had been stormed by the legions in AD 43. *(Photo: RCHME.)*

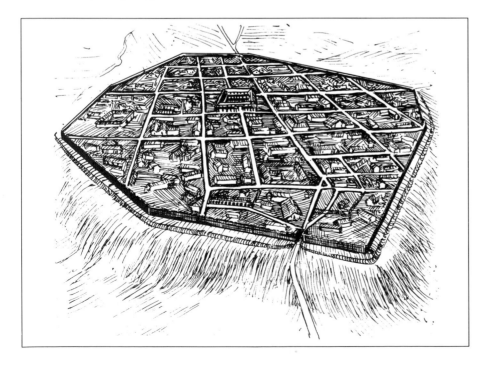

61 A reconstruction of *Calleva*, modern Silchester (Hampshire; 394) a new town founded to serve the Atrebates tribe. At the heart of the town is the forum, the main market place, and the basilica that served as the seat of local government.

occupied the town centre. Chief among them was the *forum*, a wide open space, that served as a marketplace surrounded on three sides by colonnades which housed shops. The fourth side of a forum was occupied by a *basilica*, the Roman version of a town hall. Here, the council offices were located, the councillors held their meetings and the elected magistrates held courts. The local worthies who occupied these offices were also encouraged to pay for such necessities of civilized life as public baths, theatres, amphitheatres, and on a more mundane note aqueducts, sewers and public latrines. Less important settlements lacked such embellishments and tended to have rather haphazard streets that owed more to serendipity than to deliberate planning.

The houses that filled the town blocks were a mixture of the well-appointed residences of the rich, the simpler, but still comfortable, homes of the middle classes and the shacks of the urban poor. Some, especially in the fourth century, occupied entire blocks and were built like miniature villas, complete with fine wall paintings, mosaics, under-floor central heating and bath suites. Others occupied narrow strip-like plots reminiscent of the houses later occupied by medieval merchants and craftsmen, with a shop opening on to the street and behind it a yard in which crafts were practised. Both types were constructed of wattle and daub over a timber framework erected on stone foundations.

The roads that led to Rome

Towns were not the only item missing from the infrastructure of the new province. Proper roads were needed to connect up the new forts and towns in place of the old tracks – roads that made travel easier than at any other time

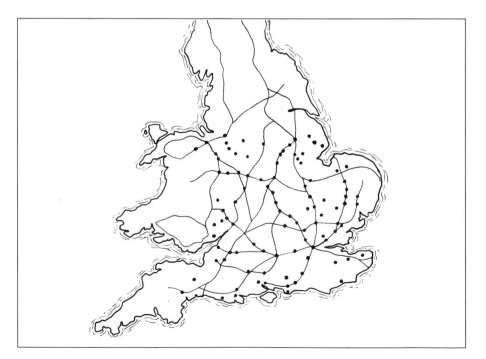

62 The distribution of towns and roads in Roman Britain.

of the island's history before the modern era. Post-houses, known as *mutationes*, were located every 16–24km (10–15 miles) along the arterial roads to provide a change of mounts for travellers on official business. Overnight accommodation was available at the *mansiones*, rest-houses that were to be found at intervals of 32–48km (20–30 miles). Their maintenance was a heavy burden on the local population, although occasionally they acted as the nuclei around which towns formed (62).

The first roads were primarily constructed for military reasons. Along them supplies and reinforcements could be quickly moved to wherever they were needed. Only later were roads commissioned by the civil authorities or land-owners, in order to connect them to the provincial network. Most of the materials needed to build the roads were simply extracted on the spot from the ditches that flanked either side of the roads. They were made up from layers of rammed gravel, which had to be constantly renewed due to wear and tear, laid on a firm stone foundation. To improve drainage many were raised on an embankment. Where rivers had to be crossed, paved fords, timber or stone bridges were provided.

Life on the land

Prehistoric farmers had been part of a subsistence economy which gave little incentive to produce more food than their families could consume. But after the Roman Conquest a true market economy began to operate in the country, which generated a demand for agricultural surpluses that had never existed in Iron Age Britain. The administrators, craftsmen and traders of the towns all had to be fed and the government imposed taxes in coin and kind to support the army and administration.

In any pre-industrial society town-dwellers are very much in the minority, usually accounting for no more than 10 per cent of the total population. The vast majority of the British continued to live in the countryside with their traditional lifestyles hardly disturbed. Excavations have shown that their settlements were little different from those of the Iron Age, especially in the less Romanized highland zone. Often the only tangible evidence of the influence of the new masters is the presence of pottery and ornaments produced by the new mass industries, together with coins. On a larger scale, the traditional round-houses were replaced by rectangular one- and two-room buildings with stone wall foundations. Similarly, storage pits were superseded by more substantial granaries and barns (63). Generally, settlements were varied in type; while most remained little more than farmsteads or hamlets there were also a few larger villages.

Farmers are, of course, notoriously conservative and continued to work the land much as their ancestors had done. But at some sites there is evidence for the use of the true plough – that could turn the sod in addition to simply scoring a furrow – in place of the ard. This would have made the cultivation of heavier clay soils much easier. Improved strains and new vegetables, fruits and herbs were introduced that appealed to Roman palates. Serious attempts were also made to establish vineyards, although not without stiff opposition

63 Romanization down on the farm. The foundations of the stone barn belonging to the villa at Lullingstone (Kent; 289). *(Photo: RCHME)*

from the traditional wine-growing areas of the Empire fearful of the competition. Most farmers, however, would have continued to grow the same staple cereal crops; though they might at the same time take advantage of Roman technology to prevent their corn from germinating during storage by drying the grain in stone or brick ovens. Yet for most farmers the major stimulus to change remained the development of the market economy, rather than the introduction of new crops and technologies.

Stimulated by peace, stable government, a new economic structure and technology that allowed more land to be brought into cultivation, there seems to have been a population explosion. Recent studies, combining the results of field surveys and aerial photography, have shown that Roman Britain was far more intensively farmed and densely occupied than was previously thought possible. In the Nene Valley (Northamptonshire) for example, the mere 36 settlements recorded by 1931 had been raised to 434 by 1972. This is an average of one settlement to every 2.5 sq. km (1 sq. mile), although not all may have been occupied at once. Current estimates of the total population of the province place it at least as high as 2 million, possibly double that.

64 The distribution of villas in Roman Britain, note how they are concentrated in the fertile lowlands close to the major towns and arterial roads. (See also 62.)

Overall, little may have changed for the peasant farmers under Roman rule, but their landlords quickly adopted a more Romanized lifestyle. They built villas for themselves in which they could enjoy all the amenities of civilized life, such as central heating, baths and fine interior decoration. Surrounding the mansion house were the barns, byres, stables, workshops and all the other varied buildings expected on a working farm. One thing seems to have been missing, quarters for the large numbers of agricultural labourers who would have been required to work the land. Possibly they resided in hamlets on the villa estates.

All this magnificence was probably paid for from the profits gained by sending agricultural surpluses to the new towns. A glance at the distribution map of known villa sites shows that they were concentrated on the rich farmlands of the lowland south and east of England (64). Particularly dense concentrations can be seen around important towns, such as Cirencester and Bath; this has in turn led to the suggestion that, like eighteenth-century gentlemen, anyone who prospered in Roman Britain aspired to a country estate. On the poorer, and less Romanized, lands of the north and west villas are extremely rare.

Some villas are much more impressive, in both size and the quality of their decoration and workmanship, than others. In Italy it is known that villas ranged from working farms, run by slaves under a bailiff, to the luxurious villas which were the country retreats of the rich. Something similar may have been true of Roman Britain. To draw once more on the eighteenth-century analogy, the luxurious villa may represent the mansion of the landowner, the less well-equipped the working farms of his tenants. In this respect it is interesting to note that the great age of the villa in Britain was the first half of the fourth century – a time when contemporary writers describe a situation in which wealth and power were being concentrated in fewer and fewer hands as the rich enlarged their estates at the expense of the peasants.

Trade and industry

With the Roman Conquest, Britain was brought into the first 'European Economic Community'; a union that might be envied by many a modern enthusiast. Throughout the Empire there was one official language, one currency, one set of laws, one central government. Under the *Pax Romana* trade both within and between provinces flourished. In Britain the new towns provided a ready market for the produce of the countryside. Romanized lifestyles and a rising standard of living created a demand for luxury goods.

Trade was made much easier by the existence of a common coinage in gold, silver and bronze. By the second century the numbers of coins found on some urban sites demonstrate that a simple monetary economy had developed over much of the province; not only for high value transactions made in gold and silver but also for the more everyday purchases involving bronze. Indeed during times when the central government was unable to provide sufficient small change, the British took matters into their own hands and minted enough bronze coins to keep the economy running.

Many imports were perishables and have left few traces behind in the archaeological record. The main exception is pottery. Amphorae, the all-purpose containers of antiquity, were shipped across the Channel in some numbers holding wine, fish sauce and other Mediterranean foodstuffs for the homesick legionary or civil servant. Fine wares destined for the tables of the middle classes were imported in vast quantities before the native industry could be organized. Chief among these wares was the ubiquitous glossy red samian ware, mass produced in Gaulish factories. Exports can be equally hard to track down; for Britain was then in the position of an undeveloped 'Third World' country, exporting raw materials and importing finished goods. Isotope analysis of plumbing at Pompeii reveals that British lead was being used in Italy well before the famous eruption of AD 79. However, the fledgling industries of the new province were, on the whole, never to be a threat to the established market leaders on the continent of Europe.

In the wake of the Conquest new technologies and methods of production were introduced. Alongside the simple domestic production of the individual master craftsman inherited from the Iron Age, larger labour forces were created and organized into workshops in which goods were mass produced. Roman industry, however, was not as labour intensive as that of the present day, and had no use for large workforces residing in industrialized towns. In fact, although a wide range of craft activities took place in the towns, factories tended to be located in the countryside.

At the most basic level the extractive industries were well organized. Iron, copper, lead and gold were all mined on a commercial scale and many quarries were opened up to supply the new demand for building stone. All mineral reserves belonged to the Emperor and were administered on his behalf by the provincial government. As the only source of the necessary know-how, many of the mines were first worked by the army, presumably with the use of captives as slave labour. Later, mineral rights were leased out to individual entrepreneurs and syndicates.

Immigrant craftsmen, possibly attached to the legions, introduced the potter's wheel, permanent kilns and the techniques of mass production into the British pottery industry, although the coarse kitchen wares produced by the new technology continued to be made in Iron Age shapes. Most of the smaller centres, with just a few kilns, only supplied their immediate catchment area, for it was not economic to transport these cheap and bulky goods far. These potteries may have been worked by farmers, during the off-periods in the agricultural year, to supplement their income. Other centres clearly belonged to highly-organized professionals, making tiles and bricks for the building trade, bulk containers for the army or quality tablewares. By the third century the latter had succeeded in capturing most of the domestic market from the formerly imported market leaders.

Religion and ritual

The Romans showed tolerance towards all faiths – so long as they did not threaten the political and social values they held dear. After the Conquest Britons, unless they were Druids, were free to worship their gods in any way they saw fit. But the ancient priestly order was quickly supressed; for in

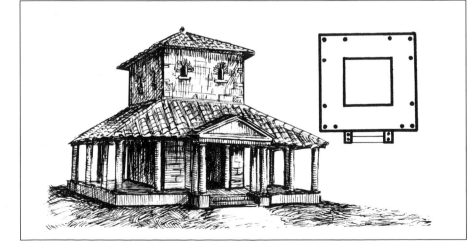

65 Reconstruction of a Romano-British temple based on excavated foundations. Pagan temples were not intended for congregational worship, therefore they did not have to be large, only the cult image and votive offerings had to be accommodated.

addition to their notoriously barbarous practices, they wielded far too much influence over the population at large. Otherwise the worship of the old Celtic gods continued quite unhindered.

Although many of native gods were identified with Roman deities, even assuming some of their functions and attributes, they were mostly not worshipped in grand Classical stone temples but in far humbler quarters. A typical shrine consisted of a small square central room, the *cella*, to house the deity's cult statue, surrounded by an ambulatory. Similar temples are also to be found across the Channel in the Celtic areas of northern France and the Rhineland (65).

Pagan temples were not intended for congregational worship, but as the homes of their divinities. Services, including sacrifices, were designed for the sustenance of the deity, although individual worshippers were free to make votive offerings in the hope that the god or goddess would grant a request, to fulfil a vow or in an act of thanksgiving. Coins were popular gifts, but others included personal ornaments and small idols; some offerings may even have been specially made by workshops attached to the temple. The canny worshipper, however, left nothing to chance and to avoid misunderstandings had his or her petition scratched on to lead plaques and deposited where the deity could read them. Most such petitions seem to be concerned with recovering stolen property.

The official divinities of the Roman State, including the genius of the ruling emperor, were worshipped by administrators and the army as a matter of patriotic duty, but they made little impact on the hearts and minds of the man in the street. Roman customs, however, had far more influence on burial rites. Cemeteries, in line with imperial law, were laid out outside the town limits along the roadside. Initially cremation was the dominant practice, the ashes being placed in a glass or pottery urn, together with a few coins, a lamp or a small pot as grave goods. Inscribed gravestones were often used to mark the graves of the middle classes. In time, for no discernible reasons, inhumation grew in popularity until it completely replaced cremation. The corpse was laid out fully clothed and shrouded in a wood, lead or stone coffin.

Exotic eastern mystery cults promised what the cold, impersonal state religion could not. Many of these cults were introduced by soldiers, foreign traders or craftsmen into the cosmopolitan towns. At first Christianity would have seemed little more than another of these popular cults – except for the fact that adherents refused to take an oath of loyalty and sacrifice to the emperor. In the eyes of officialdom Christians were thus a potentially dangerous and subversive secret society which had to be rooted out. Until, that is, in AD 313 when the unthinkable happened – the Emperor Constantine converted and made Christianity the state religion.

Despite official recognition there was no mass conversion, the worship of the pagan gods and goddesses was not even formally banned until late in the fourth century. The new religion had its strongholds in the towns. Several large late Roman extramural cemeteries, such as that recently excavated at Poundbury (Dorset), consisting of thousands of east–west orientated inhumation burials, without grave goods, may be those of flourishing Christian communities. But out in the countryside new temples were built, and old ones refurbished, long after the Empire had become nominally Christian. In fact the destruction and abandonment seen at many pagan shrines during the latter part of the fourth century is probably to be attributed more to the general recession rather than to the vigour of Christians.

Personal possessions marked with the chi-rho (the monogram composed of the first two letters of Christ's name written in Greek) or Christian inscriptions have been found scattered throughout the province, mostly on town and villa sites. Actual church buildings, however, have proved more elusive. Many communities of the faithful must have worshipped in private houses or, after AD 313, in converted pagan temples and public buildings. At Lullingstone (Kent) four rooms belonging to a villa were remodelled in the mid-fourth century to form a self-contained suite that may have functioned as a house church. The main room was decorated with frescoes featuring the chi-rho and figures with their arms outstretched in the position used by early Christians to pray. Near the villa at Icklington (Suffolk) a small fourth-century building orientated east–west may have been a purpose-built church since it had a detached baptistery equipped with a pewter tank inscribed with the chi-rho, as well as a cemetery.

Bangs and whimpers

During the early fourth century, *Britannia* had never been more prosperous. As the economy boomed, conspicuous consumption was the order of the day as landowners competed to build luxurious villas and town houses. Central government retained every confidence in the future. When, in the latter part of the third century, the rich lands of the south and east of England came under increasing threat from raiders from across the North Sea the response was a

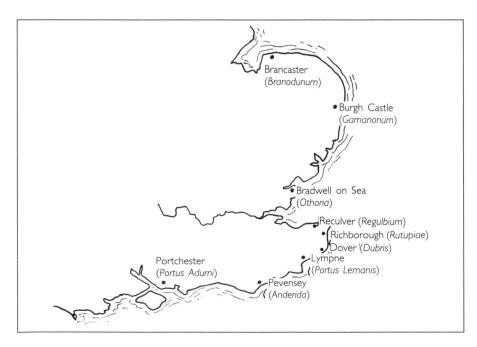

66 Forts of the Saxon Shore, the front line of defence against the highly mobile Germanic invaders of the fourth century.

vigorous campaign of defensive works, the Forts of the Saxon Shore (66). These substantial installations were surrounded by thick stone walls up to 9m (30ft) high, complete with towers strong enough to support the catapults that were the ancient equivalent of heavy artillery. Similar walls replaced the existing earthwork defences of towns at about the same time (67). As part of the reorientation of defences, the old legionary forts at Caerleon, Chester and York seem to have been largely abandoned, their troops moved out to more vulnerable regions. On the north-west frontier there was a complete reorganization of fort interiors and the old barracks were replaced by 'chalet'-style buildings that may have been family quarters. Both the walls and the forts continued to be maintained, but garrison sizes seem to have fallen.

Guarded by such defences it is hardly surprising that there is little evidence that Britain was destroyed by mindless hordes of rampaging barbarians. These

67 A sign of the times, the fourth-century town walls of *Venta Silurum*, modern Caerwent (Gwent; 81). *(Photo: courtesy of the Welsh tourist Board.)*

forts and walled towns would have been relatively easy to defend against any casual raiding party and it is unlikely that the barbarians had the experience, discipline or even the numbers to mount a successful siege; in any case they aimed to take a share in the good life of the Empire, not to destroy it out of hand. Imperial policy sought to exploit this fact in order to solve a manpower crisis, by recruiting mercenaries from beyond the frontiers. The problem may have been acute, for the later Roman army in Britain is estimated to have been no more than 12,000, down to a fifth of its former strength. Not only individual men and small units but entire tribes were resettled in vulnerable areas to take care of their defence in return for land and self-determination. A case of poachers turned gamekeepers.

Despite all these efforts to contain the barbarian problem, by the last quarter of the fourth century there is every indication that Roman Britain was a society in the process of disintegration. Most industries stopped production. The supply of coinage dried up and forts were abandoned by their defenders, or turned into farming communities, when their pay failed to arrive. In towns the grand public buildings that epitomized civilized living were not replaced as they were accidently destroyed, allowed to become dilapidated or given over to more utilitarian uses (68). Rather than the urban population swelling due to the unsettled conditions prevailing in the countryside it appears to have sharply fallen. More and more of the private houses were abandoned and the number of burials made in the extramural cemeteries declined rapidly. Within the circuits of still-impressive walls much of the land was probably derelict.

At a few sites there is admittedly good evidence for continued occupation well into the fifth century. Philip Barker, for example, discovered that at Wroxeter (Shropshire), after the *basilica* had been demolished its site was covered with a bed of gravel that was used as the foundation for a series of timber buildings. To his surprise he found that these were not the expected squatters' shacks but comparatively sophisticated structures. Some used such typical features of Classical architecture as porticoes and colonnades, translated into timber. Another structure bore a close resemblance to a Germanic hall. Such discoveries, however, seem to be the exception rather than the rule. They are possibly indicative, not of true urban continuity, but of the establishment of high-status complexes within otherwise deserted towns.

Out in the countryside recession also seems to have struck the landlords at the close of the fourth century. No more luxurious villas were built and the existing examples were not maintained in the style to which their owners had become accustomed. Richly decorated rooms were put to more mundane uses, with furnaces and corn dryers inserted through mosaic floors. Finally the villas were abandoned, allowed to fall down or demolished. Once it was suggested that their wealthy owners had retired to the safety of the walled towns, leaving a bailiff in charge and the formal reception rooms redundant. Given the contemporary decline in the towns this now seems unlikely. A simpler explanation would be that as the economy declined and towns shrank, the market for agricultural produce dried up. Whatever the truth of the matter there is no evidence that the land itself was deserted. Only villas, and all they had once stood for, had become redundant.

As evidence from recent excavations has mounted, archaeologists have

68 Urban decay:
columns from the
legionary headquarters
building excavated
under York Minster
that was patched up
and used by the Saxons
until the ninth
century. *(Photo:
RCHME)*

recognized that the end of Roman Britain came not with a bang, but with a whimper. The Empire simply exhausted itself in the face of barbarian invasions, military coups d'état and economic recession. Finally in AD 410 the Roman central government told the British that they were on their own. In reality there was no grand apocalyptic orgy of destruction, merely a slow decline until all attempts to keep up appearances were abandoned. The way of life enjoyed by the privileged minority in towns and villas simply passed away and everyone reverted to a lifestyle that had much in common with that of their Iron Age ancestors.

8 ANGLO-SAXON ATTITUDES

Germanic settlers began to arrive in substantial numbers from the mid-fifth century. They probably crossed the North Sea in ships similar to the one discovered in the royal ship burial at Sutton Hoo (Suffolk). This was a large open rowing boat 27m (89ft) long, 4.3m (14ft) wide at its greatest width and some 3m (10ft) deep. It was clinker built, constructed from nine rows of overlapping oak planks rivetted together and secured with 26 ribs. Despite the lack of a mast it was a sturdy vessel more than capable of braving the open seas for the short crossing.

Britain was not invaded by a single people under one ruler but by bands led by Germanic chieftains drawn from many different tribes, principally the Saxons, Angles and Jutes. What all these people had in common, apart from sharing a similar cultural tradition, was that they came from lands outside of the former Empire and had therefore not been so exposed to Romanization. Some may, as tradition records, have been invited by the Britons to help with their defence, others were freelance adventurers in search of new opportunities. By the sixth century the early settlements had coalesced basically into seven main kingdoms: Kent, Wessex, Surrey, Essex, Northumbria, East Anglia and Mercia. There was as yet no concept of common nationhood – at the most one of the local kings might become powerful enough to force the others to acknowledge his overlordship.

For generations archaeologists and historians let their imaginations run riot when they came to describe the arrival of the Saxons. Like a plague of locusts they were thought to have descended upon a defenceless land pillaging, burning and killing all that stood in their path. Any Britons who survived were ruthlessly enslaved, or, if they were very lucky, were able to flee to the western highlands. Their barbarous vanquishers then settled down on an almost unpopulated land to enjoy the fruits of victory. But as evidence from recent excavations and fieldwork has mounted, a very different picture has begun to emerge. This is one in which the transition from post-Roman Britain to Saxon England involved a considerable degree of continuity rather than a complete break with the past.

Another widely believed myth was that as the majority of village place-names in England derive from Germanic, not Celtic roots, the Saxons had settled a sparsely populated and heavily wooded land. Like American Pioneers they were supposed to have cleared the dense forest and established the nuclei of modern villages. Yet recent research has also shown that Roman Britain was so intensively farmed and densely populated that there was little virgin land left uncultivated. Neither would a few tens of thousands of immigrants have had the capability systematically to massacre and enslave millions of natives. Only in east of the land that would become England, where most of the early Germanic cemeteries and settlement sites have been found, may the transition have involved a genuine folk movement. Elsewhere there seems to have been no more than a 'hostile' takeover by a small ruling group. One set of masters may have been forcibly substituted for another, but everyday life went on much as before, only under new management. For the Saxons came not to destroy, but to share in the good life.

Life on the land

The Saxons has no option but to adapt themselves to the existing landscape. On the Continent Germanic tribesmen were frequently settled on Roman estates as 'guests' and given a share of the land; something similar may have occurred in Britain. In some regions the early Saxon settlement pattern even seems to have respected that of the original Roman land use. Elsewhere settlements were laid out without any reference to what had gone before. Often it was the marginal land that had been left unused, on the fringes of villa estates or villages, that was occupied by the Saxons. Villa estates may also have been taken over as viable concerns and continued to be run as a single unit. Some excavations have produced evidence that long after the Roman stone buildings were abandoned, a series of timber structures was erected that extended the life of a site well into the fifth and sixth centuries. Detailed studies of modern parish boundaries or the estate boundaries described in extant Saxon charters also seem to imply that existing estates remained intact.

Saxon settlement was mostly dispersed, taking the form of scattered hamlets and isolated farmsteads, rather than concentrated in nucleated villages. Surveys among the fields around modern villages, for example, often come across many small scatters of early Saxon sherds that mark the sites of these temporary settlements; for although the boundaries of the estates may have been fixed the settlements themselves tended to be short lived. They were regularly abandoned and rebuilt on a new site as houses decayed or the land needed to be left fallow. A process which some archaeologists rather irreverently refer to as the 'Saxon shuffle'.

Early Saxon settlements show little of the regular planning of later medieval villages and most are little more than a random cluster of huts. On the Continent, Germanic villages consisted of three main types of structures: aisled longhouses that were partitioned to provide accommodation for humans and beasts; the so-called 'sunken-featured buildings' (SFBs) erected over a pit; and settings of six to nine posts that are generally interpreted as raised granaries. In Britain, longhouses and granaries are absent but SFBs are common. There is also a new type, a hall with opposing doors in the middle of each of the long sides, which has no parallel across the North Sea and may owe something to British traditions. Settlements made up of SFBs and halls are commonest in eastern and southern England, the region which seems to have received the largest number of new settlers, but are rare in the Midlands, the North and the West Country.

At West Stow (Suffolk), the site of an early settlement has recently been excavated and some of the buildings reconstructed (69). In Roman times the surrounding area had been intensively farmed and there was a large villa that was occupied well into the fifth century. The Saxon settlement itself was established on marginal land on the fringes of the Roman settlement that occupied

69 Reconstruction of an early Saxon settlement in part based on the excavation at West Stow (Suffolk), showing typical SFBs. The large hall is a type found at other sites.

the best agricultural land. Pottery and metalwork suggest that the first houses were built *c.*400 and that occupation continued at the site until the late seventh century. Most of the 67 excavated structures were SFBs of various sizes and shapes. Not all were contemporary. Some were certainly designed for domestic occupation but the majority may have been outbuildings used for workshops, storerooms and animal houses. Hut 15, for example, was clearly a weaving shed for a hundred loomweights were found scattered on its floor. In addition to the SFBs there were also halls marked by shallow, evenly spaced post-holes. One typical example measured 8.2 by 4.3m (27 by 14ft), another was a little larger and more elaborate, featuring a partitioned off end and a central hearth. Some were rebuilt several times on the same site. Together with the SFBs they probably represent the living-quarters and associated outbuildings to support three or four extended families.

When first discovered SFBs were thought to be primitive 'pit-dwellings' in which our ancestors lived in unbelievable squalor. But none of the recently excavated floors of these pits actually show any signs of the stratified occupation deposits or of hearths that would be expected if they were living floors. Neither have any tell-tale traces of timber or wattlework retaining walls, necessary to prevent the collapse of the pits' sides, been discovered. From the evidence of charred timbers found clearly stratified beneath the other contents of some huts it is now thought that a wooden plank floor was placed above the pit. Such a raised floor would have had the practical advantage of rotting less quickly than if it were in contact with the ground.

In addition to farmsteads and hamlets many of the important administrative centres of early Saxon England were to be found in the countryside. 'Dark Age' kings were peripatetic, with no fixed capital or palace – they were constantly on the move from one royal estate to the next. Complexes of large, well-built halls, together with associated outbuildings of the right age and scale to have served as royal centres, have been discovered at Yeavering (Northumberland) and Cheddar (Somerset). Lower down the social scale the hall was also adapted for the residence of a lord. At Goltho (Lincolnshire), for example, a hall 24m (80ft) long and 6m (20ft) wide had a raised dais at its eastern end and a cobbled open hearth running down its centre. Together with its associated outbuildings this hall made up three sides of a courtyard surrounded by substantial defences (see Chapter 10 for details).

Defence of the realm

For such a supposedly bloodthirsty people the relative lack of Saxon defences comes as something of a surprise. Before the Viking raids the Saxons seem, for the most part, to have felt little need to construct defences. Where Roman walls continued to shelter some form of settlement they might be maintained. At a few new foundations, such as Tamworth (Staffordshire) or Hereford, clay ramparts and ditches were constructed in the eighth century. But the most characteristic of defences belonging to this period are to be found in the countryside, not around settlements. They take the form of long linear earthworks known as dykes. Much of the evidence for their date and purpose is ambiguous. Excavations uncover few finds, but weathered Roman sherds and other material show that they belong to the post-Roman 'Dark Ages'. Whether they were intended by the Britons as defence against the alien invaders, or by one of the Saxon states to guard against the aggression of its neighbours it is difficult to be certain. The best-known examples are found along the Welsh Marches, where the English kingdom of Mercia made uneasy contact with the Welsh principalities.

In the eighth century this defensive network culminated in Offa's Dyke (70), which marked out most of the frontier line from the Dee to the Bristol Channel,

70 Offa's Dyke (338), the great earthwork constructed to control the frontier between Mercia and the Welsh principalities in the eighth century.

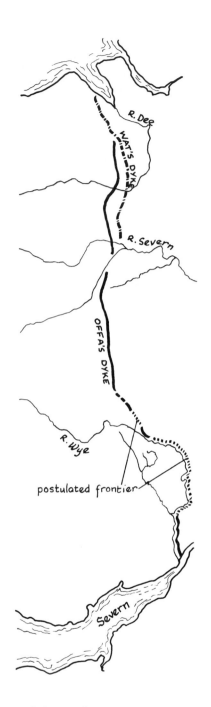

a distance of some 240km (149 miles). The Dyke consisted of a steep bank, faced with a ditch, that may have been crowned with a timber palisade or drystone wall in places. On average it measured 7.6m (25ft) from the bottom of the ditch to the crest of the bank. Unlike the Roman frontier works no forts were associated with the Dyke so it is impossible to tell how it might have been patrolled or garrisoned. What is clear is that it would have been a formidable barrier to any raiding party. No contemporary accounts of the building of the Dyke exist, but tradition is probably correct in attributing it to Offa, greatest of the Mercian kings, who ruled from 757 to 796. But whoever conceived of the Dyke, the degree of planning and organization involved is an impressive testimony to the power and administrative abilities of the Mercian state.

City slickers

Historians once thought that after towns had been sacked they were then shunned by the Germanic invaders. Recent excavations have shown that while some form of settlement often continued on their sites it is doubtful whether a fraction of either the size or urban functions of the old Roman towns was maintained. At most, administrative, and later ecclesiastical, centres may have existed within the walls. At Winchester (Hampshire), for example, the Roman walls were maintained in the early Saxon period but the area they enclosed was mostly open space, with a few scattered compounds belonging to the king, church and nobles.

Urban life began to revive in England during the eighth century when trading and manufacturing centres developed on virgin sites or in the largely deserted Roman towns. In 1985 archaeologists discovered the remains of one such settlement at York, 2km ($1\frac{1}{4}$ miles) downstream from the Roman walled city. This was no mere village but had covered an estimated area of 25ha (62 acres). In the excavated portion eight large timber halls were discovered and two gravel-surfaced streets. The small finds suggest that the inhabitants were craftsman and merchants. Waste from metalworking, bone carving and weaving imply production on a greater than domestic scale. Pottery, together with lava querns from the Rhineland, provided evidence for widespread trade links across the North Sea and there were many seventh- and eighth-century coins, balances and weights.

During the late ninth and tenth centuries Saxon towns came into their own. Administrative centres that had existed in shrunken Roman towns expanded and diversified their roles into true urban centres and new foundations grew up in which craft industries and trade flourished. In the tenth and eleventh centuries the urban population expanded to such an extent that suburbs grew up outside the city walls. By the Norman Conquest one hundred towns were in existence, more than in Roman Britain. Much of the stimulus towards urbanization was the pressing need for defence against Viking raids.

The early Saxon landscape was largely undefended and vulnerable to the mobile raider. The solution hit upon by Alfred the Great, King of Wessex (ruled 871–99), was to found a series of fortified towns, the burhs (71), right across his kingdom. As land was regained from the Vikings in the following reigns the burh system was extended and they are evidence of the considerable administrative control which must have been required to plan and impose the standard design throughout the state. As a whole the system was easily the most impressive set of public works carried out in England since the Romans. Yet burhs were not created to be forts only, they were rather intended as

71a Blueprint for a burh, one of the fortified towns planned by Alfred the Great and his immediate successors to defend against Viking raids which spearheaded the urban revival in Saxon England.

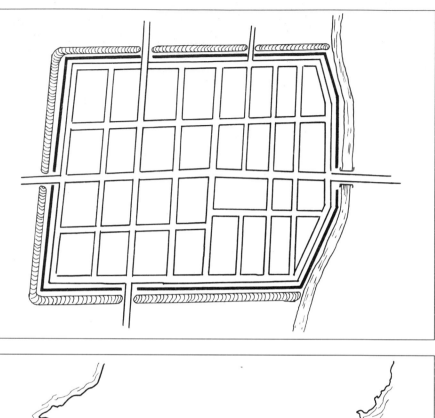

71b Distribution of burhs in southern England.

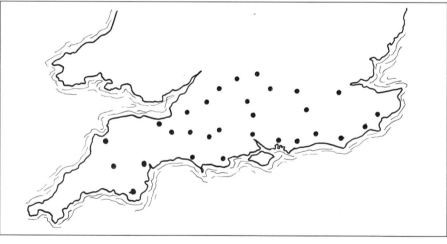

fortified towns with a permanent civilian population. Land was allocated to each site in proportion to the number of men needed for its defence. Settlers were probably attracted by such concessions as freedom of tenure, low rents and tax cuts. In addition to the regular inhabitants, when danger threatened villagers from the surrounding countryside, together with their animals, could find refuge behind the ramparts.

Burhs were all laid out according to a basic plan, featuring a rectangular grid of streets (71). Some foundations were made within the existing circuit of a Roman town wall; otherwise ramparts were made up of turf and earth dumped to form a bank, reinforced with timber and crowned with a palisade. On

average the ramparts were 12m (39ft) across and 3m (10ft) high. Gates were probably of timber. Outside the bank were usually two flat-bottomed ditches. Running around the perimeter of the rampart was a road which connected all the major streets to make the ramparts easily accessible from any part of the town. Few details are known about how land was used within the blocks of the street plan. At Winchester the excavations of Martin Biddle showed that the interior had been reorganized in a grid plan of gravel surfaced streets that bore little relationship to those of the Roman town. Along the street frontage one-room post-and-plank built houses were erected.

Trade and industry

In the Rhineland and Gaul the Germanic invaders found Roman pottery and glass factories still in operation and maintained them. But in Britain the technologies and production methods introduced by the Romans had largely been forgotten. Industry reverted once more to the level of craft production designed to meet domestic demands. Only the revival of urbanism in the eighth century stimulated trade and industry. At Winchester, for example, the recorded street

72 Urban renewal: an aerial view of the Saxon burh of Wareham (Dorset; 448). The original planner's grid still underlies the modern street-plan and the defensive earthworks are visible on the sides. (*Photo: courtesy of the University of Cambridge Committee on Aerial Photography.*)

names imply that by the eleventh century there was a considerable degree of craft specialization. Tanners, shield makers, butchers, goldsmiths and many other trades all seem to have practised their professions in their own distinctive areas of the city. Under the influence of new technologies reintroduced from Europe, local pottery industries also grew up at Ipswich, Stamford and Thetford (Suffolk, Lincolnshire and Norfolk respectively) which once more used the techniques of mass production involving the potter's wheel and well-designed kilns.

Large-scale trade, both on a domestic and an international level, had mostly disappeared by the fifth century. Contacts with Europe, however, were never entirely severed. Finds from early Saxon cemeteries demonstrate that a limited trade in luxuries was maintained with France, involving pottery, metalwork, glass, ivory and semi-precious stones. Frankish merchants also probably acted as middlemen dealing in exotic artefacts from the East, such as the Byzantine silver found in the Sutton Hoo burial.

What may be the remains of a Saxon merchant vessel were discovered near the site of a tidal creek at Graveney (Kent). As found it measured 10m (33ft) long (possibly 14m (46ft) long when complete), 3.4m (11ft) wide, and was clinker-built of oak planks, but with no mast. In the broad bottom of the craft which would have been ideal for stowing a cargo was a ballast of pebbles and Kentish ragstone. A few sherds from French wares of the tenth century were also discovered. Two C^{14} dates were obtained from the timbers: 1080 ± 40 years bp (*c.*AD 870) and 1064 ± 54 years bp (*c.* AD 886).

As trade expanded, coins were reintroduced into England. The first English coins were minted in the early sixth century. Initially they were struck in gold but when the supply of this precious metal was insufficient to meet demand England had to come off the gold standard and use silver. Mints existed at many sites, mostly in the south, including London, Rochester and Canterbury, as well as York, although it is likely that their products were mainly used by merchants and the nobility. It is unlikely that an ordinary Saxon, especially in the countryside, handled many coins.

Religion and ritual

Not much is known about the religion that the pagan English brought with them. Idols housed in temples and served by priests, holy trees, stones and springs are all mentioned by later Christian writers but without sufficient detail to allow the underlying belief system to be reconstructed. Archaeology has been able to do little but add to the details of funerary customs.

As pagans, the cemeteries of the Saxons (73) were once thought to have been entirely different from those of the Christianized Britons. Both cremation and inhumation were practised, sometimes in the same cemeteries, and a range of grave goods was provided depending on the age, sex and status of the deceased. Recent excavations have shown that the reality was less simple. At Wasperton (Warwickshire), for example, the cemetery was in use from the late Roman period right through to the eighth century. Earlier burials were inhumations, orientated north–south and placed within an enclosure, with

73 The distribution of pagan Saxon cemeteries. Note how most are to be found in the east where the impact of Germanic settlement was the greatest. (Compare this with the distribution map of Celtic river names, 80.)

such typically Roman features as wooden coffins nailed together, decapitated skeletons and hob-nailed boots. Later burials were generally made outside the existing enclosure, orientated south–north or east–west. They included both cremations in typical Saxon urns and inhumations, some of them provided with rich Saxon grave goods. But the most interesting of all the burials were the minority with hybrid characteristics, mixing a Saxon orientation with the typically Roman features. Instead of 'Saxons' supplanting 'Romano-Britons' it seems likely that the same people used the same cemetery over a period of centuries, merely choosing to bury their dead in different ways.

New technologies that enable scientists to examine traces of DNA (the material of inheritance that is found in all our cells) may soon allow these theories to be tested conclusively. Already such techniques have been used to try to show significant differences between the DNA of individuals buried with and without weapons in Saxon cemeteries in the Reading area.

The Celtic church that flourished in the West showed little inclination to convert the heathen, although it is possible that some form of Christian presence may have lingered within the area of Germanic settlement. In any case the serious work of evangelism was only begun when a mission was sent direct from Rome in 597 under St Augustine, and within a century England was once more a Christian land. Monasteries and churches were built and endowed throughout the Saxon kingdoms by royal and noble patrons. Many of the first churches were built of wood; only a single example, however, the tenth-century church of Greenstead (Surrey) survives. Originally it was 9m (29½ft) long by 5m (16½ft) wide. The walls were of split oak trunks, fastened by wooden pegs, set between a sill beam on the ground and a plate beam at roof level. Post-holes belonging to similar structures have been discovered during the excavations of

74 Saxon architectural features to look out for when exploring churches:
a long-and-short work;
b narrow, semicircular window of reused Roman tile,
c herring-bone masonry,
d decorative pilaster work.

75 All Saints, Brixworth (Northamptonshire; 64), the only large Saxon church to escape complete rebuilding under the Normans. The basic fabric is seventh-century, with later additions. Note the typical round-headed windows and reused Roman tile. *(Photo: RCHME.)*

many other churches. By the tenth century the church was wealthy enough, and the English masons sufficiently experienced, to rebuild in stone (74–5).

Monasticism flourished in the early Christian centuries, nowhere more so than in the sister houses of Monkwearmouth and Jarrow, in Tyne and Wear. Excavations to the south of the monastery church at Jarrow, founded in 681, by Dr Rosemary Cramp have uncovered the foundations of two substantial buildings. Both were constructed of fine dressed stone, plastered inside and out. The floors were of *opus signinum*, made from pebbles, concrete and pink brick dust in the Roman tradition. Limestone tiles, secured by iron nails, and lead sheets formed the roof. Scatters of glass indicated the former positions of two or three windows in Building 'A'; those in the south were of a plain blue-green glass, but the northern windows had a greater range of colours.

76 A reconstruction of the church and domestic buildings belonging to the early Saxon monastery at Jarrow (Tyne and Wear; 233), based on the excavations of R. Cramp.

As 'A' had an annex with two settings for vats in its floor the excavator suggested that it had served as the refectory of the community. Further to the south a series of artificial terraces sloped down to the river (76). The buildings that they had supported had left only slight traces, but fragments of glass and metalworking debris suggest that the monastery workshops were located here. Some were doubtless inspired by the Frankish masons, glassmakers and other craftsmen imported by an early abbot to teach the monks skills that had long been lost in England.

The fury of the Northmen

While England was enjoying the first flowering of Christian culture, in Scandinavia the climate was deteriorating, the population rising and royal power was curbing the autonomy of fiercely independent local chieftains. Factors that

77 The distribution of Norse place-names in England. Note how most are concentrated north and east of the dotted line which represents the frontier agreed between Alfred the Great and the Viking leaders following their defeat in AD 880.

were to contribute to the Viking onslaught that all but overwhelmed the Saxon kingdoms. The earliest raids were small-scale opportunistic attacks on exposed coastal sites. From bases in the Hebrides, the Isle of Man and Ireland hit-and-run attacks were made all over the coast of the British Isles during the spring and summer sailing season. Meeting little effective resistance the Vikings began to arrive in greater numbers intent on conquest.

One by one the English kingdoms were overwhelmed, until Wessex stood alone. Then, against all the odds, Alfred the Great, King of Wessex, defeated the Viking army and proved strong enough to impose a peace. According to the agreed treaty England was partitioned in AD 880 along the Roman road known as the Watling Street (77). All the land to the east and north of this line was ceded to the Vikings; a settlement that neither side intended to be final. In the following two centuries the English gained back all their lost ground and in the process achieved nationhood.

Evidence of Viking raids, to say nothing of the alleged atrocities, is difficult to find. Both the buildings recently excavated at Jarrow, for example, were covered with a thick destruction layer of charcoal. This is tempting to attribute to the documented Viking attack of AD 875, but there is no hard evidence that it was anything other than an accident. Mounts from reliquaries, book covers, caskets and other decorative metalwork of Irish and English manufacture are found in Viking graves in Norway and are presumably loot. The huge quantities of tenth-century Saxon coins that have been discovered in Scandinavia formed part of the danegeld, later extorted as protection money.

Settlers followed close on the heels of the raiders. Indeed they may have been one and the same. In any case during the ninth and tenth centuries large numbers of Danes settled in eastern and northern England. Norwegians preferred the coasts of north-west England, Man, Ireland and the Western Isles. This actually proved to be less of a disruption than might be thought. For the Danes were a people with a similar culture, lifestyle and language to the English. Only in adhering to the old Germanic gods were they substantially different. Once converted they readily assimilated into the melting pot of England. Even when their leader, King Cnut of Denmark, seized the English throne in 1014 they continued to respect English customs and made no effort forcibly to convert England into a Viking state.

From an archaeological viewpoint the Vikings are rather elusive. Relatively few of their settlements or graves have been discovered in England. But at Jarlshof in Shetland a typical Viking farmstead (78), similar to those in Norway, Iceland and the Faeroes, has been fully excavated and placed on display. At the centre of this farm was a longhouse, 21m (70ft) in length, constructed early in the ninth century from undressed stone and turf. An internal partition wall divided it into two main rooms, probably a living room and a kitchen, each

78 Reconstruction of a Viking farmstead at Jarlshof (Shetland; 232), showing the typical Norse longhouse commonly encountered in Norway, Iceland and the Faeroes and its associated outhouses. (*After Hamilton.*)

with a separate entrance. A long hearth ran down the centre of the kitchen; next to it was a cooking pit. The living room was also dominated by its hearth, on either side of which was a stone platform that had supported the bench beds. From the farmhouse a paved pathway lead to the outhouses. These probably served as a byre, barn, smithy, servants' quarters and a bath house.

Only one object suggestive of loot, a fragment of an Irish harness mount turned into a brooch, was found at the site. From the available evidence it seems these Vikings supported themselves by raising sheep, cattle and pigs, growing cereals, fishing and snaring wildfowl. It appears they prospered, for a second longhouse complex was added in the middle of the ninth century and a third towards its end, perhaps to accommodate the growing family.

In contrast to the lack of hard material evidence over much of the British Isles, place-name studies have revealed that numerous modern villages in the region of the former Danelaw bear Norse names. Any glance at the map will uncover many examples of the typical Scandinavian roots such as '-by', '-thorp' and '-thwaite'. It is interesting to observe that pure Norse names are commonest on poorer agricultural land, suggesting that the indigenous population was left largely undisturbed while new settlements were made on underutilized marginal land. The English, like the British before them, were not massacred on driven out, but continued to live on their land, even if forced to recognize a Viking overlord.

Recent excavations in York have shown that the Vikings could adapt themselves to being merchants and craftsmen just as easily as warriors and farmers and under Viking rule towns were not wantonly destroyed but developed into prosperous centres for trade and craft industries. Indeed in Ireland, where towns were lacking, the Vikings founded the first towns.

At Coppergate in York, (incidently a Norse name that means 'the street

79 Urban renewal, a tenth-century street scene based on the well-preserved remains of wooden houses found during excavations at Coppergate, York (465).

of the smiths'), four new plots were laid out in the early tenth century and houses erected along their street frontage. Fortunately waterlogged conditions preserved much of their superstructures which were composed of wattle-work laid on posts (79). Inside each house was a central raised clay hearth, surrounded by blocks of limestone and reused tile. On either side of the hearth, along the walls, benches for working, sitting and sleeping were supported by rows of stakes. An additional row of stakes, designed to support the roof, ran down the centre of each house. The surviving evidence did not allow archaeologists to determine if the houses were thatched or roofed with wooden shingles. Miscellaneous pits dug into the floor may have been used for storage before being filled with rubbish, which was otherwise simply thrown out of doors where it gradually raised the ground level.

Two of the houses seem to have been occupied by metalworkers as they contained crucibles to which splashes of gold, silver, copper and lead still adhered. These may have been the raw materials needed to make the jewellery that was cast in moulds of clay or stone. An iron coin die, used to strike Viking coins of *c.*920–7, together with folded lead strips used to test dies of coins locally minted in the names of Saxon kings, suggests that one of these smiths was connected with the mint. On a more mundane level iron was also smelted on the site in small quantities.

Natural deterioration meant that the houses had to be periodically rebuilt on a slightly higher level with each passing generation. Then late in the tenth century all four sites were reorganized and the houses rebuilt on a more substantial scale. Instead of the crude wattle walls they were given good plank walls and entrances with stone revetted passages. On average these new-style longhouses were 7.5m (25ft) long and 4m (13ft) wide. One point of interest is that their floors were partially sunken and, in contrast to the earlier Saxon SFBs, occupation debris was found stratified *in situ*, so the pits had not been covered with planks. Despite the improved domestic conditions the site continued to be the focus of craft production. Behind two of the houses were workshops – one was used by a jeweller working in jet and amber, the other was occupied by a carpenter who produced lathe-turned wooden bowls.

In addition to metalworking and carpentry many other crafts were practised at the site. Cloth was woven using many different techniques, some requiring a high level of skill. Bone was worked into pins and combs. Ice skates were fashioned from the foot bones of sheep or cattle. Leatherworkers also did a brisk trade in shoes. Most of the finds uncovered during the excavation were made locally, though some were imported, indicating the existence of quite wide-reaching trade routes. The imports included wine jars and lava querns from the Rhineland, soapstone bowls and whetstones of banded schist from Norway, Baltic amber and even silk.

All the evidence from Coppergate points to a quarter occupied by specialist craftsmen and merchants selling their wares from stalls along the street front. How typical this was of the city as a whole will not be known until the work of excavation is extended. But although these recent excavations have allowed a more balanced picture of the Vikings to be built up, these peaceful traders, craftsmen and farmers should not entirely blind us to their less respectful, free-booting cousins.

9 CELTIC TWILIGHT

The unity imposed on Britain by Rome did not outlast the break-up of the Empire. After the Roman withdrawal from Britain the power vacuum was quickly filled by numerous petty rulers. Each strove to carve out and maintain their own sphere of influence, fighting alike against Germanic settlers and local rivals. Of higher loyalties there are hints – of an overlord called Vortigern, the 'High-ruler', and a national resistance organized behind the shadowy figure of Arthur. But one by one, the squabbling states were simply absorbed by the expanding Saxon kingdoms until the principalities of Wales alone retained their cultural identity and political independence. This chapter will consider what was happening in these parts of the British Isles immediately after the Romans withdrew.

Anyone who sets off in quest of 'Arthur's Britain' soon discovers that the reality behind the myth is far different from the enchanted world of medieval poets. Once the thin veneer of Romanization was stripped away the Britons reverted to a simpler way of life, which had more in common with that of their Iron Age ancestors than that of the heroes of medieval myths.

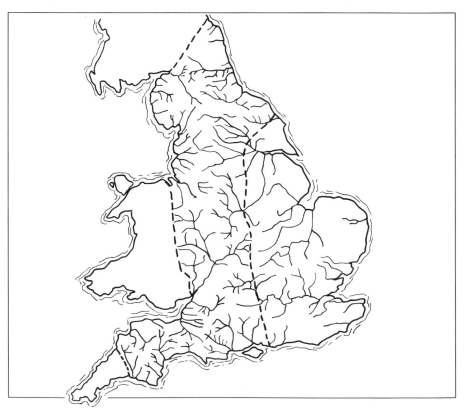

80 The distribution of Celtic river names in England, an illustration of how the impact of Germanic settlement decreased from east to west. Note how it falls into two main areas: *East*: only a few of the largest rivers retain Celtic names; *West*: most of the major rivers and some of the minor rivers have Celtic names. (Compare with 73, the distribution of pagan Saxon cemeteries.)

Given the unsettled conditions of post-Roman Britain defence might be expected to have been a priority. It therefore comes as a surprise that the defended sites of the period throughout Wales and the south-west and north of Britain were far less impressive than those of the Iron Age. They tend to be small, 1ha (2½ acres) or less, and although carefully sited to take full advantage of natural strongpoints their artificial defences are relatively weak, no match for a really determined enemy. However, the surviving literary sources imply that attacks on strongpoints played little part in British warfare. Obviously these enclosures were intended to perform very different roles from the average hillfort. Instead of housing a substantial settlement, or even providing an emergency refuge for an entire community, they were probably designed to serve as the defended household of a lord.

At Dinas Powys (Glamorgan) the remains of one such enclosure were excavated by Professor Leslie Alcock. The site chosen was a small, isolated promontory on which were the unfinished remains of an Iron Age fort. Here an area of some 60 by 30m (195 by 100ft) was enclosed on the south and east sides by a low bank and a ditch 3.35m (11ft) wide and 1.2m (4ft) deep. On the north and west sides the natural defences of the promontory were utilized, possibly with the addition of a palisade. All told not a very serious deterrent to a determined enemy. Within the enclosure all that remained of the buildings were two gullies that represented drip-trenches from the eaves of two buildings, measuring 8.2m (27ft) by 15.2m (50ft) and 6.7m (22ft) by 7.6m (25ft), that made up two sides of a yard. In addition to debris from craftsmen working in iron, leather and bone, there was also evidence that a skilled jeweller had been at work using gold and glass bosses made from fine imported *millefiori* sticks or scrap glass from Germanic vessels. This strengthens the case for considering Dinas Powys a high-status site, the seat of a chieftain who had the necessary wealth to patronize craftsmen.

Celtic sites such as Dinas Powys are notoriously difficult to date. With the disappearance of the coinage and mass-produced pottery of Roman Britain archaeologists are deprived of their most reliable material. This leaves only the objects in everyday use that often altered little over the centuries. Only the decorated metalwork and imported pottery found on high-status sites are distinctive enough to base a chronology on. Two groups of pottery, one from North Africa and the East Mediterranean, the other from south-west France, are among the most useful finds for this purpose. At Dinas Powys, for example, such finds suggest the site was occupied between *c.* AD 450–750. They also show that western Britain was not entirely isolated, although the total quantity of sherds recovered is so small that the social significance of this trade must have been far greater than its economic importance.

At South Cadbury (Somerset) Professor Alcock excavated another defended site of the period that utilized the pre-existing earthworks of a large hillfort that had been abandoned since the first century. The line of the inner circuit of defence, a total length of 1200m (3930ft), was remodelled and a substantial new rampart erected on top of the old bank. This consisted of a timber-framed rampart revetted at the front and back by drystone walls, similar to many of Iron Age date. But the post-holes that marked out the south-west gate suggested something rather more sophisticated. Their size and depth indicated

81 The Caractacus Stone (Somerset), a Romanized memorial to a sixth-century Celtic chieftain who ironically bore the same name as one of the greatest heroes of the British Resistance to the Romans. *(Photo: courtesy of the Archaeology Department, City of Bristol Museum and Art Gallery.)*

that they had once supported a timber tower identical to those found in Roman forts. Yet a Germanic brooch found sealed in the surface of a road associated with this gate implied that it had been erected *c.* AD 500. Within the ramparts a large timber hall was erected on the summit of the hill. This measured *c.*19m (63ft) by 10m (33ft) wide and was divided a third of the way down by an internal partition. Sherds of imported pottery indicated a sixth-century construction date. Clearly the site, if hardly legendary Camelot, had been the seat of an important British chieftain.

The undefended sites from lower down the social scale have been rather elusive. Although pollen studies give every indication that the land continued to be intensively farmed, very few settlement sites belonging to this period have been identified. One that has been discovered was laid out in the middle of the fifth century on the site of the former Christian cemetery at Poundbury (Dorset). It consisted of a few rectangular timber buildings, which while clearly not Germanic in character were also not very Roman, together with six very basic corn dryers of Roman type and a threshing floor. Obviously these represent remains of a small farmstead operating on the subsistence level.

One major way in which the 'Dark Age' Celts differed from their Iron Age ancestors was in religion. Unfortunately the churches and monasteries are far less easy to identify than the defended households of the rulers for they were simple structures very different from the later monumental stone buildings of medieval times. At Glastonbury (Somerset) part of what may have been the boundary of the Celtic monastery, a ditch 7.6m (25ft) wide and 3m (10ft) deep, together with the eroded remains of a bank, was discovered running below the ruins of the medieval stone church. Elsewhere in the monastic precinct the foundations of four small oratories, similar to the ancient churches with wattle walls mentioned by medieval writers, were uncovered, together with a cemetery.

As Christians the British were buried without grave goods in graves with an east–west orientation. High-status individuals were often commemorated by freestanding memorial stones with Latin epitaphs. A small number, intended for Irish settlers, are bilingual, featuring a translation of the Latin into Gaelic. One of the largest British cemeteries was excavated at Cannington (Somerset) where 500 inhumations survived quarrying from an original total that may have numbered several thousands. Radiocarbon dates imply that it was in continuous use from the second to the eighth century, the earlier inhumations having grave goods and a different orientation. Located near a hillfort the site may have served as the central burying place of a local tribe.

Ireland's Golden Age

The Romans knew little and cared less about the largest island off their province. No attempt was ever made at conquest and even trading contacts seem to have been few and far between. Traditional life simply continued, undisturbed by foreign intervention, and the ancient oral law codes, myths and legends that were written down after the conversion of Ireland to Christianity are a mine of information. They depict a highly structured society based on the *derbfine*, an extended family that held land in common and reckoned their descent in the male line from a common great-grandfather. A number of these *derbfines* made up a tribe (*tuath*), each of which was ruled by a king (*ri*). Tribal kings in turn acknowledged the overlordship of provincial kings right up to the High King of all Ireland.

Irish kings were not vested with absolute power. Their actions were limited by customary laws and the obligation to seek guidance from consultative assemblies. Kingship was even elective to a certain extent, a candidate qualifying through his individual prestige and wealth in addition to descent from royal kindred. Below the kings were the nobles (*flaithi*), who exercised a wide influence through a system of patronage (*celsine*) reminiscent of medieval feudalism in which a noble patron gave his clients protection, land and cattle in return for service and a tithe. A small, but thriving, 'middle class' (*oes dana*) included the Druids and skilled craftsmen. Most of the people, however, were commoners, ranging in status from prosperous yeoman farmers, to agricultural labourers and slaves.

Ireland has few hillforts that can compare with those of Iron Age Britain. Most earthworks, called ring-forts or raths (**82**), are constructed on a far humbler

82 The raths at Budore (Co. Antrim; 69), typical examples of the earthworks occupied by the yeoman farmers of Early Christian Ireland. The smaller has an internal diameter of 27.4m (90ft).

scale; a typical example is circular, surrounded by one or more low banks and ditches, ranging from 15 to 150m (49 to 492ft) in diameter. Once thirty to forty thousand of these enclosures existed and despite the depredations of modern farmers, many have survived to the present. Many raths were clearly not sited to take advantage of natural strongpoints. A fact which combined with the relative weakness of some of their earthworks suggests that they were intended as homesteads rather than as forts; their banks and ditches probably serving as a mark of status and to keep out raiders, thieves or animals. Others seem to have been designed with defence as a priority, carefully sited to dominate the surrounding land and equipped with well-defended entrances.

In the east of Ireland, where soils are thin but there is an abundance of good building stone, the earthen raths were translated into stone cashels surrounded by thick drystone walls. Small artificial islands, called crannogs, took the place of more conventional raths or cashels in many Irish lakes. At some sites a natural island was extended, at others it was built up from scratch from the lake bottom with stakes driven into the soft silts to form a circular enclosure. Alternatively, if the bottom of the lake was too hard for this a stone and gravel foundation might be piled up. Either way, the outline was then filled in with layers of diverse materials such as logs, branches, gravel, clay and rubble. Access was via a wooden gangway placed on piles or a stone causeway, often interrupted for security. Around the perimeter a palisade was erected and outside this further posts acted as a breakwater to protect the crannog from erosion.

Smaller raths, cashels and crannogs were presumably the residences of the tenant farmers, equivalent to the yeomen of medieval England. Larger examples, which featured multiple rings of earthworks may have belonged to the more powerful chieftains and tribal kings; a theory that is supported by the fine metalwork and other high-quality goods often discovered during their excavation. The ordinary tribespeople presumably lived in unenclosed settlements that leave few traces above ground to attract the attention of archaeologists. They may have been similar to the traditional clusters of farmsteads called clachans that remain typical of much of the modern Irish countryside. Larger, nucleated villages, were mostly the product of later, Anglo-Norman influences.

Many of the largest enclosures in Ireland seem not to have been the sites of settlements and may have functioned as assembly places for religious rituals and social activities. At these sites continuity can often be demonstrated back to the later Bronze Age, if not further. But these links with the past do not seem to have extended to the enclosed settlements. Almost all the raths, cashels and crannogs were constructed during the Early Christian Period, between c.500 and 1000. Ulster crannogs, for example, have been dated by dendrochronology to the late sixth and early seventh centuries AD. Unfortunately their Iron Age predecessors are almost completely missing from the archaeological record; a fact that has prompted some scholars to seek the origins of these forms of settlement in the Iron Age enclosures of western Britain and the crannogs of south-west Scotland. But while they are certainly similar it might just be a case of structures built by societies at a similar level of organization. Hard evidence of direct influences is harder to track down.

Domestic arrangements inside raths, cashels and crannogs were very similar, typically featuring several houses built up against the sides of the enclosure. Initially these tended to be round, but by the eighth century square and rectangular houses had become the fashion. Houses utilized the same range of materials as their enclosures – wood, wattle, clay and stone. A recent excavation at the small rath of Deer Park Farms (Co. Antrim), directed by Chris Lynn, has revealed an unusually detailed glimpse of ancient Irish life in the eighth century. The earthworks formed an enclosure 25m (85ft) across and occupying the centre was the largest of five structures, consisting of two round rooms joined together to form a 'figure-of-eight'. One of the rooms contained a central hearth flanked by brushwood bench-beds, the other a hearth and trough. On either side of this central house were two smaller one-room structures linked by stone paths. A second figure-of-eight building lay behind the first.

Due to waterlogging of the site sufficient organic material survived to allow a typical house to be reconstructed on paper. It would have been between 5 and 7m (16½ and 23ft) in diameter with the walls woven from hazel rods to create a tough wattlework structure rather like a giant basket. Each wall was double, with a strong inner skin, a less substantial outer one and a layer of grass-like packing material in between. They were constructed by inserting sticks into the ground at intervals of about 25cm (63½in), then weaving other rods between them in a technique that would be familiar to any basketry class. When the tops of the sticks were reached, a new set of rods was simply incorporated into the growing wall and the process began all over again. Up to five series of vertical rods were used, giving a height of up to 2.5m (8ft). All the cut ends were placed facing into the wall, so that the interior surface was quite smooth, but no daub was used. A single gap in the structure was left to serve as the entrance, provided with a timber frame to which a wattle door was attached. Unfortunately no evidence for the roof survived. Similar houses, known as clochans, are found inside the cashels but they were constructed of drystone masonry using corbelling. Some were roofed in stone, giving the typical 'bee-hive' appearance, others had a roof of turf or thatch supported on four posts. Clochans demonstrate the same change in fashion from round to square types as houses constructed from more perishable materials. As on earlier British Iron Age sites not all of these structures were necessarily houses, there is some evidence that they were also used as workshops, byres and stores. Additional outbuildings may also have existed outside the enclosures, but these have mostly not been looked for during excavations. Circular or rectangular huts, similar to those excavated within enclosures, have been discovered, either singly or in groups, in the open, presumably representing the homesteads of the ordinary tribes-people.

In addition to the houses long, narrow underground passages, called souterrains, are often found within raths and cashels, and even at unenclosed farmsteads. Some were tunnelled from the solid rock, while others were built as a trench lined with timber or stone. The most elaborate feature a series of chambers strung along a passage that twists, turns and changes level. At strategic points they were provided with 'creeps' where the ceiling was lowered, the walls narrowed or there were sudden drops to act as pit-falls to the un-initiated. Souterrains may have been of foreign inspiration for although in Ireland they date to the Early Christian Period, across the sea in Cornwall and Scotland similar structures were constructed during the late Iron Age. Just what souterrains were used for is debatable. As they are clearly unsuitable for permanent occupation the most popular theory has always been that they served as refuges. But they were hardly 'secret passages', the roofs of many examples would have been clearly visible, often raised above the ground. Once inside, the people would have been trapped and easily smoked or starved into submission – a fact that may explain why some have second entrances linked to escape tunnels and vents to admit fresh air. On a more practical note it has also been suggested that souterrains were simply storehouses designed to keep dairy products cool. In practice they may have served all these, and many other, functions.

Around some raths and cashels the remains of the contemporary field systems can occasionally be discerned. At Cush (Co. Limerick), for example, fields were laid out down a hillside between two small groups of raths. A typical field was rectangular in shape, some 200 by 50m (656 by 165ft), outlined by a bank and ditch. Many of these fields are larger than those previously encountered in Ireland, possibly due to the introduction of the true plough from Britain. Areas of 'ridge-and-furrow' produced by the plough, typical of medieval England (see Chapter 10 for details), have been discovered at Cush and elsewhere. The introduction of the plough may also account for the steep decline in tree pollen noticeable in samples for the third quarter of the first millennium AD. At about the same time the simple mechanical water-mill was also introduced from the Continent. Recent fieldwork has thus gone some way to redress the balance of the evidence of the texts, which emphasizes the importance of stock breeding. Bones from sites show that cattle were mostly kept either for dairy produce or as a form of wealth. Analysis of bones from excavations shows that most cattle were killed around two years of age, presumably males excess to breeding requirements, although there are also smaller numbers of mature females that may have passed their best milk-producing years. Sheep and pigs are also commonly found.

Rome may have had little impact on Ireland during the days of its imperial greatness, but after the decline and fall of the empire the efforts of Romano-British missionaries brought Ireland into the mainstream of European civilization. Within a century or so of the kidnapping by Irish raiders of the boy we now know as St Patrick, traditionally in AD 432, Ireland had been bloodlessly converted. The country eagerly assimilated all that the new religion had to teach, and learning and the arts flourished as nowhere else in Dark Age Europe. There was just one problem, however, Christianity in the Roman world tended to be based on bishoprics located in cities, but in Ireland nothing resembling a town existed at this time. Instead, the newly invented monasteries became the main administrative centres for the new religion. It should not be overlooked, however, that in addition to the monasteries many non-monastic churches were also founded to care for the spiritual needs of the people.

Monastic sites were very different from the medieval ruins familiar to the modern traveller. Early monastic sites, enclosed by bank, ditch or wall, bore a close resemblance to secular raths and cashels. Indeed some of these enclosures may simply have been handed over to the Church by their original owners. Within the innermost enclosure there might be several small churches, cemeteries, high crosses, a refectory and scattered all around the simple cells of the monks. From the tenth century onwards many sites were dominated by the tall free-standing round-towers (83) which served the dual functions of belfry and

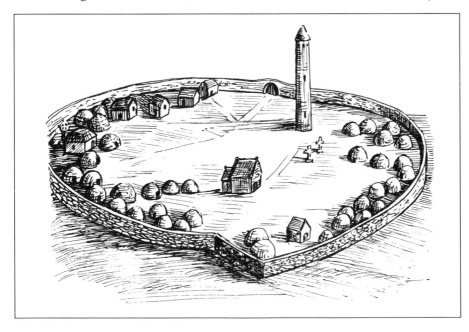

83 Reconstruction of a Celtic monastery. Instead of the claustral plan typical of the Middle Ages (see 99), the typical Irish monastery consisted of several small churches, a round-tower, beehive huts and other domestic buildings scattered within a circular enclosure wall or bank.

refuge in case of attack. Outside this consecrated land might be one or more additional enclosures, for the workshops, schools, guest quarters, homes of lay workers and the domestic buildings of the estates. In the fullness of time the larger monasteries may even have come to fulfil some of the functions of towns for the surrounding countryside.

In view of the importance of monasteries to Irish culture it is surprising that none of the major sites has been scientifically excavated in recent years. Archaeologists have, however, excavated several smaller ecclesiastical sites that may in any case have been more typical of the early church. At Reask (Co. Kerry), for example, the earliest occupation, dated by C^{14} to between 260 and 650, was represented by a spread of clay, a stone-covered drain, pits, hearths and the post-holes of a small circular structure. These rather uninspiring remains were subsequently built over by a stone enclosure 45m (148ft) in diameter, within which were two stone beehive huts, a cemetery of stone-lined graves, some with tombstones, a stone shrine and possibly a wooden church. Sherds of imported Mediterranean pottery allowed this phase of occupation to be dated to the fifth or sixth century. Later, more beehive huts were erected, a stone wall was used to divide up the enclosure, creating a sanctuary in which a small stone church, measuring 3.5 by 2.7m (11 by 10ft), was constructed, partly over the earlier cemetery.

During the Early Christian Period most crafts were practised at the domestic level of production typical of Iron Age Britain. Spindlewhorls and ironworking debris encountered during most excavations imply that communities, both secular and ecclesiastical, made such basic necessities of life as clothes and tools for themselves. Crannogs also yield evidence that the Irish were skilled in carpentry, making lathe-turned bowls and stave buckets, and leatherwork. But little pottery was used, most of Ireland, apart from a small area in the northeast, was aceramic. The number of finds also implies that some communities may have specialized in certain crafts to supplement their farming. Full-time, skilled craftsmen, especially the smiths who made high-quality status symbols and other luxuries, were supported by nobles and the church. At Armagh, for example, excavations on the site of the important early monastery provided evidence for craftsmen working in lignite, bone, antler, amber, glass and metals. Finds such as Mediterranean and Gaulish pottery, English and continental glass or decorative metalwork, discovered during the excavation of high-status sites, demonstrate that Ireland participated, if only in a limited way, in the long-distance trade in luxuries. But only in the tenth century did trade take off on a large scale, when the Vikings founded the first urban communities on the south-east coast.

Scotland before the Scots

The Roman campaigns in Scotland seem to have had few lasting effects on the indigenous population, leaving behind little but a taste for luxuries that could be acquired through trading or raiding. Left to their own devices everyday life for the inhabitants continued unchanged as it had for centuries. Iron Age Scotland, just like contemporary England and Wales, was essentially a defended

84 A prime candidate for vitrification: a timber-framed rampart of the type found at Scottish Iron Age forts. Once the wood was set alight sufficient heat would be generated to melt the silica-rich rocks, which on cooling would set into a glassy slag.

landscape, but one which contained relatively few large hillforts to compare with the great English examples. What small number there were can be found in the Lowlands, south of the Forth–Clyde line, a region culturally identical with northern England. Instead, in the Highlands and Islands, there are the duns, small circular forts, similar in scale to the Irish raths and cashels, marked out with drystone walls or simple enclosures surrounded by bank, ditch and palisade (84). Many of these enclosure walls have been vitrified – the stones fused into a glass-like slag by high temperatures when the timber-laced ramparts were set on fire. This has been variously interpreted as the work of enemy action or a deliberate feature of the design, intended to strengthen the defences.

In contrast to the unimpressive nature of Scottish forts, free-standing stone towers, called brochs (85), are among the most remarkable of all the many and

85 A tower of strength, Dun Carloway Broch, Isle of Lewis (Highlands; 165). *(Photo: courtesy of Highland and Island Enterprise.)*

varied prehistoric monuments of the British Isles. In appearance they are rather reminiscent of modern power station cooling towers, their walls, 3–4.5m (10–15ft) thick, gently taper upwards to a height of 12–15m (40–50ft). A single, narrow passage gave access to the interior via a low door, often flanked with guard chambers. Within, there was an open air courtyard, *c.*6m (20ft) in diameter, equipped with hearths, drains, wells and storage tanks of stone. Doors gave access to corbelled chambers at ground level and a stone staircase led to a series of galleries, one above the other, built into the thickness of the wall. Wooden galleries may also have been erected at some brochs projecting over the courtyard like balconies (86).

At one time brochs were widely believed to have been a reaction to Roman aggression. This theory is discredited by the fact that relatively few brochs are to be found in the southern lands that were most vulnerable to Roman activity; the vast majority are instead located on the northern mainland, Orkney and Shetland. It is more likely that the brochs served much the same function in society as the less spectacular duns or the tower-houses of late medieval Scotland, acting as the seats of local chieftains. The fashion for building brochs owes nothing to Roman influences, they probably evolved from the 'galleried duns' of the Hebrides, which also feature chambers built into the thickness of their drystone walls. It has also been suggested that the brochs were the work of a highly-skilled group of peripatetic craftsmen. What is clear is that brochs were constructed for a relatively brief period, peaking *c.*100 BC–AD 100. By the third century AD, however, all had been abandoned and left to decay.

Apart from the brochs most Scottish Iron Age homes were little different from the English round-houses. As most were constructed of perishable materials they have left few traces behind. But in the Isles an abundance of good building stone, coupled with a lack of timber, means that many well preserved examples survive. Here, in the shadow of the brochs, which were often used as

86 Reconstruction of the broch at Clickhimin (Shetland; 119), cut away to show the internal galleries within the thickness of the drystone walls. (*After Hamilton.*)

convenient quarries, large circular 'wheelhouses' were laid out. A typical example consists of a central room, around the perimeter of which is a series of stone piers that once supported the turf and timber roof. Often these piers are attached to the exterior wall only at one point, their lintels creating a continuous 'aisle'. Otherwise they were completely filled in to form a series of up to eight small cells roofed with stone slabs. Both types were left totally undefended.

The problem of the Picts

Dark Age Scotland was dominated by the people now known as the Picts. From their heartland in the east of the country, above the Forth–Clyde line, their influence extended throughout the Highlands and Islands. By the fourth century AD their power had grown to such an extent that they presented a very real threat to Roman Britain. Yet they remain an elusive race, only mentioned in a few scattered entries in the histories of other nations, and their origin is still obscure. In the absence of any evidence to the contrary, however, it seems likely that the Picts represent a regrouping of indigenous Iron Age tribes into a larger political unit, possibly a confederation. Even the name they called themselves is unknown; for the name by which history knows them is nothing more than a nickname coined by Roman writers in the late third century. It means 'the painted people', and probably refers to complex designs painted or tattooed on their bodies.

The Picts are just as difficult to track down in the archaeological record, for they made or built little that was distinctive or unique. In common with the other peoples of Britain, the Picts reused Iron Age hillforts or utilized natural strongpoints as sites for the defended households of their chieftains. Some larger, permanent forts may also have existed. At Burghead (Grampian), for example, three strong lines of timber-framed ramparts, with their accompanying ditches, cut off a promontory enclosing an area of 3ha ($7\frac{1}{2}$ acres). This acted as a substantial focus for settlement (unfortunately damaged by the construction of a new town on the site) that was occupied between the sixth and tenth centuries AD. Apart from these defensive sites little more than a few stone houses from Orkney have been discovered. Pictish graves are difficult to identify with certainty as they mostly lack grave goods. The dead were generally buried in a stone-lined grave, called a long cist, covered with a low circular or rectangular cairn of stones.

One unique feature of Pictish culture are the mysterious symbols, perhaps the same as those painted on their bodies, which are found carved on stones. They include motifs based on animals, both real and imaginary, everyday objects and strange abstract designs (87). Over 250 carved stones have survived to mark out Pictish territory. Most are found concentrated in Grampian and Tayside, regions which seem to have formed the heartland of the Picts, but others are scattered widely over the Highlands and Islands as far afield as Shetland. No one can now be certain as to precisely what message the symbols were meant to convey, but there is no shortage of suggestions. Among the most popular is the theory that they were used to mark out the boundaries of tribal and clan territories. At Burghead, for example, many slabs engraved with a

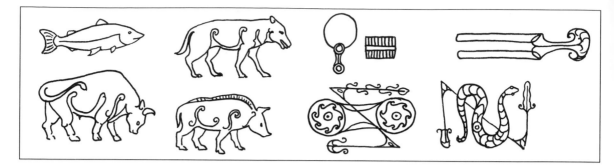

87 Signs of the times. A few of the many and varied designs used, for whatever esoteric or mundane purpose, by Picts on their symbol stones.

bull, thought to be the symbol of the ruling chief or clan, have been discovered. Other slabs may have been erected to commemorate battles, treaties, marriages or any other important event in the life of an individual or tribe. A few picture stones mark the positions of graves. Whatever functions the symbols fulfilled, their standardization over such a wide area argues for a high degree of cultural homogeneity.

A few of the later sculptured stones bear inscriptions. Several of these use the Latin alphabet, but on the whole the Irish Ogham script was preferred. Unfortunately, although it is relatively easy to read the individual letters, the language they were used to write has defied translation. Not even the most accomplished of linguists has been able to make much out from such accumulations of alphabet soup as *ettocuhetts ahehhttann hcvvew nehtons, irutuddourens, nehtetri* or *besmeqqnanammovoez iddarrnonn vorrenn ipour*! What is very clear is that despite the presence of a few loan-words and personal names, by no stretch of the imagination could Pictish be considered to be 'Q' Celtic (see p. 82), such as the Gaelic spoken by the Scots, or 'P' Celtic (although place-name studies demonstrate that 'P' Celtic dialects were spoken in the Lowlands).

The Picts finally lost their cultural identity not through invasion, conquest or massacre but by a political takeover at the highest levels of society when in AD 843 Kenneth Mac Alpin, King of the Scots (themselves originally Irish settlers on the Isles and coast of Argyll), inherited the Pictish throne by virtue of his descent from their royal house in the female line. As a consequence, the Picts were gradually absorbed into the melting pot of peoples who have become the modern Scots. In the process Gaelic language and culture rapidly eclipsed the more ancient traditions of the existing population.

10 1066 AND ALL THAT...

If archaeologists were not aware of the date of the Norman Conquest from other sources it is highly unlikely that they could have deduced it for themselves. For many of the major factors that distinguish late Saxon from medieval England do not become apparent until the twelfth or thirteenth century. After 1066 life in town and country alike continued much as before, only under new management. But in the long term the Conquest set into action forces that intensified wide-ranging social, economic, political, technological and cultural changes that were destined to transform Britain. The introduction of the castle, feudalism, the encouragement of urbanization, closer contacts with Europe, the reform of the church and the expansion of monasticism would change the face of the land.

Defence of the realm

To defeat a nation on the field of battle is easier by far than establishing a permanent occupation of the conquered land. With the death of King Harold, together with many of his leading nobles, organized resistance on a national scale might have ceased, but the threat of local rebellions remained very real. For the Normans could never be more than a tiny minority – even including civilians they numbered no more than ten thousand compared to a native population of two million. It therefore comes as no surprise that the first priority of the new masters was to consolidate their hold on a potentially hostile land. As a consequence, within a few short years of the Conquest castles dominated strategic points throughout the kingdom. These castles served functions different to those of most of the previous defensive installations of the British Isles. Unlike Roman forts, which were garrisoned by a standing army, or the Saxon burhs that provided a place of refuge for an entire community, medieval castles were intended to defend the residences of a small elite – an alien lord and his armed retinue.

Until recently it was generally accepted that castles were an entirely new concept to the Saxons and had been introduced fully developed by the Normans. Only a few scattered references are made to castles by pre-Conquest historians, and those were constructed by the Norman favourites of Edward the Confessor only a few years before 1066. Recent excavations directed by Guy Beresford at Goltho (Lincolnshire), however, have forced archaeologists to reassess these assumptions. For underneath the earthworks of a quite ordinary Norman castle were the remains of a Saxon fortification. The first phase of these defences consisted of a ditch, 5.4m (10ft) wide and 3–4m (7–8ft) deep, placed outside a bank 3.6m (12ft) thick; earthworks every bit as formidable as those that surrounded any burh. Enclosed within them was an area 48m (160ft) square,

88 The late Saxon enclosure at Goltho (Lincolnshire), one of the rare examples of pre-Conquest private fortifications. *(After Beresford.)*

89 A hostile takeover? The motte and bailey, typical of the many small castles thrown up after 1066, which the new Norman landowners built to replace the existing Saxon complex at Goltho. *(After Beresford.)*

containing post-holes belonging to a hall and its associated outbuildings (**88**). On the basis of the pottery sequence Beresford suggested a date of *c.*850 for this phase of the site, but others would prefer a tenth-century date. Later, *c.*1000, these defences were levelled and replaced by new earthworks which enclosed an even greater area. Goltho was clearly a high-status defended site that fulfilled many, if not all, of the functions later served by castles (**89**). What is more it may not be just an isolated curiosity, for one contemporary writer records that a nobleman was expected to possess a 'gatehouse' to defend his hall.

The Normans built two main types of castle, the ringwork and the motte and bailey. Ringworks consisted of a circular bank, crowned by a palisade, with an external ditch, pierced by a more strongly defended timber gatehouse. In scale these were not so different from Goltho. But the monument that has come to symbolize the Conquest is the motte and bailey castle. This consists of a conical mound, the motte, and an oval enclosure, the bailey. Between 1066 and

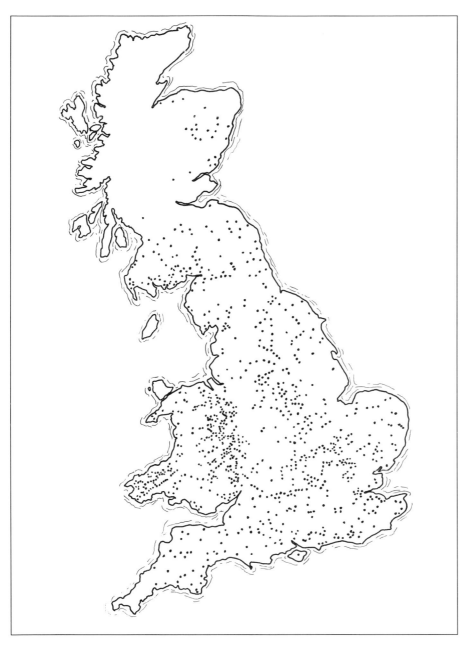

90 The distribution of motte and bailey castles in Britain, note the dense concentration along the Welsh Marches in much the same region that had been defended by Offa's Dyke. *(After Regan.)*

1215 an estimated 700 motte and bailey castles (90) and 200 ringworks were constructed in England. To build an earthen castle few specialist skills or materials were needed, only a supply of labour and raw materials. Often they were the work of a matter of months, if not weeks. Excavations have shown that some mottes consisted of no more than a heap of unconsolidated soil piled up from the surrounding ditch. But others were carefully constructed from layers of soil, turf and rubble, faced with clay or planks to prevent soil creep. On the summit of a motte, which was surrounded by a palisade, was a wooden tower.

This was intended as a combined look-out, fighting platform and ultimate place of refuge for the garrison. The bailey was surrounded by a bank, palisade and ditch. Excavations at Hen Domen (Powys) and elsewhere have shown that the bailey was crowded with often short-lived timber buildings. These included high-status halls for the lords and officers, barracks for their men, storehouses, workshops, stables and chapels. In short all the many and varied buildings that a small, self-contained community might need but for which there was no room on the motte.

Timber and earthwork castles were an efficient and cost-effective solution to the immediate security problems facing Norman lords after the Conquest, for it was expensive and time consuming to build in stone, although timber castles were not necessarily temporary or second-rate. Even once the Normans had established themselves it was beyond the means of all but the wealthier landowners to reconstruct in stone and take advantage of the subsequent advances of military engineering. Lower down the social scale, once the status quo was accepted, the need for defence receded and many a humble earthwork and timber castle was abandoned for the comforts of a manor house. In the later medieval period some new castles were founded and existing manors fortified, but they were intended more as status symbols than as serious fortifications. The same is probably true of the thousands of moated sites, as their defensive value would have been strictly limited. In fact they may have been more use to their proud owners as drains, cisterns or fishponds.

Life on the land

Duke William considered all land as the spoils of war and he dispossessed the Saxon landowning class in its entirety. A portion of the land was kept back to form the royal estates, but the majority, as much as three-quarters of the available agricultural land, was parcelled out to his main supporters. They in turn sublet part of their lands to their retainers according to the order of the feudal system. Simply stated this was a way of organizing society based on service and loyalty. Each man, from peasant to monarch, had a rigidly defined role; he received his livelihood in exchange for military service or agricultural labour. This was a system that was not entirely alien to the Saxons, as there were some comparable elements present in native society even before the Conquest.

Timeless as the familiar pattern of the English countryside might seem, it is in reality relatively recent. Much is a consequence of the Parliamentary Enclosure Acts of the eighteenth and nineteenth centuries which broke up the large open fields that had surrounded medieval villages into smaller units, creating the typical patchwork of fields outlined by hedges seen today. From the air, signs of a very different landscape can be seen, or could be until destroyed by deep ploughing in recent years. Underlying the modern countryside are the ghosts of long, strip-like fields, defined by the marks that archaeologists call 'ridge and furrow'. These patterns were scored into the land by the heavy medieval plough. When ploughing, a medieval farmer started in the middle of a strip of land, then moved back and forth on alternate sides. As the

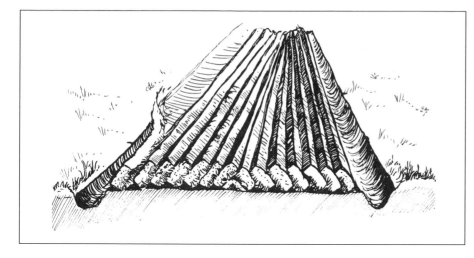

91 The formation of ridge and furrow marks in medieval fields. Note how the plough being used on alternate sides of the strip turned the sods to form ridges with corresponding furrows in between.

heavy plough cut the furrow its mouldboard turned the sod towards the centre of the strip. In time the soil that was heaped up accumulated to form a ridge, leaving a corresponding furrow between the strips (91). Many 'ridge and furrow' marks are not straight lines but follow a reversed 'S' shape caused by the ploughman swinging his team outwards just before the end of the field to make the turn easier.

Each of these large fields was open, with no internal physical divisions such as hedges. But it was nevertheless divided up into notional strips for the purposes of cultivation. On average a strip was a chain wide (5m (16½ft)) and a furlong (200m (660ft)) long. This size was not chosen at random but represented the distance that an ox team could be expected to plough without needing to rest. Smaller private fields were not unknown, especially those carved out from pasture or woodland by individuals for their own use.

Between a quarter and a third of a manorial estate might be farmed directly for the benefit of the lord using the labour due to him from the peasants under the feudal system. Most men were tied to the land as serfs, in return for which they were allocated land of their own. The average serf holding was 12ha (30 acres), not in the form of a continuous block, but scattered throughout the open fields in many small strips. Each man, however, was not free to do as he wished with his plots, all had to abide by the decision of the community on what to plant and how to work the land. A medieval village was frequently surrounded by three great open fields in which crops were grown in rotation. First there might be wheat, then pease (peas, beans or other leguminous vegetables) and finally the land was left fallow for a year. In addition to the open fields part of the land of a manor was set aside as grazing, the rights to which were also held in common (92). Not all of the villagers, however, were fortunate enough to have a share in the communal fields. Cottars, who at one time made up a quarter of the population, had nothing but the produce of their garden plots and had to rely on hiring out their services as jobbing labourers.

The origin of the open field system is steeped in controversy. Once it was thought to have been introduced by the Saxons but it is now known that in their Continental homeland they farmed small enclosed fields similar to the

92 A medieval
landscape. Surrounding
the village is common
land, woodland and
three great open fields
divided into strips.

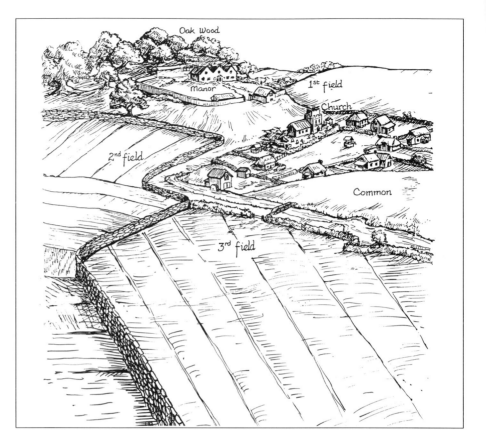

Celtic fields of Roman Britain. Yet open fields certainly existed by the time of
the Norman Conquest, for the typical 'ridge and furrow' marks have been
found in late Saxon strata underlying the earthworks of early Norman castles.
It appears that open fields may represent another aspect of the reorganization
of the countryside that began in late Saxon England at the same time as the
scattered hamlets were being gathered together into villages. This system of
communal farming seems an unlikely one for communities to adopt unprompted,
so it can be suggested that owners of estates imposed the change for economic
reasons.

Forests did not cover as much of medieval England as is popularly believed
– probably amounting to no more than 15 per cent. Almost all the natural
woodland had been cleared away during millennia of intensive farming and
only a little had regenerated. As the population rose in the early medieval
period, the forests then came under renewed pressure. Small plots, called assarts,
were cleared and privately used for pasture or arable farming. The medieval
forest was a very different place from the primeval 'wildwood'. It was in effect
a carefully managed renewable resource. Trees were coppiced – cut back to the
ground at regular intervals – or pollarded – cut at a height above the reach of
grazing animals. Both these techniques stimulated the growth of numerous
thin poles which had many and varied uses. To provide larger timbers trees
were allowed to grow undisturbed for up to a century.

Hearth and home

Many a village's proudest boast today is of a mention in Domesday Book. Once it was widely believed that English villages had pre-dated the Norman Conquest by a long time but recent excavations, combined with fieldwork, have forced a complete reassessment of the origins of the village. It is now known that the Saxons tended to live in dispersed hamlets and farmsteads that constantly shifted their sites, not in permanent nucleated villages. The Domesday Book might seem to describe a rural England full of villages, many of which can still be identified, but the reality may have been very different; the same terminology is indiscriminately applied to regions where villages have never existed. Domesday manors may in fact have been estates which included one or more settlements, some of which later developed into a medieval village bearing the same name. Precisely when the transition was made is controversial. The new settlement pattern may already have begun to emerge in the tenth century, but the process was by no means completed until the thirteenth century. Even then the village was only one aspect of the medieval settlement pattern, which continued to feature large numbers of hamlets and farmsteads.

93 Crisis and continuity, Old Sarum (Wiltshire; 341), successively the site of an Iron Age hillfort, Saxon burh, Norman castle and cathedral town. Abandoned in the thirteenth century in favour of the new town of Salisbury. *(Photo: RCHME.)*

In some regions villages never became established – and not just the less favoured upland regions that could only support a dispersed population.

At present the evidence for the origins of individual villages is mixed. Some appear to have grown organically from one or more nuclei of Saxon settlement, but equally there are others which cannot be directly linked to previously existing settlements. Many have such a regular layout that they must have been imposed on the landscape in a single planned act, whether on a virgin site or not. Where dates are available these planned villages seem to originate mostly in the eleventh and twelfth centuries. The rationale for the changeover is even less clear than its date. No individual social, economic, political or racial reason can be singled out as the sole cause. But it may be significant that the open field system was evolving at about the same time. The medieval village, no more than earlier settlements, was not frozen in time, they often changed format and layout over generations. New additions, planned or unplanned, were made as the population expanded, and other areas were abandoned as the population declined or houses were rebuilt on other sites. Only in recent centuries, with the erection of substantial stone and timber houses, have villages become fixed in one form.

Many medieval villages are the sites of flourishing communities today. In these circumstances archaeologists can hardly expect to dig under the floorboards and in the gardens of the cottages. Fortunately such a sacrifice to the greater glory of science is not necessary, for fieldwork, combined with aerial photography, has succeeded in locating the sites of hundreds of other, now deserted, medieval villages. Their excavation is a relatively recent phenomenon, for they are rich only in information, not in objects suitable for display in museums. The pioneering work was only begun in 1952 by Maurice Beresford and John Hurst at Wharram Percy on the Yorkshire Wolds.

Above ground the village of Wharram Percy, in common with other deserted medieval villages, is represented by a series of low banks that mark out the positions of the house plots that faced each other across the village street (94). Each household occupied a plot of land enclosed by a bank, ditch or fence. Within this plot the houses were generally erected at the front, facing on to the street; behind them were the outbuildings and vegetable gardens (95). This particular village seems to have been laid out in the twelfth century, then extended a hundred years later. Previously there had been several small settlement foci scattered through the valley and when Domesday Book was compiled the land was divided between two manors.

Two of the house plots at Wharram Percy have been completely excavated down to virgin soil. They show that the typical medieval house was very different from the timber-framed structures beloved of chocolate box illustrators and postcard sellers. For the substantial late medieval buildings were the residences of the prosperous few, merchants, yeoman farmers and skilled artisans; the majority lived in far humbler style. Instead of large, expensive timbers their houses were cobbled together from offcuts, wattle and daub and rubble – flimsy structures that needed to be constantly repaired and were probably entirely rebuilt once in every generation.

Of the oldest houses at Wharram Percy only a mass of superimposed postholes survived. The excavators suggested that these represent the remains of

94 *(Opposite)* Life on the land, an aerial view of earthworks marking the site of the deserted medieval village at Wharram Percy (North Yorkshire; 450). *(Photo: RCHME.)*

95 A reconstruction of the deserted medieval village of Wharram Percy (North Yorkshire; 450). Note how each house has its own individual plot fronting on to the village street.

small, one-room cottages, together with their associated outbuildings. Evidence for later housing was better preserved, in part due to the fact that in a damper climate more use was made of stone foundations and wall footings. From the thirteenth century onwards, in addition to the small one-room cottages which were probably the homes of the less prosperous peasants, larger longhouses were common. This is a type of dwelling that remained popular in parts of Scotland and Ireland well into the nineteenth century. A typical example

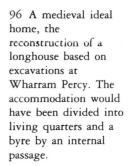

96 A medieval ideal home, the reconstruction of a longhouse based on excavations at Wharram Percy. The accommodation would have been divided into living quarters and a byre by an internal passage.

97 Lower Brockhampton Manor (Hereford and Worcester; 287), a fine example of a half-timbered fifteenth-century moated manor house. *(Photo: RCHME.)*

measured 30 by 5m (32 by 16½ft) with the interior usually divided into two rooms by a narrow passage that led directly from the door. One room was occupied by the family, the other was often used to stable the animals, for storage or even to conduct a real cottage industry (96).

At the other end of the social scale was the manor (97), the residential complex of the lord, or his bailiff. At some sites, such as Goltho or the royal estate at Cheddar, existing centres continued in use for generations after the Conquest. Other manors were administered from newly-founded sites, including castles. Excavations of early medieval manors show that they differ little from their Saxon predecessors, being based on the timber hall, which doubled as estate office and court room, together with associated outbuildings. Later many manors were rebuilt in stone according to the wealth and taste of the family concerned. A few of the stone halls of the late twelfth and thirteenth centuries still stand. Some are translations of the time-honoured plan of a ground-floor hall divided into nave and aisles; others placed the hall above a vaulted undercroft. Additional private accommodation consisted of a living room, with chapel and bedchamber *en suite*, built over an undercroft.

During the early medieval period the population, stimulated by a warm, dry climate, steadily rose from *c.*2 million to an estimated 4–5 million. To feed all these extra mouths marginal land that had not been farmed for centuries was brought back into cultivation. Forests, parks and pasture were all ploughed up; villages expanded and new settlements were founded. But by the early fourteenth century a crisis was looming: the climate had once more become colder and wetter; crop yields fell; over-exploitation of the land led to exhaustion and erosion of the soil. Then came the Black Death of 1348 in which as many as one in three people may have died. The combined effect of these disasters was to limit severely the population, which remained fixed at about 2.5 million for centuries to come.

Once the desertion of every medieval village was directly attributed to the Black Death. Although its effect was dramatic, it should not be exaggerated – it is now known that while this epidemic aggravated many of the social and economic problems experienced in late medieval England, the roots of these problems extended back well before 1348. The real story behind the deserted medieval villages is far more complex. Historians, working with archaeologists, have now established that desertions actually peaked in the early fifteenth century and continued at a high level well into the sixteenth. Indeed most of these desertions were not on marginal land but in the fertile lowlands of the Midlands, South and East.

What in fact is apparent is the crude application of market forces, a medieval version of monetarism. Landowners realized that there were vast profits to be made by enclosing their estates to use as pasture for sheep or cattle and as a result they no longer needed so much labour, so the villagers were simply evicted and left to fend for themselves. Wharram Percy survived the Black Death, but in the following two centuries slowly declined. More and more house plots were left vacant until by *c.*1500 the village had shrunk to the vicarage and two cottages.

City slickers

The revival of urban life, which had begun in the tenth century, continued undisturbed by the Norman Conquest. Although most people continued to live on the land, towns provided a wide range of services as centres of administration, industry and commerce. In the medieval period towns flourished as never before, established settlements expanded and others spontaneously sprang up at strategic spots, or were founded by lords, for although they stood outside the feudal system towns could be a rich source of profit (98).

Most medieval towns have remained prosperous urban centres. Only the havoc wreaked by destruction during the Second World War and modern redevelopment have allowed the archaeologist to explore what lies beneath the streets of many towns. All too often this has had to take the form of quick rescue excavations before everything is destroyed. Time and resources generally

98 The medieval urban revival, the distribution of towns in the eleventh century *(left)*; in the thirteenth century *(right)*. *(After Heighway.)* (Compare this with the distribution of towns in Roman Britain (62).)

allow only a small area to be completely dug, and this may reveal incomplete plans which are difficult to interpret. The problem is aggravated by the fact that medieval sites are complicated to dig, honeycombed with pits that have caused one excavator to compare them to a black-forest gateau used for pogo-stick practice. In the absence of waste-disposal facilities and reliable water supplies that are now taken for granted, each medieval household had to dig its own wells, rubbish pits and cess pits.

Land in medieval towns was divided into long, thin sections called burgage plots, the influence of which can often still be traced in modern street plans. An average plot might be 5m (16½ft) wide and 50m (164ft) long. This shape probably evolved because street frontage was at a premium. Each unit would have contained a house fronting on to the street, and behind it a yard with outbuildings. Houses were mostly built of wood, although from the thirteenth century stone foundations became common. The constant repairs and rebuildings have often destroyed all traces of the early houses on a site, except for a few post-holes. A few stone houses of the late twelfth century have survived, but generally the oldest domestic buildings that can be seen in English towns today are the substantial half-timbered houses of the fifteenth century. Combined with the evidence from excavations and documentary sources they provide a good idea of what the home of a prosperous merchant or craftsman might have looked like.

On the ground floor most of the street frontage was taken up by a shop, often constructed over a vaulted cellar. But while they might have lived 'over the shop' the bourgeois enjoyed comforts equal to the gentry. Private quarters consisted of a hall, either directly over the shop on the first floor or behind it on the ground floor, together with several smaller chambers. Workshops, for the variety of crafts that were practised in the heart of medieval towns, would have been situated in outbuildings in the yard behind the house. There was also sufficient space in the yard to keep a few animals and lay out a garden plot for growing produce.

The rubbish and cess pits dug into backyards have proved a rich source of information about the medieval diet. A wide variety of meat, game, fish and shellfish was available. To enhance the flavour of the food there were exotic herbs and spices, such as mustard, poppy seeds, fennel, coriander and pepper. For dessert there was fruit, both domestic and imported, such as strawberries, raspberries, figs, raisins, cherries, plums and nuts. The beer, ale and mead that washed it all down left behind residues of pollen from the honey, bog myrtle and hops. But just as might be expected from the poor hygiene – with wells and cess pits in close proximity – the presence of the eggs of a wide variety of parasitic worms and flukes indicates that most of the population was infected with such debilitating, if not life threatening, organisms. The stagnant water of the pits also provided ideal breeding conditions for flies, many of whose pupae are found during excavations.

Religion and ritual

At the heart of every medieval community, whether urban or rural, was the parish church. The first churches, built after the conversion of the Saxon kingdoms to Christianity, were mostly monastic or were minsters. Minsters were designed to serve a large area and were staffed by a college of priests. They were often founded on royal estates where the local administration could make the best use of literate clergy. In time, a network of smaller, dependent churches grew up which looked to the minster as the mother house. Many of these were endowed by lords, who could expect a substantial return on their investment from the tithes that everyone had to pay. In fact a contemporary definition of nobility makes it clear that anyone with social pretensions was expected to have their own church. As a consequence, the parish system, though slow to evolve, was already well established by the Norman Conquest and may have played an important role in the fixing of settlement sites. The Domesday Book records 2000 churches serving the 13,000 settlements, although many may not have been included.

Excavations in and around parish churches have shown that many were first founded in the late Saxon period. At St Mary's, Tanner Street, in Winchester one of the rare secular stone buildings was directly converted into the first of a series of churches on the site. More often a simple wooden church was provided, later replaced by a small stone building divided into nave and chancel. After 1066 a vigorous programme of reconstruction replaced most of the Saxon buildings, from cathedrals to parish churches, and throughout the medieval period they continued to be rebuilt. In fact the fortunes of a community, from prosperity to dereliction and back again, can often be traced through the structure of its parish church.

Even where it is not possible to excavate much can be learnt about the history of a church by a careful study of the above-ground structure. Changing architectural styles often allow phases of activity to be dated to within decades. The method used is to draw accurate scale plans showing the position of every stone on both external and internal walls; this brings out hidden details, such as blocked doors and windows, aisles, roof lines, different building stones and mortars. At Rivenhall (Essex), for example, the application of this technique showed that what was thought to be an uninspiring Victorian structure actually preserved substantial medieval and even Saxon work.

Monasticism had been introduced into England at the same time as Christianity, for St Augustine and the first missionaries were all monks. From the seventh century monasteries flourished throughout the Saxon kingdoms. The Viking raids of the ninth century contributed to a decline, but from the tenth century a growing reform movement revitalized religious life. After the Conquest old foundations were everywhere rebuilt and enlarged and new ones founded, until by the time of the break with Rome the 50 houses and 1000 religious had increased to 900 convents and 17,500 monks and nuns.

Medieval monasteries are very different in plan from their earlier Saxon and Celtic predecessors; for now many of the most important buildings, such as church, chapter house and refectory, were grouped around a cloister (99).

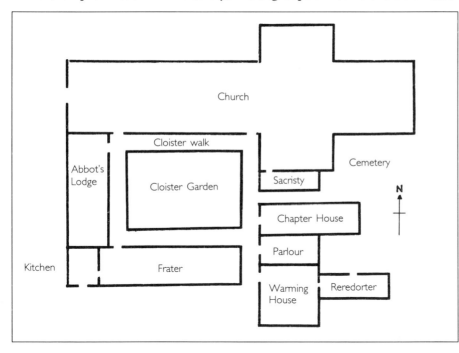

99 Blueprint for a medieval monastery. The church and all the most important domestic buildings were arranged around a cloister. (Compare with the reconstruction of a Celtic monastery, 83.)

Earlier monasteries were less well organized, although the cloistered plan was not unknown in late Saxon England, as excavations at St Augustine's Abbey Canterbury and the New Minster, Winchester have shown.

From the eighth century it had been illegal to be buried anywhere but in consecrated ground around a church. Due to their lack of grave goods medieval cemeteries have tended to be neglected by archaeologists; but the pioneering study carried out by the York Archaeological Trust on the site of the long demolished church of St Helens-on-the-Walls has demonstrated that in the hands of experts the dry bones are capable of revealing many interesting facts about the life and death of the population at large.

As expected child mortality was high, a quarter of the population dying between the ages of six and ten. Studies based on X-rays of a sample of limb bones showed that growth had been interrupted by an average of two serious illnesses in childhood. Intermittent bouts of malnutrition also left their marks in the notched appearance of tooth enamel. It is interesting, however, to note that, from a general examination of the bones, there appears to have been no difference in the treatment accorded to boys and girls.

Over half of the women died before the age of 35; by contrast only a third of the men died young, many surviving into their fifth or sixth decade. Few of the skeletons showed any signs of wounds and most of those that were found were due to accidents rather than acts of violence. The bones also provided evidence for possible cases of rickets, tuberculosis, syphilis and leprosy. Rheumatism and arthritis were even more common within the population than at present.

The skulls provided the biggest surprise, for when they were compared to those from Anglo-Scandinavian and Roman burials from York they showed a marked change in characteristics in the early medieval period, from being long and narrow to broad and short. This trend seems not to have been an isolated quirk, for it has also been recorded elsewhere, for instance in the countryside at Wharram Percy. The cause is not known, but what is certain is that it was not due to few thousand French settlers after the Norman Conquest.

GAZETTEER

Introduction

Gazetteer entries are arranged alphabetically. Sites are located with reference to the Ordnance Survey 1:50,000 series of maps. For example, if a site is at SX 259688 the two letter prefix (or in Ireland a one letter prefix) indicates which of the hundred-kilometre squares into which Britain is divided the site lies in. The six figure number can then be used to locate the exact position of a site. Many, but by no means all, sites are held in public custody. If in doubt it is best to check. Access to sites privately owned is generally granted on reasonable terms if prior permission is sought, but visitors should not abuse this courtesy and ought to remember at all times to observe the Countryside Code. On no account should anyone attempt to dig, use metal detectors or otherwise hunt for souvenirs.

Note: Numbers in captions to illustrations denote gazetteer entries.

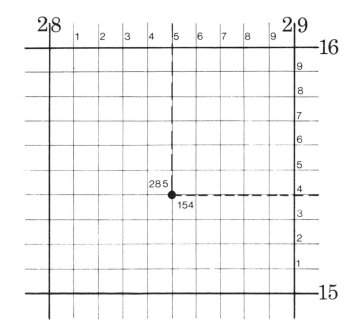

100 How to locate a site on an Ordnance Survey map. The first two figures of a reference indicate which of the vertical grid lines to follow, the third figure refers to the notional subdivisions between these lines. Likewise the third and fourth figures indicate a horizontal grid line, the sixth its subdivision.

Southern England

At Kent's Cavern (Devon) excavations have uncovered some of the earliest evidence for humans in Britain. The many caves and rock shelters of the Mendips around Cheddar Gorge (Somerset) were also lived in by Upper Palaeolithic hunter-gatherers.

Southern England contains many of the most impressive ceremonial and burial sites constructed by the first farmers. Well preserved chambered long barrows can be seen at West Kennet (Wiltshire), Wayland's Smithy (Oxfordshire) and Stoney Littleton (Avon). Erosion has left other tomb chambers open to the air, such as the 'quoits' of Cornwall at Lanyon, Chun and Zennor.

One of the few causewayed camps that offers anything to the casual visitor can be explored on Windmill Hill (Wiltshire). Far more impressive are the henges at Avebury and Stonehenge (both in Wiltshire), Knowlton and Maumbury Rings (both in Dorset). Finally on Shapwick Heath a section of one of the timber trackways across the Somerset Levels has been reconstructed.

Dartmoor is littered with settlements and ritual sites of the Bronze Age abandoned after the climate deteriorated late in the second millennium BC. Grimspound, Merrivale and Riders Rings are among the best examples. Round barrows are also widely distributed throughout the region, good clusters can be seen at Lambourn Seven Barrows (Berkshire), Oakley Down (Dorset), Treyford (Sussex) and around Stonehenge on Salisbury Plain. The best collection of finds from these burials is displayed in Devizes Museum (Wiltshire).

The unsettled conditions of the Iron Age have left a great legacy of hillforts. Maiden Castle, Hambledon Hill and Hod Hill (all in Dorset), to name but a few, are among the finest in England. For a different experience of life in the Iron Age go to the experimental farm at Little Butser (Hampshire).

At Richborough (Kent) traces of the Roman invasion bridgehead of AD 43 are exposed. The Romans changed the face of Britain by founding towns such as Silchester (Surrey). Recent excavations at Dover (Kent) have uncovered the remains of a luxurious town house, complete with frescoes, and at Bath (Avon) there is the sumptuous bathing and shrine complex dedicated to Sulis Minerva. In the countryside a Romanized elite built themselves luxurious villas, the greatest of which, at Fishbourne (West Sussex) may have been the palace of the collaborator King Cogidubnus. Other well preserved villas with fine mosaics can be visited at Bignor (East Sussex) and Lullingstone (Kent). When Saxon raiders threatened the rich lands of the south the Saxon Shore Forts were constructed in the third and fourth centuries AD, of which there are substantial remains at Lympne (Kent), Pevensey (East Sussex), Portchester (Hampshire), Reculver and Richborough (both in Kent).

The invading Saxons established several small kingdoms in southern England. Of these, Kent maintained close links across the Channel, and these links eventually brought the first missionaries to British shores in AD 597. The foundations of a series of small Saxon churches can be traced on the site of St Augustine's Abbey in Canterbury, and the church of St Martin in the same city may have been used for Christian worship even earlier. One of the finest remaining examples of Saxon architecture, a tenth-century church, can be seen at Bradford-upon-Avon (Wiltshire).

As the Saxons expanded, the native British sphere of influence shrank until only the kingdom of Dumnonia in Cornwall held out. The impressive earthwork known as the Wansdyke that meanders through Wiltshire and Avon was probably built at this time. Excavations at the hillfort of South Cadbury (Somerset) have revealed it to have been an important fortified centre in the sixth century. Celtic memorial stones, such as King Doniert's Stone, Men Scryfa and the Tristan Stone in Cornwall provide further tangible evidence for the region's Celtic culture.

Wessex alone of the Saxon kingdoms was able to withstand the Viking onslaught, although even her king had to seek refuge in the dense marshes at Athelney (Somerset). After his eventual victory Alfred and his successors founded many of the fortified burhs. Good examples can be explored at Cricklade (Wiltshire), Wallingford (Berkshire) and Wareham (Dorset).

Champions of lost causes will enjoy refighting the fatal events of 1066 at Battle (West Sussex), but the region is not rich in castles. At Exeter, however, the stone gatehouse remains from a castle erected by the Conquerer himself. There are also good examples of shell keeps on the mottes at Launceston and Restormel (both in Cornwall). Dover Castle is almost perfectly preserved, and as an added bonus also contains a Saxon chapel and Roman lighthouse, while the remains of Corfe (Dorset) form as romantic a ruin to explore as anyone could wish for.

At Old Sarum (Wiltshire) the earthworks and foundations of castle, cathedral and town readily evoke the Middle Ages, as does the half-deserted cinque port of Winchelsea. Late Norman stone houses that once belonged to the wealthy merchants or craftsmen can be seen at Southampton, where a later half-timbered house has been reconstructed complete with all its fixtures and fittings. At the other end of the social spectrum the deserted village at Hound Tor on Dartmoor should not be neglected and there are reconstructions of the homes of peasants and yeoman at the Downs and Weald Open Air Museum at Singleton (West Sussex). Although many rich monasteries once existed in southern England their remains have mostly been quarried away. But at Cleeve Abbey (Somerset) the buildings that surrounded the cloister are almost perfectly preserved and the ruins at Netley (Hampshire) are also impressive.

Central England

Palaeolithic hunters occupied the rock shelters of the Creswell Crags (Derbyshire). From the first farmers there is a fine group of chambered long barrows on the Gloucestershire Cotswolds, namely Belas Knap, Hetty Pegler's Tump, Notgrove and Nympsfield. Otherwise this region cannot match the glories of the Wessex Downlands, although the stone circle, the Rollright Stones (Oxfordshire) and the henge at Arbor Low (Derbyshire) are both well worth a visit. The adventurous can also explore a Neolithic flint mine at Grimes Graves (Norfolk). Another must for visitors is Flag Fen (Cambridgeshire), where excavations continue and the waterlogged timbers of extraordinary Bronze Age structures can be seen.

Hillforts abounded on the hills of the Welsh border country. Fine examples include Caer Caradoc, Old Oswestry, the Wrekin (all in Shropshire), and the Herefordshire Beacon (Hereford and Worcester). Dykes belonging to the tribal centres of the Catuvellauni, the dominant power immediately before the Roman Conquest, can also be traced at Colchester (Essex) and Wheathampstead (St Albans; Hertfordshire). The unique White Horse of Uffington (Berkshire) located on on a hillside beneath a small hillfort may also have been cut during this period.

The Romans founded numerous towns in the region. At St Albans (Hertfordshire) can be seen the well preserved earthworks of a Roman theatre. Leicester and Wroxeter (Shropshire) have substantial remains of walls belonging to a bathing complex, and at Lincoln one of the city gates, the Newport Arch, survives almost intact. Beneath the Norman castle that houses Colchester Museum are the vaults of a temple dedicated to the official cult of emperor worship. Lydney Park (Gloucestershire) houses a very different temple, dedicated to the Celtic god Nodens in the last days of Roman Britain. In the surrounding countryside a Romanized elite lived in elegant villas such as those visible at Chedworth and Great Witcombe (both in Gloucestershire), or North Leigh (Oxfordshire). Less is visible of the military presence, though exceptions are the reconstructed timber buildings of the fort at Baginton (The Lunt; Warwickshire) and the Saxon Shore fort at Burgh Castle (Norfolk).

Saxon settlement was heaviest in East Anglia, where typical domestic buildings have been reconstructed at West Stow (Suffolk). The royal burial mounds of East Anglian kings can also be seen at Sutton Hoo (Suffolk). To the west the power of the kingdom of Mercia is demonstrated by Offa's Dyke that once guarded the Welsh frontier. The region has many fine Saxon churches. At Brixworth (Northamptonshire) is the only survivor of a large Saxon church, often considered to be the best of its period north of the Alps. The excavated remains at North Elmham (Norfolk) provide an idea of what Saxon cathedrals may have looked like. On a more modest scale is the small church built within a Roman fort at Bradwell-

on-Sea (Essex). Finally there is the parish church at Deerhurst (Gloucestershire), where there is also the added bonus of a small Saxon chapel. Unlike these examples many Saxon churches must have been built of wood, but Greenstead-juxta-Ongar (Essex) is the sole survivor.

After the Norman Conquest many castles were constructed. East Anglia, in particular, contains many fine examples. At Thetford (Norfolk) is the largest motte in Britain. Impressive stone tower keeps of the twelfth century can be seen at Castle Rising (Norfolk), Hedingham (Essex) and Orford (Suffolk). At Castle Acre (Norfolk) there are also the ruins of a priory. A unique glimpse into the landscape of medieval England can be obtained at Laxton (Nottinghamshire), one of the few villages to have maintained the open field system of cultivation. The late Norman stone manor houses at Boothby Pagnell (Lincolnshire) and Burton Agnes (Humberside) also bring the past alive. Town houses of the same date can be seen at Lincoln and Bury St Edmunds (Suffolk). Finally the late medieval moated manors at Stokesay (Shropshire) and Lower Brockhampton (Hereford and Worcester) are good examples of fortified manors.

Northern England

Good examples of megalithic tombs are rare in this region, but two earthwork henges can be seen at Penrith (Cumbria) and Thornborough (North Yorkshire). Neither of these henges is associated with a stone circle, but at Keswick (Cumbria) there is a small, but well preserved, stone circle. The Rudston monolith (Humberside), however, at 8m (26ft) tall is the largest standing stone in England. The three standing stones together known as the Devil's Arrows (West Yorkshire) are also well worth a visit. Many of the mysterious cup-and-ring marks are to be found engraved on rock outcrops of the region. Fine examples exist at Ilkley Moor (West Yorkshire), Dod Law and Roughting Linn (both in Northumbria). There is also a chance to explore the site of a Neolithic axe factory at Great Langdale (Cumbria), whose finished products were widely traded throughout Britain.

During the Iron Age many a natural strongpoint of the highland zone was crowned by a hillfort. In addition to their defensive ramparts, at such sites as Mam Tor (Derbyshire), Dod Law and Yeavering Bell (both in Northumberland), many foundations of houses can be traced in the interiors. Stanwick (North Yorkshire), although occupying a low-lying site, is the largest earthwork enclosure in Britain.

The northern frontier of the Roman Empire was eventually drawn across Northumbria and Cumbria, along the Tyne–Solway line and heavily defended by Hadrian's Wall. Parts of the wall are still impressive to this day and many of the associated forts, such as Chesters, Corbridge and Housesteads vividly summon up the life of the common soldier. To the north of Hadrian's Wall the outposts of Hardknott Castle (Cumbria) and High Rochester (Northumbria) are also well preserved while at Rey Cross (Durham) are the finest examples of marching camps to survive in Britain. There were few towns in the region. At Vindolanda an example of the civilian settlements that grew up outside the gates of some forts can be seen. York still has part of the fourth-century town wall, complete with bastions, and at Aldborough (North Yorkshire) there are the mosaics produced by a local workshop.

For a brief period the Saxon kingdom of Northumbria that emerged from the wreck of the Roman province was the dominant force in English politics. Her kings ruled all England north of the Humber and were recognized as overlord far to the south. After the conversion to Christianity the region experienced a cultural renaissance based on monasteries such as those at Jarrow and Monkwearmouth (both in Tyne and Wear), where parts of the monastic churches in which the Venerable Bede worshipped still survive. The relics of St Cuthbert can be seen in Durham Cathedral.

Divided by dynastic strife and civil war, Northumbria was easily conquered by the Vikings in the ninth century. These supreme opportunists not only destroyed but also created a thriving trading centre in the old Roman city of York which has been vividly brought to life in the Jorvik Viking Centre. Elsewhere Viking influence can be seen in the hybrid Anglo-Scandinavian styles of stone carving seen on the crosses at Gosforth and Dearham (both in Cumbria). An almost intact late Saxon church at Escomb (Durham) is also well worth visiting.

After the Norman Conquest many fine castles such as those at Conisborough and Richmond (both in South Yorkshire), were constructed throughout the region. The reformed religious orders also sought out the isolated highland zone in order to return to the original purity of the monastic life. In the process some became rich enough from wool to build monasteries such as Fountains Abbey and Rievaulx (both in West Yorkshire), which remain magnificent even in ruins. At Wharram Percy (North Yorkshire) a deserted medieval village is coming to life again as a result of recent excavations.

Wales

In the National Museum of Wales at Cardiff the finds from the Pontnewydd Cave and the Red Lady of Paviland are displayed. In the south-east there is a group of chambered cairns, at Parc Cwm, St Lythans and Tinkinswood (all in Glamorgan), similar to those of the Cotswolds. Cromlechs, or portal dolmens, solitary tomb chambers revealed by the loss of their cairn, can be seen at Bodowyr (Gwynedd) and Pentre Ifan (Dyfed). But the finest of all the Welsh

megalithic tombs are the two passage graves at Barclodiad y Gawres and Bryn Celli Ddu (both in Gwynedd) which have the closest match across the Irish Sea. Other ritual monuments are not so impressive as those of England. Stone circles, such as that at Cerrig Duon (Powys) tend to be small and there are no grand henge monuments. Ysbyty Cynfyn (Gwynedd), however, provides an interesting example of a later Christianization of one of these pagan sites. From the Iron Age are the forts of Tre'r Ceiri, Holyhead Mountain and Dinorben (all in Gwynedd), where the stone walls of the ramparts and the foundations of houses are well preserved.

After fierce resistance by the hill tribes, encouraged by Caratacus, Wales was conquered by the Romans. Anglesey, the last bastion of druidism, holding out until AD 69. At Y Pigwn (Powys) earthworks belonging to a temporary marching camp, laid out during one of these campaigns, are still visible. Among the spoils of victory there was the gold mined at Dolaucothi (Dyfed). The Second Legion was stationed at Caerleon (Gwent), where the amphitheatre, barrack blocks, part of the baths and a first-class museum allow the life of a legionary to be vividly reconstructed. Numerous smaller forts were built throughout the region and garrisoned by auxiliary troops. At Brecon Gaer and Llandrindod Wells (both in Powys) there are substantial remains of the second-century rebuilding of these forts in stone. Of the coastal forts erected against the Irish raiders of the fourth century the ruins at Caer Gybi on Anglesey are well preserved, and at Cardiff the outer wall of the Roman fort has been reconstructed around the later medieval castle. The Romanized culture of villas and towns, however, made little impact on everyday life in Wales; although at Caerwent (Glamorgan) the impressive remains of the town wall of *Venta Silurum*, the capital of the Silures tribe, can be seen.

The thin veneer of Romanization quickly disappeared during the Dark Ages. Some of the old Iron Age defended sites such as Dinas Emrys (Gwynedd) and Dinas Powys (Glamorgan) were reoccupied, but on the whole little is visible above ground except in museum showcases. The ruling elite, however commemorated themselves with Latin epitaphs on their memorial stones and crosses. Good collections of these monuments can be seen at Carmarthen (Dyfed), Margam (Glamorgan) and Penmachno (Gwynedd).

Alone of the Celtic successor states, the Welsh principalities were able to hold out against the Germanic settlers who seized power in the rest of Roman Britain. Indeed Offa's Dyke had to be built by the English to keep out Welsh raiders. Saxon England had little influence on Wales, but all this changed with the arrival of the aggressive and highly opportunistic Normans. By a never relenting war of attrition the Normans gradually took over Wales, leaving behind them a rich legacy of castles, such as Caerphilly (Glamorgan) and Pembroke (Dyfed) to name but two. Finally only mountainous Gwynedd held out until forced to give up the unequal struggle when Edward I was determined to place the entire island of Britain, Wales and Scotland included, under his rule. In 1282 Llywelyn the Last was killed in a skirmish, and Wales was reorganized to suit her new masters. As part of this plan a series of castles was built all over north Wales, their remains, as at Beaumaris, Caernarfon, Conwy and Harlech, are among the finest surviving monuments from medieval times. Two other contrasting views of life in medieval Wales can be observed at the well-preserved abbey of Tintern and the reconstructed buildings of the deserted village at Cosmeston (both in Glamorgan).

Scotland

The everyday life of the first farmers can be vividly imagined amongst the remains of their stone village at Skara Brae on Mainland, Orkney. At Stanydale (Shetland) there is another stone house, which, from its size, may have been that of a chief, or possibly a meeting place. Many fine examples of megalithic tombs belonging to several different classes can be seen, mainly in the west and north. Some, such as the long chambered cairns at Cairnholy (Dumfries and Galloway) and the magnificent passage grave at Maes Howe (Orkney), show close links with similar examples across the Irish Sea. Others, such as the stalled cairns at Unstan and Midhowe (both Orkney), represent local developments.

At Callanish (Isle of Lewis) the impressive stone circle with four attached avenues is second only to Stonehenge. Other fine henges can be visited at Inverurie (Grampian) and the Ring of Brodgar (Orkney). Excavations at Cairnpapple Hill (Lothian) have revealed that this site had a long and complex history extending from the Neolithic to the Iron Age. Among the remains now visible is a Beaker burial preserved *in situ* under a modern cover. At Kintraw (Strathclyde) those interested in the astronomical theories of Professor Thom may want to see the artificial platform that could have been used to make astronomical observations by far sighting on the Island of Jura. Good examples of the mysterious cup-and-ring marks, together with many Bronze Age cists, are to be found in the Loch Gilphead region (Strathclyde).

Only a few large hillforts, such as Eildon Hill (Borders) and Traprain Law (Lothian), were constructed in Scotland. Most, such as the duns, were on a humbler scale consisting of one or more banks or walls surrounded by ditches; many of the walls subsequently became vitrified. Scattered over the Highlands and Islands, however, are the free-standing towers called brochs, still impressive in ruins. That on the Isle of Mousa (Shetland) is almost perfectly preserved and other fine examples can be see at Clickhimin (also Shetland), Gurness (Orkney) and Dun Carloway (Isle of Lewis). After the brochs were abandoned wheelhouses

were built from their stones as at Jarlshof (Shetland). Some peoples of Scotland also constructed souterrains such as those at Ardestie (Tayside) and Rennibister (Orkney).

In AD 80 Scotland was invaded by the Roman legions under Agricola. The Lowlands were quickly occupied and even the Highlands subdued before the order arrived to evacuate. Apart from a few forward listening posts all the new gains were abandoned, although the Lowlands were to be reoccupied in the mid-second century. At that time the Antonine Wall was constructed across the country from the Forth to the Clyde. As it was built of turf on stone foundations generally only the outer ditch has been well preserved. More can be seen of the forts, such as Rough Castle (Central), which accompanied the Wall. Other fine forts used to garrison the Lowlands can be seen at Ardoch (Tayside), the Birrens (Dumfries and Galloway) and Raedykes (Grampian). The strategy of the Roman army can be followed at the native forts at Burnswark (Dumfries and Galloway), which was used for target practice, and at Woden Law (Borders) where there are the remains of practice siege-works, temporary camps and a military road.

In the final analysis the Romans had little influence upon the Scottish tribes. During the early first millennium AD the people known as the Picts emerged from the anonymity of prehistory. They took advantage of a declining empire to raid deep into Roman Britain. But it is through their inscribed picture stones, such as those at Aberlemno, Fowlis Wester and Glamis (all in Tayside), rather than forts that they make their presence felt in the land.

Scotland was first evangelized by British missionaries from northern England. Some of their priests and converts are commemorated by the Early Christian memorial stones found in the south-west at Govan (Strathclyde), Kirkmadrine and Whithorn (both in Dumfries and Galloway). Then came the Irish, who from their base on Iona, converted the Picts. What may be one of their monasteries may be seen at Eileach-an-Naoimh (Strathclyde). One of the finest examples of Saxon art, the high cross at Ruthwell (Dumfries and Galloway), reminds us that much of the Lowlands received Germanic settlers during this period. Northumbrian architects may also have built the church towers at Restenneth (Tayside) and St Andrew's (Fife).

The first Scots settled the country that would bear their name in the sixth century AD, but the real genesis of modern Scotland came when their king, Kenneth Mac Alpin, ascended the throne of the Picts in 843. At about the same time Vikings were settling the islands and mainland of the north and west. A typical Norse farmstead can be seen at Jarlshof (Shetland) and at the Brough of Birsay (Orkney) an important ecclesiastical and administrative centre of the Earls of Orkney.

The Normans had no territorial claims on Scotland, but under David I (1124–63) large numbers of knights were invited to settle in the country. At Inverurie (Grampian) the motte of one of their castles is still impressive. At the same time the Celtic church was reformed to bring it into line with European trends. New monasteries were endowed by the crown and the nobility, such as the abbey of Jedburgh (Borders), and staffed by members of the Continental orders.

Ireland

The first farmers made their mark on the land with numerous megalithic tombs and ritual centres. Often the stones of the burial chambers stand alone, their surrounding cairns stripped away, to form dolmens, stone tables, similar to those of Wales and Cornwall, such as those at Legananny (Co. Down), Poulnabrone (Co. Clare) or Proleek (Co. Louth). Court cairns, such as Audleystown (Co. Down) or Knockoneill (Co. Derry), featured forecourts partially or completely enclosing a stage for rituals outside their entrances and facades of tall uprights linked with panels of drystone walling. The wedge tomb is exclusively Irish. Named after their characteristic shape, these mounds, such as Labbacallee (Co. Cork), were erected at the very end of the megalithic building period during the early Bronze Age.

The finest of all the megalithic tombs are the passage graves. These consist of circular mounds entered by a single passage ending in a corbelled burial chamber in the heart of the mound. Among the stone slabs that line the passages are many decorated with the abstract designs that form what is known as 'passage grave art'. The group of mounds in the Boyne Valley – Dowth, Knowth and Newgrange (all in Co. Meath), form one of the finest assemblages of prehistoric monuments in the entire British Isles.

Irish ritual monuments are generally smaller and less impressive than their British counterparts. There are a few equivalents to British henges, such as the Giant's Rig (Co. Down), a circular enclosure surrounded by bank and ditch. Stone circles, such as those that are continually being found during peat cutting at Beaghmore (Co. Tyrone), are composed of short stones and enclose only a small area. But the Punchestown monolith (Co. Kildare) is the largest standing stone in the British Isles.

There is less to see of the everyday life of the Neolithic peoples. Some circular stone house foundations are exposed at Lough Gur (Co. Limerick). An axe factory whose products were traded widely over Northern Ireland and Scotland can be visited at Tievebulliagh (Co. Antrim). At Lyles Hill (Co. Antrim), there is a late Neolithic hilltop enclosure similar in some respects to the English causewayed camps.

During the Iron Age only a few hillforts, such as that at Mooghaun (Co. Cork), were constructed that can compare with those of Britain. Rather than serving as forts or settlements the largest earthworks of this period, such as those at Garranes (Co. Cork), Navan (Co. Antrim) or Tara (Co. Meath), were intended mostly as tribal assembly places. Recent excavations have shown that activity at these sites often stretches back without a break into the later Bronze Age. In contrast there are some superb stone forts in the west of the country such as Dún Aengus (Co. Galway). One of the finest examples of pre-Christian sculpture can be seen at Turoe (Co. Galway) on the mysterious ritual stone of the first century AD.

The Roman occupation of *Britannia* had few repercussions across the Irish Sea. But by the fourth century AD the Irish had acquired the idea of writing and developed their own script, Ogham, which was used to write brief epitaphs on memorial stones. Traditional life continued undisturbed. The nobles lived in raths, such as those at Ballycatteen (Co. Cork, Cush (Co. Limerick) or Lissue (Co. Antrim). Where there was good building stone cashels were constructed, such as those at the Grianán of Aileach (Co. Donegal), Knockdrum (Co. Cork) and Staigue (Co. Kerry). In the lakes the equivalent was the crannog, and artificial island such as can be seen at Lough-na-Cranagh (Co. Antrim). Full-scale reconstructions of a crannog and a cashel can be seen at Craggaunowen (Co. Clare). Examples of the intriguing souterrains can be visited at Donaghmore (Co. Louth) and Drumena (Co. Down).

The Early Christian Period was the Golden Age of Irish culture. Learning and the arts flourished in the monasteries. The typical Celtic monastery consisted of several small stone churches and a scattering of monks' cells within an enclosure wall or bank. Good examples can be seen at Inishcaltra and Scattery Island (Co. Clare), Inishmurray (Co. Sligo) and Nendrum (Co. Down). Magnificent high crosses and tomb slabs mark the site of monasteries at Clonmacnoise (Co. Offaly), Kells (Co. Meath) and Monasterboice (Co. Louth) to name but a few. Other sites, such as Ardmore (Co. Waterford) and Devenish (Co. Fermanagh), are dominated by round towers. Finally there is Skellig St Michael (Co. Kerry), a community on a rock far out into the Atlantic for those who wished to retreat from the world, where the beehive cells and oratories survive almost intact.

The brilliant promise of the Early Christian Period failed to come to fruition as the squabbling petty kingdoms were incapable of uniting to form a nation. One made the fatal mistake of inviting the help of Norman knights. In their wake the Anglo-Norman invaders built castles, at first motte and baileys, later such impressive stone fortresses as Roscommon Castle (Co. Roscommon) and Trim (Co. Meath). Another of the major changes of the period was the reform of the Church to bring it into line with the rest of Christian Europe. In the process new monasteries belonging to the Continental orders were founded and endowed with buildings on the claustral plan, as can be seen at Mellifont (Co. Louth) and Jerpoint (Co. Kilkenny).

Sites

1 Aberlemno (Tayside)
Pictish symbol stones.
Location: 8km (5 miles) east of Forfar at NO 523559.
Description: Two fine Pictish stones can be seen in an enclosure by the side of the B9134. Another is in the churchyard at NO 523555.

2 Abernethy (Tayside)
Round-tower.
Location: 9.7km (6 miles) south-east of Perth at NO 191165.
Description: One of only three round-towers outside Ireland. Nearby, at NO 183153, is the hillfort of Castle Law.

3 Abinger (Surrey)
Mesolithic camp site.
Location: 6.5km (4 miles) south-west of Dorking at TQ 112459.
Description: In the grounds of the manor house a modern shelter (apply to the manor for the key) covers a small pit that formed part of a camp site. Nearby, at TQ 114460, is the small motte of a Norman castle.

4 Ackling Dyke (Dorset)
Roman road.
Location: 22.5km (14 miles) south-west of Salisbury at SU 015163.
Description: The raised agger of this minor road can be traced for several miles along a public right of way.

5 Aghanaglack (Co. Fermanagh)
Megalithic tomb.
Location: 11.3km (7 miles) from Enniskillen at H 098436.
Description: A good example of a court grave. Nearby at H 113462 cup-and-ring marks can be seen on the Boho Stones.

6 Ahenny (Co. Tipperary)
High crosses.
Location: 7.2km (4½ miles) north-east of Carrick-on-Sear at S 4129.
Description: Two fine high crosses are to be found in the churchyard.

7 Aldborough (North Yorkshire)
Roman town.
Location: 35.4km (22 miles) from York at SE 405665.
Description: *Issurium* was founded early in the second century AD to serve as the tribal capital of the Brigantes. Part of the late Roman town wall is preserved in a public park in the south-west area of the town. Two mosaics belonging to the flourishing local workshop can be seen *in situ* on the site of a fourth-century town-house now occupied by the Aldborough Arms. Others are on display in Leeds City Museum.

8 Alice Holt (Hampshire)
Roman kiln.
Location: 3.2km (2 miles) south of Farnham at SU 808403.
Description: A reconstruction of a kiln typical of those used in the important New Forest pottery industry. Many overgrown dumps of kiln wasters, pots spoiled during firing, can also be seen in the region.

9 Anaghmore (Co. Antrim)
Megalithic tomb.
Location: 2.2km (1½ miles) north of Crossmaglen at H 905178.
Description: A good example of a court grave.

10 Andreas (Isle of Man)
Viking sculptures.
Location: 6.4km (4 miles) north of Ramsey at SC 411993.
Description: The church houses a small collection of tenth-century sculptured stones showing mixed Celtic and Norse influences, including scenes from Viking mythology.

11 Anglesey (Gwynedd)
See: Barclodiad y Gawres, Bodowyr, Bryn Celli Ddu, Caer Gybi, Din Lligwy and Llangadwaladr.

12 The Antonine Wall (Central and Strathclyde)
Roman frontier.
Location: Between the Clyde and Forth estuaries.
Description: The Antonine Wall was not actually a wall at all, but was mostly turf laid on a stone foundation. As a consequence it is not as well preserved as Hadrian's Wall and often only the line of the ditch can be traced. At Watling Lodge, 2.4km (1½ miles) south of Falkirk at NS 865798, the wall itself has mostly disappeared but the ditch, 12m (20ft) wide, is still well preserved. In the same general area at the Tenfield Plantation, NS 855798, the ditch is also well preserved and much more of the wall itself has survived, including beacon platforms. Of the auxiliary forts Rough Castle (see separate entry) is the best preserved. A good collection of material from the Wall, including inscriptions, can be seen in the Hunterian Museum of Glasgow University.

13 The Aran Isles (Co. Galway)
See: Dún Aengus and Dún Oghil.

14 Arbor Low (Derbyshire)
Henge and stone circle.
Location: 4.8km (3 miles) west of Middleton at SK 161636.
Description: A bank and internal ditch form an enclosure 76m (250ft) in diameter inside which 50 prone stones are arranged in a circle.

15 Arbory Hill (Strathclyde)
Iron Age fort.
Location: 1.6km (1 mile) north-east of Abington at NS 944238.

Description: A small but well preserved fort consisting of three concentric rings of defences, an inner drystone wall within two pairs of banks and ditches.

16 Ardestie (Tayside)
Souterrain.
Location: 9.6km (6 miles) north-east of Dundee at NO 502344.
Description: A fine example, lacking only the original roofing slabs. Another, with multiple entrances, can be visited nearby at Cairlungie (NO 511359).

17 Ardmore (Co. Waterford)
Round-tower.
Location: 8km (5 miles) east of Youghal at X 188773.
Description: An almost perfectly preserved example, standing to its full height of 29m (95ft).

18 Ardoch (Tayside)
Roman fort.
Location: 19.3km (12 miles) north of Stirling at NN 839079.
Description: The defensive ditches, dating to the early second century, are well preserved on the northern and western sides of the fort.

19 Ardwell (Dumfries and Galloway)
Broch.
Location: 16km (10 miles) south of Stranraer at NX 066466.
Description: Foundations of one of the few brochs in south-west Scotland can be seen within a promontory fort. Nearby, at NX 107455, is a well preserved motte from a twelfth-century Norman castle.

20 Arran (Strathclyde)
Prehistoric sites.
Location: 24km (15 miles) by ferry from Ardrossan.
Description: Among the most interesting of many prehistoric sites is the complex of six stone circles, together with standing stones and cist graves, on Machrie Moor at NR 011325. Cairn Ban (NR 991262), the Giants Graves (NR 043246) and Tormore (NR 9033109) are all chambered cairns. Finally at Auchagallon (NR 893349) is a good example of a Bronze Age round cairn surrounded by a stone circle.

21 Athelney (Somerset)
Historic site.
Location: 12.9km (8 miles) north-east of Taunton at ST 346293.
Description: Alfred the Great, King of Wessex, founded a monastery here at the place where he had taken refuge after being surprised by Vikings. The site is marked by a modern monument. The most famous find, the Alfred Jewel, is on display in the Ashmolean Museum, Oxford.

22 Audleystown (Co. Down)
Megalithic tomb.
Location: 1.2km ($\frac{3}{4}$ mile) west of Strangford at J 56505.
Description: A fine example of a court cairn.

23 Avebury (Wiltshire)
Neolithic henge.
Location: 11.25km (7 miles) west of Marlborough at SU 100700.
Description: The village of Avebury shelters within the enclosure of a giant Neolithic henge. The bank and internal ditch which surround this circular enclosure of 4.8ha (12 acres) are still impressive. Around the perimeter was once a stone circle, two smaller circles were also placed in the centre. Only 27 megaliths survive, but the positions of many others are marked with concrete pillars. The stone used was sarsen sandstone from the nearby Marlborough Downs, where natural sarsen boulders can be seen on National Trust land at Piggle Dene (SU 142686) and Lockeridge Dene (SU 143673.) The Alexander Keiller Museum in the centre of Avebury houses an important collection of locally excavated material.

24 Badbury Rings (Dorset)
Hillfort.
Location: 4.8km (3 miles) north-west of Wimbourne Minster at ST 964030.
Description: A medium-sized hillfort defended by three concentric rings of ramparts.

25 Baginton (Warwickshire)
Roman fort.
Location: On the southern outskirts of Coventry at SP 344752.
Description: Full-scale reproductions of Roman timber military buildings, dating from c.AD 60–80, have been made on their original sites. They include the east gate, a granary that serves as the site museum and a curious circular stockade that may have been used for training horses. Also known as The Lunt.

26 Balladoole (Isle of Man)
Viking ship burial.
Location: 1.6km (1 mile) west of Castletown at SC 246682.
Description: The position of this pagan ship burial is outlined within the ramparts of a hillfort. The rich grave goods are on display in the Manx Museum in Douglas.

27 Ballycatteen (Co. Cork)
Rath.
Location: 12km ($7\frac{1}{2}$ miles) south-west of Kinsale at W 582459.
Description: A fine example of a rath enclosed by three circuits of defences within which are the foundations of huts and three souterrains.

28 Ballymacdermot (Co. Armagh)
Megalithic tomb.
Location: 3.2km (2 miles) south-west of Newry at J 063238.
Description: A good example of a court cairn.

29 Ballynoe (Co. Down)
Stone circle.
Location: 4km ($2\frac{1}{2}$ miles) south of Downpatrick at J 481404.

Description: A good example of one of the smaller stone circles formed from 50 small stones.

30 Bamburgh Castle (Northumberland)
Castle.
Location: 38.6km (24 miles) south-east of Berwick at NU 184350.
Description: The rock of Bamburgh, now occupied by a twelfth-century keep, was an important centre for the early Saxon kingdom of Bernicia.

31 Barclodiad y Gawres (Anglesey, Gwynedd)
Megalithic tomb.
Location: 14.5km (9 miles) south-east of Holyhead at SH 329709.
Description: A fine example of a passage grave, containing the best passage grave art outside of Ireland.

32 Barmekin of Echt (Grampian)
Hillfort.
Location: 24km (15 miles) south-west of Aberdeen at NJ 725070.
Description: A small, but well preserved, fort with five concentric rings of defences.

33 Bartlow Hills (Essex)
Roman barrows.
Location: 16km (10 miles) south-east of Cambridge at TL 587448.
Description: Four barrows of the mid-second century, finds are in Saffron Walden Museum.

34 Barton-upon-Humber (Lincolnshire)
Saxon tower.
Location: 22.5km (14 miles) east of Scunthorpe at TA 035219.
Description: A good example of Saxon stonework, featuring decorative pilasters.

35 Bath (Avon)
Roman baths and temple.
Location: 19km (12 miles) west of Bristol.
Description: The bathing complex in the city centre, fed by natural hot springs, features several large swimming pools in addition to 'Turkish bath' suites. Its reservoir doubled as a holy spring into which the faithful cast offerings. Recently the forecourt of the temple of Minerva was excavated and placed on display. The site museum has an excellent collection of votives, tombstones and sculptures.

36 Battle (East Sussex)
Historic battlefield.
Location: 9.5km (6 miles) north west of Hastings at TQ 746163.
Description: The historic battlefield is marked by the ruins of an abbey founded by William the Conqueror. According to tradition the site of the high altar marked the spot where King Harold fell.

37 Beacon Hill (Hampshire)
Hillfort.
Location: 8.9km (5½ miles) north of Whitchurch at SU 458573.

Description: Within the single rampart some hut platforms are visible. In the south-west corner there is also the grave of the fifth Earl of Carnarvon, co-discoverer of Tutankhamun's tomb.

38 Beaghmore (Co. Tyrone)
Stone circles.
Location: 13.6km (8½ miles west of Cookstown at H 685864.
Description: Many small stone circles, alignments and cairns have been exposed by peat cutting in this region.

39 Beaumaris (Gwynedd)
Castle.
Location: On Anglesey, 8km (5 miles) north-east of the Menai Bridge at SH 607763.
Description: A fine Edwardian concentric castle, consisting of two rings of walls studded with great towers and gatehouses, each a mini-keep.

40 Belas Knap (Gloucestershire)
Megalithic tomb.
Location: 2.8km (1¼ miles) south of Winchcombe at SP 022254.
Description: A fine example of a long barrow, unusual in that the chambers are in the side of the mound and not opening off a passage from the court.

41 Benwell (Tyne and Wear)
Roman temple.
Location: 3.2km (2 miles) west of Newcastle at NZ 214647.
Description: The fort and town of *Condercum* has almost disappeared under the suburbs. In Broomridge Avenue the foundations of a small Roman temple are exposed, dedicated to the god Atenocritus. Three altars from the temple, together with the head belonging to the cult statue of the god, can be seen in Newcastle Museum. Casts have been replaced on site. At the bottom of Denhill Park housing estate there is the only surviving crossing of the *vallum* that belonged to Hadrian's Wall.

42 Berkhamstead (Hertfordshire)
Castle.
Location: 45km (28 miles) north of London at SP 995083.
Description: Earthworks belonging to a late eleventh-century motte and bailey castle.

43 Bewcastle (Cumbria)
Saxon cross.
Location: 24km (15 miles) north-east of Carlisle at NY 565746.
Description: In the churchyard is one of the finest pieces of early Saxon sculpture to survive. It is almost complete, lacking only the head piece, standing 4.1m (14½ft) tall. It is carved with figures, foliage and an illegible runic inscription.

44 Bignor (West Sussex)
Roman villa.
Location: 22.5km (14 miles) from Chichester at
SU 988147.
Description: A series of six mosaics, from a fourth-
century courtyard villa, are preserved under modern
sheds. The two most interesting show Venus attended
by cupids playing at gladiators, and Ganymede being
carried off by Zeus in the form of an eagle.

45 Birdoswald (Cumbria)
Roman fort.
Location: 25.7km (16 miles) north-east of Carlisle at
NY 615662.
Description: The defensive walls are relatively well
preserved, especially in the region of the south and
east gates.

46 The Birrens (Dumfries and Galloway)
Roman fort.
Location: 1km ($\frac{1}{2}$ mile) south of Middlebie at
NY 218753.
Description: *Blatobulgium* stood on the main military
road from Carlisle into Scotland and was one of the
largest forts in the Scottish Lowlands. The turf
rampart and the ditches are especially well preserved
on the northern side.

47 Bishop Auckland (County Durham)
Saxon cross.
Location: 16km (10 miles) south-west of Durham at
NZ 220285.
Description: In the southernmost of the two churches
belonging to the town is a fine example of a Saxon
high cross carved with a classical design of figures and
a vine scroll.

48 Black Carts (Northumbria)
Hadrian's Wall.
Location: 9.6km (6 miles) north-west of Hexham at
NY 889713.
Description: A well-preserved section of the wall 200m
(656ft) in length which is part of the later narrow
building, 2.4m (8ft) wide. It incorporates the back
wall of a turret, but the front wall has been reduced
to the foundations.

49 Blackstone Edge (Greater Manchester)
Roman road.
Location: 24km (15 miles) north-east of Manchester
between SD 973170 and SD 988184.
Description: This minor road led from Manchester to
Ilkley. It is 4.9m (16ft) across, outlined with
substantial kerbstones within which the surface is now
made up of large paving stones – these originally
would have been surfaced with gravel. A stone trough
down the centre probably held turf to allow the
hooves of horses to get a grip.

50 Boa Island (Co. Fermanagh)
Stone figures.
Location: In Loch Erne, 35.4km (22 miles) north of
Enniskillen at H 085620.

Description: Two curious stone figures dating to the
early first millennium AD can be seen in the graveyard
at Caldragh.

51 Bodowyr (Gwynedd)
Megalithic tomb.
Location: On the Island of Anglesey 11.3km (7 miles)
south-west of the Menai Bridge, at SH 464682.
Description: A fine example of a cromlech.

52 Boothby Pagnell (Lincolnshire)
Medieval manor house.
Location: 8km (5 miles) south-east of Grantham at
SK 9711307.
Description: A small stone house of *c.*AD 1200
consisting of a first-floor hall and solar above a stone
vaulted undercroft. Permission to visit can be obtained
from the Hall in whose grounds it stands.

53 Boscawen-un (Cornwall)
Stone circle.
Location: 1.6km (1 mile) north of St Buryan at
SW 412274.
Description: Small but well-preserved remains of a
stone circle made up of 19 stones, with one in the
middle. A short distance north-east of the site, at
SW 425282, is a prominent standing stone, the Blind
Fiddler, which is 3m (10ft) high.

54 Bosham (West Sussex)
Saxon church.
Location: 6.4km (4 miles) west of Chichester at
SU 804039.
Description: The west tower, nave and chancel arch
survive from an eleventh-century Saxon church
illustrated on the Bayeux Tapestry.

55 Boyle (Co. Roscommon)
Medieval monastery.
Location: 48km (30 miles) north of Roscommon at
G 800030.
Description: Ruins of the church and claustral
buildings of a reformed monastery.

56 Braaid (Isle of Man)
Viking farmstead.
Location: 5.6km ($3\frac{1}{2}$ miles) west of Douglas at
SC 325766.
Description: A pair of typical boat-shaped Viking
longhouses can be seen at Braaid, belonging to a small
farmstead, together with the foundations of a large
Iron Age round-house.

57 Bradford-on-avon (Wiltshire)
Saxon church.
Location: 8km (5 miles) south of Bath at ST 824689.
Description: This tenth-century church is complete,
apart from the south porch. The exterior is decorated
with fine pilaster work. High above the chancel arch
are two Saxon sculptures of angels, all that survives
from the rood (crucifixion). A fine medieval tithe barn
belonging to a monastic grange can also be visited on
the outskirts of the town.

58 Brading (Isle of Wight)
Roman villa.
Location: On the southern outskirts of the town at
SZ 599853.
Description: Four rooms, decorated with mosaics, from
the fourth-century villa are preserved under cover. One
of the mosaics shows Orpheus playing his lyre, in the
room next door Bacchus occupies the centre, while a
variety of curious figures, including a cock-headed
being, occupy the side panels. The other two mosaics
illustrate the legend of Perseus and Andromeda.

59 Bradwell-on-Sea (Essex)
Saxon church.
Location: 11.2km (7 miles) east of Maldon at
TM 031082.
Description: A seventh-century church, incorporating
reused Roman materials, built across the west wall of
the Saxon Shore fort of *Othonia*.

60 Braunton (Devon)
Open fields.
Location: 8km (5 miles) north-west of Barnstaple at
SS 475360.
Description: Braunton is one of the rare surviving
places where the medieval open field system of
cultivation can still be seen in action. The field
divisions in use at the site today are over six hundred
years old. A small museum in the village churchyard
explains the history of the site.

61 Breamore (Hampshire)
Saxon church.
Location: 14.5km (9 miles) south of Salisbury at
SU 153188.
Description: The nave, central tower and south porch
survive from a late tenth-century minster church. The
lower courses of the Saxon chancel and north porch
can also be traced beneath the later walls. Over the
door to the south porch is a contemporary inscription.

62 Brechin (Tayside)
Round-tower.
Location: 11.2km (7 miles) west of Montrose at
NO 596601.
Description: A tenth-century round-tower is
incorporated into the medieval cathedral.

63 Brecon y Gaer (Powys)
Roman fort.
Location: 4km (2½ miles) west of Brecon at SL 002297
Description: Remains of three gates, of which the
south gate is the best preserved, two turrets and part
of the perimeter wall belonging to the second-century
rebuilding in stone survive.

64 Brixworth (Northamptonshire)
Saxon church.
Location: 11.3km (7 miles) north of Northampton at
SP 747713.
Description: The church of All Saints is the only
example of a large Saxon church to survive Norman
rebuilding. The 36.6-m (120-ft) long nave was built

in the late seventh century. As is typical in this early
period large amounts of Roman materials were reused
in the fabric. Blocked arches in the walls of the nave
show that the church was once much larger, with
flanking porticii chapels on either side, which were
later knocked together to form a continuous aisle. The
lower part of the tower was once the west porch of the
original church, to which an upper storey was added
in the late tenth century.

65 Brompton, (North Yorkshire)
Viking sculptures.
Location: 1.6km (1 miles) north of Northallerton at
SE 373396.
Description: In the parish church is a fine collection of
Anglo-Scandinavian sculptures, including 'hog back'
tombstones – stylized houses, with arched gables and
muzzled bears at either end.

66 The Brough of Birsay (Orkney)
Ecclesiastical and Viking remains.
Location: 32.3km (20 miles) north-west of Kirkwall at
HY 230280.
Description: On this small island (accessible by
causeway – check the tide times) was an important
administrative and ecclesiastical centre serving the
Norse Earls of Orkney. The foundations of the ruler's
halls, the cathedral and the bishop's palace are
exposed.

67 Brunton (Northumberland)
Hadrian's Wall.
Location: 6.4km (4 miles) north of Hexham at
NY 921698.
Description: A well-preserved section of the Wall
standing up to 5.2m (17ft) high and incorporating a
turret. It is located at the point where the wall was
reduced in width, to the east of the turret it is 3m
(10ft) wide, but to the west only 1.8m (6ft) wide.

68 Bryn Celli Ddu (Anglesey, Gwynedd)
Megalithic tomb.
Location: On the island of Anglesey south-east of
Llanddaniel Fab at SH 508702.
Description: A fine example of a passage grave.

69 Budore (Co. Antrim)
Raths.
Location: 8km (5 miles) east of Crumlin at J 234762.
Description: There are two raths, the smaller, northern
example is the better preserved.

70 Burgh Castle (Norfolk)
Roman fort.
Location: 6.4km (4 miles) south-west of Great
Yarmouth at TG 475045.
Description: The perimeter wall of the Saxon Shore
fort of *Gariannonum* survives up to 4.6m (15ft) high
on three sides.

71 Burnswark (Dumfries and Galloway)
Hillfort and Roman camps.
Location: 6.4km (4 miles) south-east of Lockerbie at
NY 186788.

Description: Below this small hillfort, on the south-east and the north-west sides, are two Roman siege camps. On the northern side there are also the Three Brethren, mounds that may once have supported catapults firing lead sling-bolts. Examples of these missiles were actually found in the hillfort during excavations. Appearances, however, are deceptive, as although these earthworks are clearly designed to mount a siege, excavations have shown that they were constructed long after the hillfort had been abandoned, presumably for target practice during military manoeuvres.

72 Burren (Co. Clare)
Prehistoric sites.
Location: 19km (12 miles) north-west of Gort.
Description: Among the many sites are the dolmens at Poulnabrone (M 2400), Ballyganners (R 2294), Baur (M 2200), Derrynavahaugh (M 1805) and Parknabinnia (R 2694). The cashel at Caherdoonerish (M 1611) is a fine example of its type and at Ballykinvarga (R 2694) the outer defences include a fine strip of chevaux-de-frise.

73 Burton Agnes (Humberside)
Medieval manor.
Location: 9.7km (6 miles) west of Bridlington at TA 102633.
Description: A stone late twelfth-century manor house, disguised by a later cladding of brick, consisting of a first-floor hall above a vaulted undercroft.

74 Bury St Edmunds (Suffolk)
Norman townhouse.
Location: 37km (24 miles) west of Cambridge in the market place.
Description: Moyses Hall, which houses the local archaeological museum, is a fine twelfth-century town house. Nearby two gatehouses survive from the great medieval abbey.

75 Butser (Hampshire)
Experimental prehistoric farm.
Location: 4.8km (3 miles) south of Petersfield at SU 724204.
Description: A reconstruction of a working farm of the fourth century BC. Although the main part of the farm is not open to the general public a demonstration area is provided, which features a reconstructed Iron Age house based on the example excavated at Pimperne in Dorset.

76 Caer Caradoc (Shropshire)
Hillfort.
Location: 1.6km (1 mile) north of Church Stretton at SO 477953.
Description: A small hillfort that according to local tradition was one of the bases from which Caratacus organized resistance to the Romans.

77 Caer Gybi (Anglesey, Gwynedd)
Roman fort.
Location: On Anglesey overlooking Holyhead harbour at SH 246827.

Description: One of a series of small forts built as protection from Irish pirates. Parts of the walls, featuring three corner towers, still stand 4m (15ft) high.

78 Caerleon (Gwent)
Legionary base.
Location: 4.8km (3 miles) north-east of Newport at ST 339906.
Description: Caerleon was founded as the base for the Second Legion in AD 75. The foundations of one of three of the original 64 barracks blocks can be seen at Prygs Field together with a stretch of the rampart. To the south-east of the town, outside the area enclosed by the Roman walls, is the amphitheatre, the best preserved example in Britain. The recently excavated legionary bath-house can be visited near the the Bull Inn. The Caerleon Legionary Museum covers all aspects of army life.

79 Caernarfon (Gwynedd)
Castle and Roman fort.
Location: 16km (10 miles) south-west of Bangor at SH 478627.
Description: The great castle was built by Edward I *c.*1283–1330 as the centre of royal power in Gwynedd. It consists of a chain of towers, each a mini-fortress in its own right, linked by a curtain wall. On the outskirts of the town, at SH 485624, are the remains of the Roman fort of *Segontium*. Within the perimeter wall the foundations of the headquarters building, barracks, workshops, a bath-house and a mithraeum can be seen.

80 Caerphilly (Glamorgan)
Castle.
Location: 6.4km (4 miles) north of Cardiff at ST 155871.
Description: Caerphilly Castle, the largest in Wales, was begun *c.*1270 by an English lord. It consists of two concentric walls, studded with towers, surrounded by moats. Behind are the unfinished earthworks of an outer bailey, perhaps intended as a refuge for the inhabitants of the town.

81 Caerwent (Gwent)
Roman town.
Location: 8km (5 miles) south-west of Chepstow at ST 469905.
Description: *Venta Silurum* was founded in the late first century AD as the tribal capital of the Silures. Early in the third century it was surrounded by a wall, which was later strengthened with towers. Defences are especially well preserved on the southern and eastern sides of the modern town. Here parts of the walls stand to a height of 5m (16½ft). Within the walls foundations of houses and an octagonal temple are exposed and two inscribed stones are in the parish church. Other finds are on display in Newport Museum and the National Museum of Wales in Cardiff.

82 Cairnholy (Dumfries and Galloway)
Megalithic tombs.
Location: 6.4km (4 miles) south-east of Creetown at
NX 517538.
Description: Two long cairns, now rather eroded, but
with fine forecourts and burial chambers.

83 Cairnpapple Hill (Lothian)
Prehistoric ritual centre.
Location: 4.8km (3 miles) north of Bathgate at
NS 987717.
Description: A complex site that was the focus of
ritual from the Neolithic to the Iron Age. First the
site was marked with three large boulders, then a
typical Neolithic henge with two simple gap entrances
was laid out by cutting a ditch from the rock. An oval
ring of 24 stones was laid out around the perimeter
and three more stones placed near the centre. Two
Beaker inhumation burials were later made within the
enclosure, one of which is preserved *in situ*. Next a
large stone cairn was heaped over the western part of
the henge. A burial was made in a cist in the centre
of the cairn, then it was enlarged. Later many urned
cremations were inserted into the cairn as secondary
burials.

84 Callanish (Western Isles)
Stone circle.
Location: On the Isle of Lewis, 20km (12½ miles) west
of Stornaway at NB 213330.
Description: After Stonehenge, Callanish is perhaps the
most impressive of all stone circles in the British Isles.
The heart of the monument is formed by a flattened
circle of 13 tall stones 13m (43ft) across. Within the
circle is a single standing stone 4.6m (15ft) high and
a small round cairn. Four stone rows radiate from the
circle. A double row of 19 stones runs towards the
north-east, other single rows point to the west, north-
east and south. Two other stone circles can be seen
nearby at Cnoc Ceann, NB 222326 and Cnoc Fillibhir
Bheag, NB 226326.

85 Canterbury (Kent)
Saxon churches.
Location: 80km (50 miles) south-east of London.
Description: St Martin's Church (TR 158577) may be
the one mentioned by the Venerable Bede as a Roman
foundation in which the Christian Queen Bertha of
Kent worshipped before the arrival of St Augustine.
The western part of the chancel is of early Saxon date
and has much reused Roman material in its fabric.
The foundations of several small Saxon churches which
served the the Benedictine community founded by the
Saint can be seen at St Augustine's Abbey at
TR 155577.

86 Cardiff (Glamorgan)
Castle.
Location: 80km (50 miles) east of Bristol at
SS 190770.
Description: Cardiff Castle stands on the site of a
fourth-century Roman fort whose perimeter wall was

reconstructed in the nineteenth century. Within is a
Norman motte crowned with a twelfth-century shell
keep. Nearby is the National Museum of Wales, which
has an excellent display of archaeological finds made
all over the Principality, including artefacts from the
Iron Age ritual deposit of Llyn Cerrig Bach and many
Early Christian memorial stones.

87 The Carew Cross (Dyfed)
High cross.
Location: 7.2km (4½ miles) east of Pembroke at
SN 046037.
Description: At 4m (13ft) tall, the Carew Cross is one
of the largest and finest of the Early Christian
monuments of Wales. It is inscribed *Margiteut rex etg
filius* – 'King Margiteut, son of Etguin', possibly the
local prince Maredudd ap Edwin (died *c*.AD 1035).

88 Carlwark (Derbyshire)
Hillfort.
Location: 4.8km (3 miles) south-west of Sheffield at
SK 260815.
Description: A well-preserved hillfort defended by a
drystone wall, preserved up to 1.8m (6ft) high in
places.

89 Carmarthen (Dyfed)
Early Christian memorial stones.
Location: 80km (50 miles) west of Cardiff.
Description: The museum houses an important
collection of Early Christian memorial stones from the
area. The most interesting bears a bilingual inscription
in Latin and Ogham: *Memoria Voteporigis Protictoris*,
commemorating Votepor, a fifth-century British ruler.

90 Carn Brea (Cornwall)
Hillfort.
Location: 2km (1¼ miles) south of Redruth at
SW 685407.
Description: Within the stone banks and ditches are
the outlines of many hut circles. To the eastern side of
the hill there are also the earthworks belonging to a
small twelfth-century castle.

91 Carn Euny (Cornwall)
Iron Age settlement.
Location: 6.4km (4 miles) west of Penzance at
SW 402288.
Description: A well-preserved settlement of eight
houses, dated to the first century BC. One is associated
with a fogou, a curved underground stone-lined
passage 20m (66ft) in length.

92 Carranmore (Co. Antrim)
Megalithic tomb.
Location: 9.6km (6 miles) west of Cushendun at
D 218388.
Description: On the summit of Mount Carranmore is
a large cairn that covers a passage grave. The burial
chamber at the end of the passage features a fine
corbelled stone roof.

93 Carrawburgh (Northumberland)
Mithraeum.
Location: 6.4km (4 miles) west of Chesters at
NY 859771.
Description: Just outside the slight remains of a
Roman fort are the foundations of a shrine to Mithras.
A full-scale reconstruction of which can be seen in the
University Museum of Antiquities at Newcastle. To
the north of the fort a marshy well represents the site
of the shrine to the water-nymph Coventina, from
which 14,000 coins, together with many other votive
offerings, were recovered. Many of these finds can be
seen on display at Chesters museum.

94 Carrowkeel (Co. Sligo)
Megalithic cemetery.
Location: 24km (15 miles) south of Sligo at
G 755155.
Description: A cemetery of 14 passage graves spread
out along five low ridges, a total distance of 1.6km
(1 mile).

95 Cashel (Co. Tipperary)
Celtic monastery.
Location: 13km (8 miles) south-east of Tipperary at
S 073407.
Description: The principal ruins of this important site,
once the seat of the Kings of Munster, are those of the
medieval cathedral, twelfth-century Cormac's Chapel
and a round-tower.

96 Cashtal-yn-Ard (Isle of Man)
Megalithic tomb.
Location: 4km (2½ miles) south-east of Maughold at
SC 463092.
Description: The forecourt and tomb chambers from a
vanished long cairn.

97 Castell Collen (Powys)
Roman fort.
Location: Just north-west of Llandrindod Wells at
SO 055628.
Description: The second-century stone ramparts enclose
an area of 2ha (5 acres) in which the foundations of
the headquarters building, granaries and a bath-house
can be discerned.

98 Castle Acre (Norfolk)
Priory and castle.
Location: 19.3km (12 miles) east of King's Lynn at
TF 813148.
Description: There remains substantial parts of the
church and the eastern range of the cloister, including
the chapter house and the undercroft of the dorter.
The castle of the priory's patrons, featuring an early
twelfth-century shell keep, is located nearby.

99 Castle Dore (Cornwall)
Hillfort.
Location: 4.8km (3 miles) north of Fowey at
SX 103548.
Description: According to tradition this small hillfort
was the seat of King Mark of Cornwall, uncle of

Tristan and intended husband of Isolde. The Tristan
Stone, 3.2km (2 miles) south of Castle Dore, at
SX 0954, is an Early Christian memorial stone of
the sixth century inscribed: *Drustanus hic jacit cunomori
filius* – 'Here lies Tristan, the son of Cunomorus'.

100 Castle Greg (Lothian)
Roman fort.
Location: 4.8km (3 miles) east of West Calder at
NT 048590.
Description: A small, but well preserved, fort of the
second century AD enclosed by an earth rampart and
two ditches.

101 Castle Haven (Dumfries and Galloway)
Dun.
Location: 13km (8 miles) west of Kirkcudbright at
NX 594483.
Description: Castle Haven is a small, 'D'-shaped fort
surrounded by a drystone wall. Built into the
thickness of the wall are three sections of galleries,
entered from the internal courtyard.

102 Castle Rising (Norfolk)
Castle.
Location: 6.4km (4 miles) north-east of King's Lynn at
TF 666246.
Description: Earthworks of an oval ringwork castle
with two baileys and an impressive stone twelfth-
century keep.

103 Castle Strange (Co. Roscommon)
Cult stone.
Location: 6.4km (4 miles) south-west of Roscommon
at M 820600.
Description: A short pillar, dating to the first century
BC, engraved with curvilinear designs in the La Tène
style.

104 Cerne Abbas (Dorset)
Chalk figure.
Location: 8.8km (5½ miles) north of Dorchester at
ST 660170.
Description: A naked figure, 55m (100ft) high, cut
into the chalk. The best view can be obtained just
outside the town to the north from a lay-by on the
A352. His erect phallus makes for an obvious fertility
symbol and rumours of strange practices designed to
promote the birth of a child linger to this day.

105 Cerrig Duon (Powys)
Stone circle.
Location: 11.2km (7 miles) north-east of Abercraf at
SN 852229.
Description: A small, but well preserved, circle
consisting of 20 small stones.

106 Cheddar (Somerset)
Caves.
Location: 32km (20 miles) south-west of Bristol.
Description: Many of the caves of the Gorge were
inhabited by Palaeolithic humans. On the Mendips the
caves at Aveline's Hole in Burrington Coombe, at
ST 476587, and Soldier's Hole (ST 467538) were also
occupied. Finds are displayed in a museum above

Gough's Cave. They include the skeleton of 'Cheddar Man', dated to 7130 ± 150bp. In the grounds of the Kings of Wessex School the foundations of the Saxon palace complex are outlined.

107 Chedworth (Gloucester)
Roman villa.
Location: 16km (10 miles) north-west of Cirencester at SP 053135.
Description: The west and north wings of this fourth-century courtyard villa are exposed under cover. The main room of the west wing, probably the dining room, contains a mosaic, featuring Bacchus in the damaged central roundel flanked by the four seasons. In the north wing there was a small bath suite comprising five rooms. Water for the bath and the rest of the villa was supplied from a spring around which a nymphaeum, a shrine to the nymphs, was constructed.

108 Chepstow (Gwent)
Castle.
Location: 45km (28 miles) north-east of Cardiff at ST 533941.
Description: Within the impressive late medieval circuit of defences is a two-storeyed hall-keep, one of the earliest surviving examples of the use of stone in castles.

109 Chester (Cheshire)
Roman town.
Location: 32km (20 miles) south of Liverpool.
Description: *Deva* grew up outside the base of the XXth Legion founded in AD 85. Its amphitheatre, once the largest in Britain, is to be found outside Newgate. Unfortunately only the northern half can be seen at present, although there are plans to uncover the remainder. An interesting feature of this site is the small chapel to Nemesis, goddess of fate, at its eastern entrance, where performers in the ring would have stopped to say their prayers. The Grosvenor House Museum has an excellent Roman collection, including several interesting tombstones that were found reused as building stone during demolition work on the town walls.

110 Chesters (Northumberland)
Roman fort.
Location: 8km (5 miles) north of Hexham at NY 911701.
Description: Within the rampart of the fort of *Cilurnum* are the foundations of barrack blocks and the especially well-preserved *principia*. Outside the fort at NY 913700 the foundations of a Roman bridge that crossed the Tyne can be seen. The western abutment of the bridge is still in the water, but the eastern is on dry land. When the water level is low the piers of the bridge can also be seen on the river bed. Downstream from the bridge is the military bath-house, parts of the walls of which survive to 4.6m (15ft). The *apodyterium*, the undressing room, is particularly well preserved, the niches which served as lockers for the bathers still visible in its wall.

111 Chichester (West Sussex)
Roman town and inscription.
Location: 51km (32 miles) east of Southampton.
Description: *Noviomagus Regnensium* was founded by the Romans as the *civitas* capital of the Atrebates tribe. Before the Conquest, Chichester was the site of an *oppidum*, a tribal centre for the Atrebates. Parts of the system of earthworks, called the Devil's Ditch, which made up the *oppidum* can be seen outside the modern town at SU 825083 – 919085. Built into a wall under the portico of the Assembly Rooms in North Street is a Latin inscription that reads: NEPTUNO ET MINERVAE / TEMPLUM / PRO SALVTE DOMVS DIVINAE / EX AVCTORITATE TI CLAVDIVS COGIDVBNI REG MAGN BRIT / COLEGIVM FABROR ET QUI IN E / SVNT DSD DONANTE AF AEM / . . . ENTE PVDENTINI FIL – 'The temple of Neptune and Minerva was erected for the health of the imperial family, on the authority of the British king Tiberius Claudius Cogidubnus, by the guild of workers . . .'

112 Christchurch (Hampshire)
Norman house.
Location: 2.4km (1½ miles) east of Bournemouth at SZ 160926.
Description: Within the bailey of the castle in a municipal park is the well preserved Constable's House of c.1160. It consists of a first-floor hall above an undercroft, and it survives to roof level. The foundations of a square stone keep can also be seen on the motte of the castle.

113 Chun Castle (Cornwall)
Hillfort.
Location: 1.6km (1 mile) south-west of Morvah at SW 405339.
Description: In addition to the small hillfort there are several other interesting monuments in the area. Chun Quoit (SW 402340) is a well-preserved example of a dolmen. Men-an-Tol, at SW 427349, consists of a circular stone with a central hole standing between two small uprights that may have formed the entrance of a tomb. To the north-east, 0.8km (½ mile) away, is the Men Scryfa (SW 427353), an Early Christian memorial stone inscribed dating to the late fifth or early sixth century. It is inscribed: RIALOBRANI CVNOVALI – 'Riaolbranus, son of Cunoval'.

114 Chysauster (Cornwall)
Iron Age settlement.
Location: 5km (3 miles) north of Penzance at SW 472350.
Description: This first-century BC village consists of nine circular huts, the walls of which are preserved up to a height of 1.8m (6ft). The houses are all of the courtyard plan, the single narrow entrance opening out into a large internal courtyard surrounded by rooms set into the thickness of the walls. The remains of a ruined fogou and the garden plots cultivated by the villagers can also be seen.

115 Cirencester (Gloucestershire)
Roman town.
Location: 32km (20 miles) south-east of Gloucester.

Description: *Corinium* was founded in the first century
AD as the capital of the Dobunni and grew to become,
after London, the largest city in Roman Britain.
Fragments of the town walls can be seen laid out in
the Watermoor Recreation Ground but the finest
surviving structure consists of the earthen banks of the
amphitheatre to be found on the outskirts of the town.
The Corinium Museum contains one of the best
displayed collections relating to Roman Britain in the
country. The highlight of the collection is the series of
fourth-century mosaics from the flourishing local
school. A mosaicist's workshop, one of the state rooms
of a villa and its kitchen have been reconstructed in
the museum.

116 Cissbury (West Sussex)
Hillfort.
Location: 6.4km (4 miles) north of Worthing at
TQ 139080.
Description: In the south-west region of the enclosure
are many shallow depressions that mark the sites of
Neolithic flint mines. None of the shafts explored has
been left exposed. Finds are on display in Lewes and
Worthing museums.

117 The Clava Cairns (Highland)
Megalithic tombs.
Location: 6km (4 miles) west of Inverness at
NH 756443.
Description: The three Clava Cairns are arranged in a
row, each surrounded by a stone circle; the chambers
once covered by the cairns are now exposed. The two
outer cairns are passage graves, but there is no passage
in the central cairn. The passages seem to be aligned
to the midwinter sunset. Some cup-marked stones can
be seen among those used in the cairns.

118 Cleeve (Somerset)
Medieval monastery.
Location: 9.6km (6 miles) south-east of Minehead at
ST 047407.
Description: The monastic church has been totally
destroyed, but the domestic buildings around the
cloister are well preserved. There is also a fine
thirteenth-century painted tile pavement featuring the
heraldic shields of the abbey's benefactors preserved *in
situ*.

119 Clickhimin (Shetland Isles)
Prehistoric and Viking settlement.
Location: 1km ($\frac{1}{2}$ mile) west of Lerwick at
HU 404132.
Description: A complex site whose visible remains
include those of a Bronze Age farmstead, an Iron Age
ring fort, a broch, a wheelhouse and a Viking
longhouse.

120 Clonmacnoise (Co. Offaly)
Celtic monastery.
Location: 11km (7 miles) south of Athlone at
N 010306.
Description: One of the greatest of all Irish
monasteries, founded in AD 548. The ruins include a

later, medieval cathedral, two small stone churches, the
stump of a round-tower, magnificent high crosses and
a collection of tombstones that illustrate the
development of Irish art from the eighth to the
twelfth century.

121 Colchester (Essex)
Roman town.
Location: 80km (50 miles) north-east of London.
Description: Grym's Dyke, part of the earthworks of
the tribal *oppidum* of the Trinovantes can be followed
from TL 956267 to 956214. After the Roman
Conquest a veteran's colony was founded on the site,
intended to be the provincial capital, *Camulodunum*, in
AD 48. The Norman castle in the High Street was
erected over the Temple of Claudius. On request, the
custodian will take you into the Roman vaults. Under
the Hole in the Wall Inn on Balkerne Hill are the
remains of a first-century arch later incorporated into
the town defences. There are also the ruins of the
Norman priory church of St Botolph.

122 Conisbrough (South Yorkshire)
Castle.
Location: 8km (5 miles) south-west of Doncaster at
SK 517989.
Description: A fine example of a massive twelfth-
century keep, 23m (75ft) high.

123 Conwy (Gwynedd)
Castle.
Location: 4.8km (3 miles) south of Llandudno at
SH 784774.
Description: One of the nine great castles erected on
the orders of Edward I to dominate the newly-
conquered land of Gwynedd. The town wall is also
well preserved.

124 Corbridge (Northumbria)
Roman fort.
Location: 27.4km (17 miles) west of Newcastle at
NY 982648.
Description: Most of the visible remains of *Coriosopitum*
date to the third- and fourth-century rebuildings. They
include granaries and storerooms but the most
interesting feature of the site is the *principia*, the
headquarters building. There is a good site museum.

125 Corfe (Dorset)
Castle.
Location: 8km (5 miles) north-west of Swanage at
SY 958823.
Description: Corfe was founded as a simple motte and
bailey castle, then strengthened with the stone
defences that, despite Civil War slighting, are still
impressive.

126 Cosmeston (Glamorgan)
Deserted medieval village.
Location: 3.2km (2 miles) south of Penarth at
SS 178690.
Description: At the Cosmeston Lakes Country Park the

site of a deserted medieval village is currently under excavation by the Glamorgan-South Gwent Archaeological Trust.

127 Craggaunowen (Co. Clare)
Reconstructions.
Location: At the village of Quin, close to Shannon International Airport.
Description: Reconstructions of a crannog and cashel. At nearby Bunratty Castle a fifteenth-century structure has been well restored and furnished to illustrate life in the Middle Ages.

128 Craig Phadrig (Highlands)
Vitrified fort.
Location: 2.4km (1½ miles) west of Inverness at NH 640426.
Description: Two drystone walls enclose this important fort. The outer, and less well preserved, shows clear signs of vitrification.

129 Creswell Crags (Derbyshire)
Palaeolithic inhabited caves.
Location: 8km (5 miles) south-west of Worksop at SK 530740.
Description: A series of caves and rock shelters, once occupied by Palaeolithic humans, located in the limestone cliffs of a narrow valley. For safety reasons the interiors are barred. Good visitor's centre.

130 Creevykeel (Co. Sligo)
Megalithic tomb.
Location: 8km (5 miles) north of Grange at G 721546.
Description: At the broader eastern end of this long cairn is an impressive forecourt from which runs a passage, divided into two chambers. In the side of the mound there are another two chambers with separate entrances.

131 Cricklade (Wiltshire)
Saxon burh.
Location: 11.3km (7 miles) south-east of Cirencester at SU 10393.
Description: The modern town occupies the site of a Saxon burh. Most of the defensive circuit of earthworks survives. It is particularly well preserved on the eastern side of the town. Here the bank is still 1m (3ft) high and 18.3m (60ft) broad. Within this defensive perimeter the site was divided into a grid that still forms the basis of the modern street plan.

132 Crickley Hill (Gloucestershire)
Hillfort.
Location: 1.6km (1 mile) north of Birdlip at SO 927161.
Description: A bank, 3m (10ft) high, and ditch cut off a promontory at Crickley Hill. Recent excavations have shown that long before this Iron Age hillfort was constructed there had been a Neolithic causewayed camp on the site.

133 Cronk Sumark (Isle of Man)
Iron Age hillfort.

Location: 6.4km (4 miles) west of Ramsay at SC 392941.
Description: A small, but well-preserved, fort consisting of an inner enclosure around the summit of the hill and two outer ramparts, one of which is vitrified.

134 Cush (Co. Limerick)
Raths.
Location: 4.8km (3 miles) north-east of Kilfinname at R 698259.
Description: A cluster of six small raths, average diameter 20m (65ft), mostly with two circuits of earthworks.

135 Danebury (Hampshire)
Hillfort.
Location: 7.25km (4½ miles) south of Andover at SU 324377.
Description: For details see Chapter 6. Finds are on display in the Museum of the Iron Age in Andover.

136 Danes Graves (Humberside)
Iron Age barrow cemetery.
Location: 4.8km (3 miles) north of Great Driffield at TA 018633.
Description: Two hundred barrows of the Iron Age Arras Culture survive from a large cemetery that once numbered over five hundred. Each is between 3 and 10m (10 and 30ft) in diameter and under 1.2m (4ft) high.

137 Dartmoor (Devon)
See entries under Grimspound, Kestor and Merrivale.

138 Dearham (Cumbria)
Anglo-Scandinavian cross.
Location: 3.2km (2 miles) east of Maryport in the Parish church at NY 073364.
Description: A fine example of the tenth-century Anglo-Scandinavian school of sculpture.

139 Deerhurst (Gloucestershire)
Saxon church.
Location: 4.8km (3 miles) south of Tewkesbury at SO 8702992.
Description: The narrow western porch beneath the tower, the nave and the side chapels that have been incorporated into the aisles survive from a seventh-century monastery church. In the tenth century the upper part of the tower was added together with a semi-circular apse, whose foundations can be seen behind the modern chancel. A short distance south-west of the church is a small Saxon chapel. The original dedicatory inscription is displayed in the Ashmolean Museum in Oxford. It states that the chapel was founded by Earl Odda for the soul of his brother Aelfric and dedicated on 12 April 1056.

140 Deerness (Orkney)
Dark Age complex.
Location: On the eastern tip of Mainland, Orkney at HY 596088.

Description: A stone-faced rampart cuts off a promontory, within are the foundations of 19 small rectangular buildings. Once assumed to be the cells of Celtic monks grouped around a chapel, recent work suggests that they may have served a secular, Norse or Pictish community.

141 Denbigh (Clwyd)
Castle.
Location: 16km (10 miles) south of Rhyl at SJ 052658.
Description: A fine late twelfth-century castle. The defensive wall of the adjacent town is also well preserved.

142 Devenish (Co. Fermanagh)
Round-tower
Location: 3.2km (2 miles) north-west of Enniskillen at H 224469.
Description: The site of an early Celtic monastery on an island in Loch Erne is marked by this well-preserved twelfth-century round-tower, 25m (82ft) tall.

143 Devil's Arrows (North Yorkshire)
Standing stones.
Location: 1.6km (1 mile) west of Aldborough at SE 391665.
Description: These three stones, each taller than the uprights at Stonehenge, stand in a row orientated north–south.

144 Devil's Ditch (Cambridgeshire)
Dark Age dykes.
Location: 16km (10 miles) north-east of Cambridge between TL 5864 and 6261.
Description: Running across Newmarket Heath, the Devil's Ditch is a series of three linear earthworks. Their exact date is unknown; some think that they were erected by the Britons against the Saxons, others that the East Anglians built them for defence against the more powerful kingdom of Mercia.

145 Din Lligwy (Gwynedd)
Iron Age settlement.
Location: On Anglesey, 2.4km (1½ miles) south-west of Meolfre at SH 497861.
Description: Within the enclosure wall are two circular and seven rectangular huts, possibly a fourth-century chieftain's residence. Lligwy Cromlech is a short distance away at SH 501860.

146 Dinas Emrys (Gwynedd)
Hillfort.
Location: 1.6km (1 mile) north of Beddgelert at SH 606492.
Description: This small fort belonging to the late Iron Age is more interesting for its mythical associations than the surviving remains. Only slight traces of a double drystone rampart can be seen but legend tells how Dinas Emrys was one of the strongholds of the tyrant Vortigern, the fifth-century ruler who emerged from the collapse of Roman Britain as overlord of all the Celtic chieftains.

147 Dinas Powys (Glamorgan)
Dark Age defended homestead.
Location: 8km (5 miles) south of Cardiff at ST 145725.
Description: Site of an important excavation described in Chapter 9.

148 The Dingle Peninsula (Co. Kerry)
Prehistoric and Early Christian sites.
Location: 64km (40 miles) north-west of Killarney.
Description: The Dingle Peninsula is so rich in archaeological sites that only a few can be mentioned here. The Gallarus Oratory, a perfectly preserved small drystone church of the twelfth century is 6.4km (4 miles) north-west of Dingle. A group of interesting Ogham stones exists at Ballintaggart, 2.5m (1½ miles) south-east of Dingle. The inscriptions have been read as *Tria maqa mailagni* – 'the three sons of Mallagnos', *Cunu maqqi avi corbri* – 'Cormac, grandson of Coiurpre' and *Netta laminaua koi maqqi mucoidovins* – 'Nephew of Laminacca, son of the people of Dorvinas'. The promontory fort at Dunbeg, 4.8km (3 miles) south-west of Ventry at V 351972, is also well worth visiting. Here a massive drystone wall 45.6m (15ft) long and 3m (10ft) high cuts off the headland, outside which there are four banks and two ditches.

149 Dinorben (Gwynedd)
Promontory fort.
Location: 3.2km (2 miles) south-west of Abergele at SH 968757.
Description: This promontory fort is formed by three lines of ramparts. The inner, a substantial stone bank, is continued all the way around the perimeter of the site. Flanking the narrow entrance is a pair of guard chambers built into the thickness of the wall. Within, the foundations of over fifty hut circles can be traced.

150 Dod Law (Northumberland)
Hillfort and cup-and-ring marks.
Location: 4.8km (3 miles) south-east of Doddington at NU 004317.
Description: The drystone wall ramparts of the Iron Age hillfort are still preserved to a height of 2.75m (9ft). Within, the foundations of hut circles and cattle pounds can be seen. Bronze Age cup-and-ring marks can also be seen in some numbers scattered on the rocks of the hill.

151 Dolaucothi (Dyfed)
Roman gold mines.
Location: 14.5km (9 miles) south-east of Lampeter at SN 665403.
Description: Gold was mined at this site using both the open-cast technique and shallow shafts, although the remains of the Roman workings are difficult to distinguish from those of a later date. Part of wooden water-wheel that drained one shaft is displayed in the National Museum at Cardiff.

152 Dolebury (Avon)
Hillfort.
Location: 1.6km (1 mile) south-east of Churchill at
ST 450596.
Description: A single bank outlines a roughly
rectangular hillfort with fine views across the Mendips.
Inside the ramparts are traces of lead mining and the
mounds of a medieval rabbit warren.

153 Donaghmore (Co. Louth)
Souterrain.
Location: 3.6km (2½ miles) west of Dundalk at
J 009071.
Description: One of the finest of souterrains, consisting
of a series of five interlinked passages laid out on
different levels to a total length of 75m (246ft).

154 Doon Lough (Co. Donegal)
Cashel.
Location: On an island 8km (5 miles) from Ardara at
G 700980.
Description: Almost the entire area of this small island
is taken up by a cashel featuring well-restored walls
4.5m (15ft) high.

155 Dorchester (Dorset)
Historic town.
Location: 32km (20 miles) south-east of Yeovil at
SY 690910.
Description: *Durnovaria* was founded in the first
century AD to serve as the tribal capital of the
Durotriges. In Colliton Park the foundations of a
typical fourth-century townhouse, complete with
mosaic, are exposed. The County Museum in High
West Street contains an excellent gallery of local
archaeology, which includes finds from Sir Mortimer
Wheeler's classic excavations at nearby Maiden Castle.

156 Dover (Kent)
Historic town.
Location: 112km (70 miles) south-east of London.
Description: *Dubris* grew up in the first century AD
around the headquarters of the *Classis Britannica*, the
provincial fleet. The recently discovered painted house
of *c*.AD 200 has been preserved *in situ*. Its walls stand
up to 2.75m (9ft) high in places with 37 sq.m (400
sq.ft) of original painted plaster still intact. Within
the medieval castle is the pharos, a Roman lighthouse,
and next to it the Saxon church of St Mary.

157 Dowth (Co. Meath)
Megalithic tomb.
Location: 6.4km (4 miles) east of Slane at O 023738.
Description: A fine passage grave, 90m (295ft) in
diameter and 15m (49ft) high. Within are three stone
lined passages. Two lead to burial chambers, the other
is a later souterrain. Several of the stones lining the
passages and burial chambers are decorated with
passage grave motifs and in one a large stone basin, in
which the ashes of the dead were placed, is still *in
situ*.

158 Dreva Craig (Borders)
Hillfort.
Location: 1.6km (1 mile) south-east of Broughton at
NT 126353.
Description: An oval fort surrounded by two massive
drystone walls. Inside numerous hut circles are visible,
but the main feature of interest is outside the walls on
the south-west side of the fort. Here a hundred stones
remain of the chevaux-de-frise.

159 Drumena (Co. Down)
Cashel.
Location: 3.2km (2 miles) south-west of Castlewellan
at J 310340.
Description: A well-restored cashel, the walls are
3.3m (11ft) thick and 2.75m (9ft) high. Within, a
souterrain 15m (49ft) long is accessible via a modern
entrance.

160 Dublin (Co. Dublin)
Viking settlement.
Location: At St Audoen's, High Street.
Description: Dublin was founded *c*.AD 988, by the
Vikings not the native Irish. Excavations at the Wood
Quay site nearby have allowed a detailed
reconstruction of life in Viking Dublin to be built,
including full-scale replicas of houses, bringing the
sights, sounds and even smells back to life.

161 Dumbarton Rock (Strathclyde)
Hillfort.
Location: 0.5km (*c*.1 mile) south-west of the town
centre at NS 400745.
Description: The great rock of Dumbarton was the
capital of the Dark Age British kingdom of
Strathcylde, which explains its name–'the fort of the
British'. Although the rock itself is spectacular and
well worth a visit, little can be seen from this early
period.

162 Dumyat (Central)
Hillfort.
Location: 6.4km (4 miles) north-east of Stirling at
NS 832973.
Description: Substantial remains of the rampart walls,
some vitrified, remain from this fort which may have
been a centre of the Maeatae tribe from the late first
millennium BC to the early first millennium AD.

163 Dún Aengus (Co. Galway)
Stone fort.
Location: On Inishmore Island, one of the Aran Isles,
6.4km (4 miles) west of Kilronan harbour at
L 817098.
Description: Possibly the finest prehistoric stone fort in
Ireland, located on top of a 91m (300ft) high cliff.
Three out of an original four concentric walls survive,
although about half of the circuit has fallen away into
the sea. Just outside of the third wall is a band of
chevaux-de-frise, 9m–24m wide, consisting of
numerous pointed stones about 1m (3¼ft) high,
rammed into the natural joints of the bedrock.

164 Dún Ailinne (Co. Kildare)
Iron Age assembly place.
Location: 3.2km (2 miles) south-west of Killcullen at N 820078.
Description: A circular bank and ditch outline the site of the royal seat of Leinster. Within there is little to be seen, only a large cairn.

165 Dun Carloway (Highlands)
Broch.
Location: On the Isle of Lewis, 24km (15 miles) north-west of Stornaway at NB 190413.
Description: One of the finest examples of a broch to survive. Parts of the walls, 3.4m (11ft), thick stand to a height of 6.7m (23ft).

166 Dún Oghil (Co. Galway)
Stone fort.
Location: On Inishmore, one of the Aran Isles, 2.2km (1½ miles) north-west of Kilronin harbour at L 863068.
Description: Two concentric rings of stone ramparts make up this fort, the outer 3.7m (12ft) high, the inner 4.6m (15ft). On the inside there are terraces leading up to a rampart walk.

167 Dunadd (Strathclyde)
Scottish fort.
Location: 4.8km (3 miles) north of Lochgilphead at NR 840925.
Description: Dunadd was the capital of the kingdom of Dalriada established in Argyll and the Western Isles in the fifth century AD by immigrants from Ireland, the original Scots. The defences consist of a lower enclosure and a citadel and are formed by drystone walls linking outcrops of natural rock. Just below the summit, protected under glass, is a carving of a boar. Nearby is an Ogham inscription in the Pictish language and a footprint and bowls carved into the rock. They were probably used in the inauguration rituals of the early Scottish kings.

168 Dunalis (Co. Londonderry)
Souterrain.
Location: 5.5km (3½ miles) south-west of Coleraine at C 805305.
Description: A fine souterrain, 20.4m (67ft) long, consisting of three parts on slightly different levels connected via narrow creeps. Several of the lintel stones that make up the ceiling bear Ogham inscriptions.

169 Durham (County Durham)
Saxon sculpture and relics.
Location: 20km (12 miles) south of Newcastle at NZ 270430
Description: Saxon relics from the grave of St Cuthbert are displayed in the Cathedral Treasury. They include the pectoral cross, portable altar and comb used by the saint, together with the fragments from his original seventh-century coffin. There are also embroidered vestments donated by King Aethelstan in AD 954. In the former monk's dormitory there is an important collection of Saxon and Anglo-Scandinavian sculptured stones gathered from all over the north of England. It also includes casts of the Bewcastle and Ruthwell crosses (see separate entries).

170 The Dwarfie Stane (Orkney)
Rock-cut tomb.
Location: On the island of Hoy at NY 243004.
Description: The Dwarfie Stane is a unique British example of a tomb type commonly found in the Iberian Peninsula. It was hollowed out from a large, naturally-formed block of sandstone 6m (28ft) long, 4.3m (14ft) wide and 2.7m (9ft) deep. A passage, 2.3m (7½ft) long and 0.8m (2¼ft) high, penetrates the stone. On either side of which are two chambers in which burials were placed. The tomb was originally sealed by the block of stone which now lies outside the entrance.

171 Eamont Bridge (Cumbria)
Henges.
Location: 2km (1¼ miles) south-east of Penrith at NY 519284.
Description: The Mayburgh henge is a circular earthwork 109m (360ft) in diameter. At the centre is a large standing stone, the only survivor of four that once formed a rectangular setting called a cove. A nearby second henge, King Arthur's Round Table at NY 523283, is less well preserved.

172 Earl's Barton, (Northamptonshire)
Saxon tower.
Location: 9.7km (6 miles) north-east of Northampton at SP 852638.
Description: The parish church of All Saints has a fine late tenth-century Saxon tower decorated with ornamental pilaster work on the exterior walls.

173 Edinshall (Borders)
Hillfort.
Location: 3.6km (2¼ miles) north-west of Preston at NT 772604.
Description: An oval hillfort defended by two banks with external ditches. In the eastern sector can be seen the foundations of a broch, one of the few to be found in Lowland Scotland. Many hut platforms of an extensive settlement can also be seen in the western half of the fort, partly extending over the earlier ramparts.

174 Eildon Hill (Borders)
Hillfort.
Location: 1.6km (1 mile) south-east of Melrose at NT 554328.
Description: The largest hillfort in Scotland, capital of the powerful Selgovae people. Within the ramparts are the site of a small Roman signal station as well as hundreds of hut platforms.

175 Eileach-an-Naoimh (Strathclyde)
Monastic site.
Location: 29km (18 miles) south-west of Oban at NM 645100.

Description: This remote island is worth the effort to visit, for it contains one of the best preserved of early monastic sites in Scotland. Foundations of a chapel and three beehive huts from a simple Celtic community can be traced on the ground.

176 Escomb (County Durham)
Saxon church.
Location: 1.6km (1 mile) west of Bishop Auckland at NZ 189301.
Description: The church of St John is possibly the best preserved of all surviving Saxon churches. It is small and simple, consisting of a rectangular box-like nave and even smaller chancel.

177 Eyam (Derbyshire)
Saxon cross.
Location: 9.7km (6 miles) north of Bakewell in the churchyard at SK 218765.
Description: One of the finest surviving pieces of Saxon sculpture.

178 Eywas Harold (Hereford and Worcester)
Motte and bailey castle.
Location: 16km (10 miles) south-west of Hereford at SO 385207.
Description: The first castle on this site, mentioned in the *Anglo-Saxon Chronicle*, was erected by a Norman favourite of Edward the Confessor in 1052. Although the present motte, 15.25m (50ft) high, is probably post-Conquest in date.

179 Exeter (Devon)
Historic town.
Location: 128km (80 miles) south-west of Bristol.
Description: A unique Norman stone gatehouse seen in Rougemont Gardens, is all that survives from a castle erected by William the Conqueror. Its triangular-headed windows demonstrate that native Saxon masons were employed in the building work.

180 Finchdale Priory (County Durham)
Medieval monastery.
Location: 6.4km (4 miles) north-east of Durham at NZ 295473.
Description: Substantial remains of the church and claustral buildings survive from the priory, founded in 1237 as a 'rest home' for the monks of Durham cathedral.

181 Fishbourne (West Sussex)
Roman villa.
Location: 2km (1¼ miles) west of Chichester at SU 841047.
Description: A first-century villa built on a palatial scale and decorated in the finest Italian style using costly imported marbles and mosaics. Most of the northern wing is preserved under a modern shelter. Parts of the foundations belonging to the east and west wings are marked out on the ground, but the south wing, which contained the owner's residential quarters, is unfortunatey mostly under the A27. Part of the formal garden that occupied the courtyard has

been replanted based on the evidence discovered during excavations. The villa is generally thought to have been constructed for Cogidubnus, client king of the Atrebates, as reward for services rendered, but this is by no means certain.

182 Flag Fen (Cambridgeshire)
Bronze Age site.
Location: Outside Peterborough at TL 227989.
Description: A unique waterlogged site preserved in the peat, consisting of a timber platform and a long avenue of posts where large numbers of votive offerings were found. The excellent Flag Fen visitor centre has displays and reconstructions and visitors can also see excavations in progress. A fascinating insight into wetland archaeology. The surrounding area also contains evidence of Bronze Age field systems.

183 Flint (Clwyd)
Castle.
Location: 10km (6 miles) north-west of Chester at SJ 247734.
Description: The inner bailey of this Edwardian castle remains impressive. It consists of a square curtain wall with three towers at its corners and a fourth slightly detached, surrounded by its own moat.

184 Fountains Abbey (North Yorkshire)
Medieval monastery.
Location: 6.5km (4 miles) south-west of Ripon at SE 274683.
Description: Possibly the finest monastic ruin in the British Isles, set within an exceptionally beautiful eighteenth-century landscaped park. Fountains was founded in AD 1132 by Benedictine monks from St Mary's Abbey in York who wished to live more austere lives, in accordance with the newly-reformed Cistercian rule.

185 Fourknocks (Co. Meath)
Megalithic tomb.
Location: 27.2km (17 miles) north of Dublin at O 110720.
Description: Fourknocks consists of a group of three passage graves, the survivors of a once larger cemetery. The most interesting contains a cruciform chamber at the end of the passage which is now protected under the shelter of a modern concrete dome. Among the megaliths that line the passage are 12 decorated in the passage grave style, one of which features the rare motif of the human face.

186 Fowlis Wester (Tayside)
Pictish stones.
Location: 6.5km (4 miles) north-east of Crieff at NN 928241.
Description: One Pictish symbol stone is to be found in the village square, another inside the church on its north wall.

187 Framlingham (Suffolk)
Castle.
Location: 11.2km (7 miles) west of Saxmundham at
TM 286637.
Description: The twelfth-century curtain wall is still
well preserved, but only slight traces remain of the
original interior buildings of this castle.

188 Furness Abbey (Cumbria)
Medieval monastery.
Location: 2.5km (1½ miles) from Barrow-in-Furness at
SD 218720.
Description: The Cistercian abbey at Furness was
founded in AD 1123. What remains are the north
tower, transepts and chancel of the abbey church,
together with the east range of the cloister.

189 Garranes (Co. Cork)
Rath.
Location: 6.5km (4 miles) south-east of Crookstown at
W 473646.
Description: A large rath, 67m (220ft) in diameter,
enclosed by three concentric rings of banks and
ditches.

190 The Giant's Rig (Co. Down)
Neolithic enclosure.
Location: 6.5km (4 miles) south of Belfast at
J 327677.
Description: A bank, 3.6m (12ft) high, forms an
enclosure that is similar to the British henges.

191 Glamis (Tayside)
Pictish stone.
Location: 8km (5 miles) south of Kirriemuir at
NO 385465.
Description: A magnificent cross slab, 2.74m (9ft)
high, stands in the grounds of the Manse on the
eastern fringe of the village.

192 Glastonbury (Somerset)
Medieval monastery.
Location: 40km (25 miles) south-west of Bristol.
Description: The fine fifteenth-century courthouse of
the Abbey in the High Street has been converted into
a museum in which a selection of finds from the the
Somerset Levels and the Iron Age lake villages are
displayed. But on the actual site of the Glastonbury
lake village, at Godney (ST 492409), a mile north-
west of the town, only a few low mounds can be seen.
On the Tor overlooking the town, excavations
uncovered the site of a fifth- and sixth-century
settlement, but only the medieval tower of a ruined
chapel stands above ground. The Lady Chapel, part of
the church and the Abbot's Kitchen survive from the
medieval abbey. A good site museum displays
sculptured stones, tiles and other finds made during
excavations.

193 Glendalough (Co. Wicklow)
Celtic monastery.
Location: 40km (25 miles) south of Dublin at
T 126968.

Description: A number of small churches, dating from
the ninth to the twelfth centuries, are scattered over
the site. The most interesting is the two-storeyed
oratory with a pitched stone roof, known as St Kevin's
Kitchen. There is also a round-tower and many cross
slabs.

194 Glenelg (Highland)
Brochs.
Location: 11.2km (7 miles) south-east of the Kyle of
Lochalsh.
Description: Two of the best-preserved brochs are
south-east of Glenelg. Dun Telve (NG 829173) has an
internal courtyard, 10m (32ft) in diameter, surrounded
by walls 4m (13ft) thick and up to 10m (33ft) high
in places. Dun Troddan (NG 834172) is a little
smaller and less well preserved. Half the 7.6m (25ft)
high walls have fallen down, allowing a cut-away view
of the galleries and chambers constructed in their
thickness.

195 Gloucester (Gloucestershire)
Historic town.
Location: 64km (40 miles) north of Bristol.
Description: *Colonia Nervia Glevensium* was founded in
AD 97 on the site of a former legionary base. A section
of the Roman town wall can be seen in the Museum
and part of the east gate is accessible beneath Boots at
38–44 East Gate Street. The many finds that have
been made during excavations and building work are
well displayed in the city museum. They include the
fine tombstone of the auxiliary cavalryman Rufus Sita.

196 Gosforth (Cumbria)
Anglo-Scandinavian cross.
Location: 19km (12 miles) south of Whitehaven at
NY 072836.
Description: The cross, 4.5m (15ft) high, that stands
in the churchyard is the finest surviving example of
the Anglo-Scandinavian school. Carved in the tenth
century it features a mixture of pagan and Christian
scenes.

197 Govan (Strathclyde)
Early Christian memorial stones.
Location: 6.5km (4 miles) west of Glasgow city centre.
Description: In Govan church is displayed an
important collection of monuments of the tenth to
twelfth centuries.

198 Great Chalfield (Wiltshire)
Medieval manor.
Location: 8km (5 miles) from Melksham at
ST 860360.
Description: A fine example of later medieval domestic
architecture built by Thomas Tropnell, a successful
merchant *c*.1480. It has an H-shaped plan with a
ground-floor hall, solar above, in the central block.

199 Great Langdale (Cumbria)
Neolithic axe factory.
Location: 11.2km (7 miles) north-west of Ambleside at
NY 272072.

Description: A grey-green volcanic tuff that outcrops on the steep slopes above Great Langdale was used as a source of raw material by Neolithic axe makers. Roughouts and waste flakes from their activity have been found, but the climb is recommended only for the very experienced.

200 Great Witcombe (Gloucestershire)
Roman villa.
Location: 6.4km (4 miles) south-east of Gloucester at SO 899142.
Description: The original nucleus of this site was enlarged in the fourth century to form an impressive courtyard villa. In the west wing was a small bath-house, with fine geometric mosaics featuring marine life. These are preserved under modern cover and most of the rest of the foundations are also exposed to view.

201 Greenstead-juxta-Ongar (Essex)
Saxon church.
Location: 19km (12½ miles) west of Chelmsford at TL 538030.
Description: The parish church is the only surviving example of Saxon wooden architecture. The walls are of large timber logs split vertically and morticed into wooden beams at top and bottom. Each is connected to its neighbour by tongue-and-groove joints. The brick plinth on which the logs now rest is the result of restoration work.

202 The Grianàn of Ailach (Co. Donegal)
Cashel.
Location: 7.2km (4½ miles) north-west of Derry at C 366197.
Description: Once the seat of the O'Neill kings of Ulster the restored walls of this cashel rise to a height of 5m (17ft). On the interior face of the walls were three to four stone terraces, connected via four stone stairways, two of which are original. Two galleries were also constructed in the thickness of the wall.

203 Grimes Graves (Norfolk)
Neolithic flint mines.
Location: 4.8km (3 miles) north-east of Brandon at TL 8178898.
Description: An extensive area of disturbed ground marks the site of hundreds of shafts, spoil heaps and working floors belonging to one of the main flint-mining centres of England. One excavated shaft has been left open and can be entered, but the side galleries which extend from its bottom have been closed off for safety reasons. There is a good site museum and more finds are on display in the Castle Museum, Norwich.

204 Grimspound (Devon)
Bronze Age settlement.
Location: On Dartmoor, 12km (7½ miles) north-west of Ashburton at SX 700809.
Description: Grimspound is one of the best preserved of all the many settlements that make up the unique Bronze Age landscape of Dartmoor. The outer wall of the pound, slightly restored, still stands in part to a

height of 1.2m (4ft) and is 3m (10ft) thick. It encloses and area of 1.6ha (4 acres), in which the foundations of some thirty hut circles can be clearly traced. Stock pens can also be seen built against the enclosure wall.

205 Gurness (Orkney)
Broch.
Location: On Aikerness, at NY 383268
Description: The walls of this broch stand to a height of 3m (10ft). The outer defence works are more substantial than usual, consisting of a drystone wall with unique bastions, and three rock-cut ditches. In the courtyard are foundations from the post-broch settlements, which include courtyard houses and a Viking longhouse.

206 Hadrian's Wall (Northumberland and Cumbria)
See: Black Carts, Brunton, Poltross Burn and Walltown Crag for the better preserved sections of the Wall. For the associated forts *see:* Birdoswald, Carrawburgh, Chesters, Corbridge, Housesteads, South Shields and Vindolanda.

207 Halligye (Cornwall)
Souterrain.
Location: 6.5km (4 miles) east of Helston at SW 712238.
Description: Halligye fogou is the best preserved of Cornish souterrains, 'T'-shaped in plan and 16.4m (54ft) long.

208 Hambledon Hill (Dorset)
Hillfort.
Location: 8km (5 miles) north-west of Blandford Forum at ST 845126.
Description: Two ramparts enclose the northern spur of this hill to form the hillfort. Little can be seen of the causewayed camp described in Chapter 4.

209 Hardknott Fort (Cumbria)
Roman fort.
Location: 5.6km (9 miles) north-east of Ravenglass at NY 218014.
Description: The fort of *Mediobogdum* was constructed on this strategic site late in the first century to guard the Hardknott Pass. The outer defensive wall with four corner towers, survives in part to a height of 3m (10ft), although it has been restored in places by replacing the original stones which had fallen from the wall. Within the walls, foundations of the *principia*, part of the commander's house and granaries are exposed. Outside the east gate of the fort is the parade ground.

210 Harlech (Gwynedd)
Castle.
Location: Overlooking the town at SH 581312, 24km (15 miles) south-west of Blaenau Ffestiniog.
Description: A magnificent castle built by Edward I in 1283–9. It consists of two high curtain walls studded with impressive towers and gatehouses that are practically mini-keeps in themselves, enclosing an inner and middle bailey. A third, low wall, takes in most of the lower slopes of the hill down to the coast.

211 Hawick (Borders)
Norman motte.
Location: In the city centre in Motte Park at
NT 499141, the town is 18km (11 miles) south-west
of Jedburgh.
Description: A well-preserved motte, 7.6m (25ft) high,
belonging to a twelfth-century Norman castle. Two
other monuments in the immediate area of Hawick are
also well worth visiting, a stone circle at Burgh Hill
(NT 470062) and an Iron Age fort on Bonchester Hill
(NT 595117).

212 Hedingham (Essex)
Castle.
Location: 6.5km (4 miles) north-west of Halstead at
TL 787359.
Description: The great tower keep at Hedingham, four
storeys high, is one of the finest surviving pieces of
late Norman architecture in Britain.

213 Hembury (Devon)
Hillfort.
Location: 5.6km (3½ miles) north-west of Honiton
ST 113031.
Description: Site of a causewayed camp, hillfort and
Roman fort.

214 Hengistbury Head (Dorset)
Iron Age trading centre.
Location: 4km (2½ miles) east of Bournemouth at
SZ 164010.
Description: During the Iron Age this promontory,
which forms the southern arm of Christchurch
harbour, was an important trading and manufacturing
centre. All that is visible on site is a double rampart
that cut off the approach from the land. Within the
defended area there is also a group of thirteen round
barrows. Finds are in nearby Christchurch Museum.

215 Herefordshire Beacon (Hereford and Worcester)
Hillfort.
Location: 3.2km (2 miles) south-west of Little Malvern
at SO 760400.
Description: A fine hillfort occupies the summit of
this hill, which also contains the earthworks of a small
twelfth-century castle. In the neighbourhood the
hillfort on Midsummer Hill at SO 761375 is also well
worth visiting.

216 Hetty Pegler's Tump (Gloucestershire)
Megalithic tomb.
Location: 1.6km (1 mile) north of Uley at SO 790001.
Description: A fine long barrow. In the broader,
eastern end there is a forecourt, at the centre of which
is the entrance to the tomb. From the forecourt a
passage, 6.7m (22ft) long, leads into the mound. Five
small chambers opened off this passage, a pair on
either side and one at the very end.

217 Hexham (Northumberland)
Saxon crypt.
Location: 4.8km (3 miles) west of Corbridge at
NY 935641.

Description: The crypt of the monastery founded by St
Wilfrid in 674 survives. Beneath a trapdoor in the
choir are the foundations of the Saxon apse. In the
church there are also Roman inscribed stones, a Saxon
cross and a chalice.

218 High Rochester (Northumberland)
Roman fort.
Location: 1.6km (1 mile) north of Rochester at
NY 833986.
Description: Parts of the outer defensive wall of the
fort of *Bremenium* are well preserved, especially at the
north gate, which survives to a height of 1.8m (6ft).
In the fourth century the rampart was strengthened
with platforms designed to carry the missile-firing
ballistas. Outside the eastern wall are the remains of
several mausolea.

219 Hod Hill (Dorset)
Hillfort.
Location: 3.2km (2 miles) south of Iwerne Minster at
ST 857108.
Description: Hod Hill was an important centre for the
Durotriges tribe, and in the years preceding the
Roman Conquest it sheltered a substantial settlement
made up of 270 houses with an estimated population
of 500–1000. The foundations of many of these houses
can be seen in the south-east area of the enclosure,
which also houses a small Roman fort.

220 Holtye (East Sussex)
Roman road.
Location: 8km (5 miles) south-east of East Grinstead
at TQ 461391.
Description: A portion of a minor Roman road is well
maintained by the Sussex Archaeological Trust. Slag
from the local iron industry was used to surface the
road, in which ruts made by cart wheels can still be
distinguished.

221 Holyhead Mountain (Gwynedd)
Iron Age settlement.
Location: On Anglesey, 3.2km (2 miles) west of
Holyhead at SH 212820.
Description: Twenty circular and rectangular hut
foundations are scattered over the slope of this hill.
Nearby are a pair of standing stones at Penrhos 2.4km
(1½ miles) to the south-west at SH 227809 and the
Trefignath burial chamber 2.4km (1½ miles) to the
south-east at SH 260804.

222 Hound Tor (Devon)
Deserted medieval village.
Location: 6.5km (4 miles) from Grimspound at
SX 743790.
Description: Foundations belonging to eight medieval
longhouses from a settlement that was abandoned in
the fourteenth century with the deterioration of the
climate.

223 Housesteads (Northumberland)
Roman fort.
Location: 19.3km (12 miles) from Hexham at
NY 789687.

Description: *Vercovicium* was garrisoned by the First Cohort of Tungrians, an infantry unit from Belgium. Visible remains include of the Commander's House, the *principia*, hospital and granaries. There is also a small site museum. A special feature of this site is the well-preserved Roman public latrine. Outside the fort a few house foundations of the *vicus* are visible. To the north is a well-preserved stretch of the wall.

224 Huntingdon (Cambridgeshire)
Motte.
Location: 30km (19 miles) north-east of Cambridge at TL 240714.
Description: An impressive motte, 12m (40ft) high, with two attached baileys, survives from a castle begun by William I.

225 The Hurlers (Cornwall)
Stone circles.
Location: 6.5km (4 miles) north of Liskeard at SK 250713.
Description: A group of three stone circles that according to tradition are petrified men punished for playing ball on the Sabbath. A short walk to the north-east, at SX 260719, is the Rillaton barrow where the famous Bronze Age gold cup displayed in the British Museum was found. Trethevy Quoit, at SX 259688, is a good example of a dolmen.

226 Ilkley (West Yorkshire)
Cup-and-ring marks.
Location: 22.5km (14 miles) north-east of Leeds on Ilkley Moor.
Description: The moors south of Ilkley are rich in monuments and rocks carved with cup-and-ring marks. Two of the most interesting are the Hanging Stones at SE 124867 and the Swastika Stone at SE 094470. For the benefit of the visitor who has neither the time nor the energy to seek out these carvings *in situ* some examples have been moved to the park opposite St Margaret's church in Ilkley. Several small stone circles can also be seen on the moors, notably the Bradey Circle (SE 090440) and the Twelve Apostles (SE 126451).

227 Inishcaltra (Co. Clare)
Celtic monastery.
Location: On an island in Lough Derg, 1.5km (1 mile) south-east of Mountshannon, at R 7085.
Description: A typical Celtic monastery consisting of three small churches, cemetery, two inscribed crosses and a round-tower.

228 Inishmurray (Co. Sligo)
Celtic monastery.
Location: 14.5km (9 miles) by boat from Mullaghmore harbour at G 575538.
Description: The restored enclosure wall stands 4m (13ft) high in places. Inside there are three stone churches, some beehive huts and a well-preserved cemetery with over fifty memorial pillars and cross slabs.

229 Inverurie (Grampian)
Stone circle and henge.
Location: 29km (18 miles) north-west of Aberdeen, at NJ 779196.
Description: On the southern outskirts of the town is the Broomend of Crichie, a Neolithic henge with two surviving stones from a small stone circle and a Pictish picture stone (not *in situ*). In the town cemetery at NJ 781206 can be seen the well-preserved remains of a Norman motte and bailey castle.

230 Iona (Strathclyde)
Celtic monastery.
Location: 96km (60 miles) by ferry from Oban.
Description: Only faint traces of the boundary ditch are visible from the Celtic monastery founded by St Columba in 563. The present day cathedral of the restored Iona community dates from the Benedictine monastery established in the twelfth century. Next to the cathedral can be seen the principal relics to survive from the earlier monastery: two stone crosses of the eighth century together with a concrete reproduction of a third. A short distance from the cathedral is the Reilig Odhrain, the traditional burial place of the early kings of Scotland.

231 Islay (Strathclyde)
High crosses.
Location: 48km (30 miles) by ferry from Kennacraig.
Description: There are two fine carved crosses on the island. The first is at Kildalton, NR 459508, the other is at Kilnave, NR 286715. A well-preserved dun is also worth visiting at Dun Nosebridge NR 371601.

232 Jarlshof (Shetland)
Location: On Sumbrugh Head, 1km (*c*.½ mile) south-east of the airport at HU 399096.
Description: Seven distinct phases of occupation were identified during excavations ranging from Neolithic to post-medieval. The most interesting ruins are those of a Viking farmstead with three longhouses and their associated outbuildings in the courtyard of an earlier broch.

233 Jarrow (Tyne and Wear)
Saxon monastery.
Location: 3.2km (2 miles) west of South Shields at NZ 359652.
Description: The chancel of the parish church belongs to the original buildings of the monastery founded in 681. The central tower is also Saxon, the upper part, dating to the eleventh century, was added to a seventh-century porch. To the south of the church the foundations of the monastic buildings are marked out. Finds are in the nearby Jarrow Hall Museum.

234 Jedburgh (Borders)
Early Christian memorial stones.
Location: 32km (20 miles) north-east of Hawick.
Description: The museum attached to the abbey ruins houses an interesting collection of Early Christian sculptured stones.

235 Jerpoint (Co. Kilkenny)
Medieval monastery.
Location: 2km (1½ miles) south-west of Thomastown
at S 5740.
Description: The remains of this Cistercian monastery
make up one of the finest monastic ruins in Ireland.
The church itself preserves some twelfth-century work,
but the cloisters were rebuilt in the fifteenth century
and have been well restored. In the eastern range can
be seen the chapter house, refectory, dormitory and
kitchen.

236 Kells (Co. Meath)
Celtic monastery.
Location: 14.5km (9 miles) north-west of Navan at
N 738754.
Description: In the graveyard of the Protestant church
can be seen four stone crosses and a round-tower.
Nearby is the small twelfth-century stone church
known as St Columb's House and there is the Market
Cross in the town centre.

237 The Kempe Stones (Co. Down)
Megalithic tomb.
Location: 8km (5 miles) from central Belfast at
J 445736.
Description: A well-preserved cromlech.

238 Kenilworth Castle (Warwickshire)
Castle.
Location: 8km (5 miles) south-west of Coventry at
SP 279723.
Description: The first castle on this site was a small
motte and bailey. The great stone keep was added in
the twelfth century. Further additions were made in
the fourteenth and sixteenth centuries.

239 Kent's Cavern (Devon)
Cave.
Location: In Ilsham Road near Torquay harbour at
SX 934641
Description: One of the earliest occupied sites in the
British Isles, first lived in *c.*300,000 years ago. A
selection of the finds is displayed in the Museum of
Torquay Natural History Society in Babbacombe Road.

240 Kestor (Devon)
Bronze Age settlement.
Location: On Dartmoor 3.6km (2¼ miles) south-west
of Chagford at SX 665867.
Description: A well-preserved settlement consisting of
25 hut circles, loosely grouped together without an
enclosing pound wall. Low walls can also be seen
marking out the associated field system.

241 Keswick (Cumbria)
Stone circle.
Location: 2.4km (1½ miles) of Keswick at NY 292236.
Description: A small stone circle, with a rather
flattened shape, consisting of thirty stones. Inside are
ten stones in a rectangular setting.

242 Kidwelly (Dyfed)
Castle.
Location: 38km (24 miles) west of Swansea at
SN 409710.
Description: A twelfth-century earthwork castle later
strengthened with a stone curtain wall and towers.

243 Kildonan (Strathclyde)
Dun.
Location: 10.3km (6½ miles) north-east of Campletown
at NR 780277.
Description: A small triangular dun with walls up to
4.3m (14ft) thick.

244 Killadeas (Co. Fermanagh)
Early Christian stone.
Location: 11.2km (7 miles) north-west of Enniskillen
at H 205540.
Description: In the village graveyard can be seen the
unique eighth-century Bishop's Stone, carved with the
figure of a priest holding crozier and bell.

245 Killaloe (Co. Clare)
Ogham stone.
Location: 20km (12½ miles) north-east of Limerick.
Description: The Protestant cathedral in the town
centre shelters a unique memorial stone inscribed with
a bilingual Ogham/Runic inscription: 'A prayer for
Thorgrim who set up the stone'.

246 Killamery (Co. Kilkenny)
Cross and Ogham stone.
Location: 8km (5 miles) south-west of Callen at
S 3836.
Description: The cross is inscribed Ordo Maelsechnaill
– 'A prayer for Maelsechnaill'. Next to it are an
Ogham stone, a pillar stone and two inscised slabs
with further inscriptions.

247 Kilmacduagh (Co. Galway)
Round-tower.
Location: 4.8km (3 miles) south-west of Gort at
M 400000.
Description: A well-preserved round-tower, 30m (90ft)
high.

248 Kilnasaggart (Co. Antrim)
Inscribed pillar.
Location: Close to the border with the Republic,
0.4km (¼ mile) east of Kilnasaggart railway bridge at
J 062149.
Description: One side of this pillar is covered with ten
incised crosses, the other has one large cross and an
inscription which reads: *In locso tunimn airni ternonc mac
ceran bicercul Peter alpstal* – 'Ternohc, son of little
Ceran, consecrated this place to the protection of
Peter'. Ternohc is thought to have died *c.*AD 715.

249 King Doniert's Stone (Devon)
Memorial cross.
Location: 4.8km (3 miles) north-west of Liskeard
SX 200690.

Description: A late ninth-century cross shaft inscribed *Doniert rogarit pro anima* – 'Doniert has prayed for his soul'. Doniert was probably a Cornish king.

250 Kingston-upon-Thames (Surrey)
Consecration stone.
Location: In the town centre, which is 16km (10 miles) south-west of central London, at TQ 185696.
Description: The King's Stone, that gave the town its name, was used during the inauguration ceremonies of the Saxon kings.

251 Kintraw (Strathclyde)
Standing stones.
Location: 10.5km ($6\frac{1}{2}$ miles) north of Kilmartin at NM 830050.
Description: By themselves the small cairn and standing stone at the site are not very impressive. What makes the site worth a visit is the theory of the late Professor Thom that Kintraw was used as astronomical observatory. Standing on the platform behind the monuments, which excavations have shown is artificial, the midwinter solstice could be seen across the sea against the mountains of Jura.

252 Kirk Michael (Isle of Man)
Viking sculptures.
Location: 9.7km (6 miles) west of Peel at SC 318909.
Description: In the parish church there is a small collection of stone crosses in the typical Manx hybrid Norse-Celtic style.

253 Kirkdale (North Yorkshire)
Saxon sundial.
Location: 6.5km (4 miles) east of Helmsley SE 677857.
Description: Above the south door of this Saxon church is a sundial inscribed: 'Orm the son of Gamal, bought St Gregory's church when it was broken and fallen, and had it made anew from the ground in honour of Christ and St Gregory, in the days of Edward the King and Tosti the Earl.'

254 Kirkmadrine (Dumfries and Galloway)
Early Christian memorial stone.
Location: 13km (8 miles) south of Stranraer at NX 081484.
Description: At the western end of the parish church is displayed a small group of Early Christian memorial stones. The most interesting is inscribed HIC/ACENT / S (AN)C(T)I ET PRAE / CIPUI SACER / DOTES IDES VIVENTIVS / ET MAVORIVS – 'Here lie the holy and chief priests Ides, Vaventius and Mavorius'.

255 Kirkstall Abbey (West Yorkshire)
Medieval monastery.
Location: 4.8km (3 miles) north-west of Leeds at SE 260360.
Description: A daughter house of Fountains Abbey founded in 1152. The east range of the cloister, featuring library, chapter house, warming house, kitchen and refectory gives a good impression of the life of the community. The thirteenth-century Abbot's Lodging is also notable.

256 Kirriemuir (Tayside)
Pictish stone.
Location: 8km (5 miles) north-west of Forfar at NO 380540.
Description: Four Pictish stones can be seen in the cemetery to the north of the town.

257 Kit's Coty House (Kent)
Megalithic tomb.
Location: 4.8km (3 miles) north of Maidstone at TQ 745608.
Description: Three uprights and a capstone survive from a chambered tomb. Nearby Little Kit's Coty House (TQ 744604) is even less well preserved.

258 Knockdrum (Co. Cork)
Cashel.
Location: 1.2km ($\frac{3}{4}$ mile) north of Castletownshed at W 175315.
Description: A well-restored cashel with a fine enclosure wall surrounding a roofless stone house, which contains the entrance to a small stone souterrain.

259 Knockoneill (Co. Derry)
Megalithic tomb.
Location: 4km ($2\frac{1}{2}$ miles) west of Swatragh at C 820087.
Description: A good example of a court tomb.

260 Knowlton (Dorset)
Neolithic henges.
Location: 13km (8 miles) north of Wimborne Minster at SU 024100.
Description: The surviving example of a group of three henges is outlined with a bank up to 3.7m (12ft) high and a ditch 10.7m (35ft) wide. This important pagan ritual site was later Christianized by the addition of a Norman church in the middle of the central henge.

261 Knowth (Co. Meath)
Megalithic tomb cemetery.
Location: 3.2km (2 miles) east of Slane at N 999738.
Description: After Newgrange the finest of all the Irish passage grave cemeteries. The main mound is 12m (39ft) high and 78m (260ft) in diameter. It contains two passages arranged back to back which end in small cruciform chambers. Around it are some fifteen smaller mounds.

262 Labbacallee (Co. Cork)
Megalithic tomb.
Location: 8km (5 miles) north-west of Fermoy at R 774020.
Description: The largest of the Irish wedge tombs.

263 Lambourn Seven Barrows (Berkshire)
Barrow cemetery.
Location: 3.2km (2 miles) north of Lambourn at SU 328828.
Description: Good examples of several types of round barrow from a group that once numbered over forty.

264 Lanyon Quoit (Cornwall)
Megalithic tomb.
Location: 6.5km (4 miles) north-west of Penzance at
SW 430337.
Description: A fine example of a quoit.

265 Launceston (Cornwall)
Castle.
Location: 32km (20 miles) north-west of Plymouth at
SX 331847.
Description: An early Norman motte crowned with a
twelfth-century shell keep. In the bailey parts of the
curtain wall and a gatehouse survive.

266 Laxton (Nottinghamshire)
Open fieldsystem.
Location: 14.5km (9 miles) south-west of Stamford at
SK 722670.
Description: Laxton is one of the few places in
England that has kept the open fieldsystem of
cultivation. Three of the four medieval open fields
belonging to the village survive.

267 Leacanabuaile (Co. Kerry)
Cashel.
Location: 3.2km (2 miles) west of Cahersiveen at
V 446811.
Description: A fine, restored cashel with walls up to
1.2m (4ft) high. Within there is a single beehive hut,
in the floor of which is the entrance to a small
souterrain 10m (30ft) long which ends in a corbelled
chamber constructed in the thickness of the cashel
wall.

268 Legananny (Co. Down)
Megalithic tomb.
Location: 6km (4 miles) south of Dromar at J 294436.
Description: A fine example of a cromlech.

269 Leicester (Leicestershire)
Historic town.
Location: 64km (40 miles) north-east of Birminghan.
Description: *Ratae Corieltauvorum* was founded as the
tribal capital of the Corieltauvi. The Jewry Wall, parts
of which are 10m (30ft) high, belongs to the exercise
hall of its baths. Finds from local sites, including good
examples of mosaics and painted wall plaster, can be
seen in the adjacent Jewry Wall Museum.

270 Lewes (East Sussex)
Castle.
Location: 13km (8 miles) north-east of Brighton at
TQ 415101.
Description: Earthworks consisting of two mottes and
a bailey, with some fragments of the later rebuilding
in stone.

271 Lincoln (Lincolnshire)
Historic town.
Location: 64km (40 miles) north-east of Nottingham.
Description: *Lindum* was founded as a Roman colony
late in the first century. The Newport Arch once
formed its north gate. Some other fragments of the
defences can also be traced, especially near the

Cathedral. Lincoln Castle (SK 975718) has two mottes,
one of them crowned by a shell keep. On Steep Hill
the Jew's House and Aaron the Jew's House are late
twelfth century in date.

272 Lindisfarne (Northumberland)
Monastery.
Location: 14.5km (9 miles) south of Berwick-on-Tweed
at NU 126418.
Description: Lindisfarne, also called Holy Island, can
be reached across a causeway from the shore at low
tide (be sure to check the times of the tides before a
visit). Nothing can be seen of the early monastery,
founded in AD 634, except for memorial stones in the
museum, but the ruins of the Norman priory church
of St Peter mark the site.

273 Lissue (Co. Antrim)
Rath.
Location: 4km (2½ miles) west of Lisburn at J 227632.
Description: A good example of its type.

274 Little Salkeld (Cumbria)
Stone circle.
Location: 6.5km (4 miles) north-east of Penrith at
NY 571373.
Description: Long Meg is a tall standing stone, her
daughters an oval stone circle. A second, Little Long
Meg, can also be seen nearby.

275 Littlecote Park (Wiltshire)
Roman villa.
Location: 4km (2½ miles) north-west of Hungerford at
SU 302175.
Description: In the grounds of the sixteenth-century
mansion are exposed the foundations of a fourth-
century villa, complete with a well-restored mosaic,
featuring Orpheus and the four seasons.

276 Liverpool (Merseyside)
Megalithic tomb.
Location: In Calderstones Park at SJ 407873.
Description: The stones of this Bronze Age cist grave
are richly carved with a variety of motifs including
cup-and-ring marks, a spiral and foot prints.

277 Llandrindod Wells (Powys)
Roman fort.
Location: 9.6km (6 miles) north of Builth Wells at
SO 050620.
Description: Visible remains date to the second-century
rebuilding of the fort in stone. On the common, south
of the village, the keen-eyed visitor may be able to
trace the outlines of some of the 18 practice camps
that were dug by the troops.

278 Llangadwaladr (Anglesey, Gwynedd)
Early Christian memorial stone.
Location: On Anglesey, 35.4km (22 miles) east of
Aberffraw at SH 383692.
Description: The Catamanus stone in the parish church
probably marked the gave of Cadfan, King of
Gwynedd, who died, *c.*AD 625. Its inscription can be
translated as 'Here lies Catamanus, the wisest and
most renowned of all kings'.

279 Llantwit Major (Glamorgan)
Early Christian memorial stones.
Location: 24km (15 miles) west of Cardiff at
SS 970680.
Description: A small, but interesting, collection of
sculptured stones is on display in the parish church.

280 Lochgilphead (Strathclyde)
Prehistoric sites.
Location: 32km (20 miles) south-west of Inveraray.
Description: An area rich in prehistoric sites. Good
examples of cup-and-ring marks can be seen at
Achnabreck (NR 856907), Baluacraig (NR 831970),
Cairnbaan (NR 83910) and Kilmichael Glassary
(NR 858935). A cist within the cairn at Nether
Largie (NR 831985), accessible via a modern trapdoor,
has carvings of axes and cup-and-ring marks on the
stones. A stone circle and standing stones can be
visited at Temple Wood (NR 826979).

281 Lockleys Park (Hertforshire)
Roman bath house.
Location: Just outside Welwyn Village at TL 522316.
Description: This small third-century bath-house, once
part of a villa complex, is preserved beneath a modern
concrete vault under the motorway in the grounds of
Lockleys Park.

282 London
Historic town.
Description: Good sections of the Roman wall, with
medieval additions, can be seen on Tower Hill and in
the Barbican. The foundations of a mithraeum, moved
a short distance from their original site, can be seen in
Temple Court at 11 Queen Victoria Street. In the
crypt of All Hallows Barking, on Tower Hill, are
displayed fragments of Saxon sculpture and Roman
finds, including debris from the Boudican sack and
two tesselated pavements. Under St Brides, in Fleet
Street, the remains of a series of medieval churches
and a Roman house that preceded the modern Wren
church can be seen. The archaeology and history of the
capital are well catered for in the Museum of London
in the Barbican.

283 Longstone Rath (Co. Kildare)
Rath.
Location: 4.8km (3 miles) east of Nass at N 936206.
Description: An important rath, in the centre of which
is a standing stone, 6.4m (21ft) high, at the base of
which was discovered a cist with the cremated remains
of two adults.

284 Loughcrew (Co. Meath)
Barrow cemetery.
Location: 16.5km (10 miles) north of Kells at
N 507770–N 600780.
Description: The barrows are arranged in two groups
around the twin peaks of Cairnbone East and
Cairnbone West. The best preserved, Cairn T of the
eastern group, is 36.5m (120ft) in diameter and has
stones decorated in the style of passage grave art in
the burial chamber.

285 Lough Gur (Co. Limerick)
Prehistoric sites.
Location: 19.5km (12 miles) south-east of Limerick at
R 640410.
Description: An area rich in sites, including wedge
tombs, hut circles, standing stones, cashels and
crannogs. Consult a large-scale map for details.

286 Lough-na-Cranagh (Co. Antrim)
Crannog.
Location: 7km (4 miles) east of Ballycastle at
D 178427.
Description: A good example of one these artificial
islands. Around its perimeter the retaining wall is
clearly visible.

287 Lower Brockhampton (Hereford and Worcester)
Medieval manor house.
Location: 5.6km (3½ miles) from Bromyard at
SO 688560.
Description: A well-preserved example of a half-
timbered moated manor house dating to the early
fifteenth century, complete with the original
gatehouse.

288 Ludlow (Shropshire)
Castle.
Location: 36km (22½ miles) south of Shrewsbury at
SO 508746.
Description: A fine stone castle featuring a twelfth-
century keep and an unusual round chapel modelled
on the Church of the Holy Sepulchre in Jerusalem.

289 Lullingstone (Kent)
Roman villa.
Location: 8km (5 miles) south-east of Bromley at
TQ 530650.
Description: This villa is famous for its fourth-century
mosaics. The finest shows Europa and the bull and has
an apt quotation from Virgil's *Aeneid*: *Invida si (tauri)
vidisset Iuno natatus / justus Aeolias isset ad osque domos* –
'If Juno had seen the swimming of the bull she would
more justly have gone to the Halls of Aeolus'.

290 Lurigethan (Co. Antrim)
Promontory fort.
Location: 1.6km (1 mile) west of Waterfoot at
D 224254.
Description: A band of between four and six ramparts,
0.9m (3ft) high, together with their accompanying
ditches, extend for 0.4km (¼ mile) to cut off the
promontory.

291 Lydford (Devon)
Saxon burh and medieval castle.
Location: 14.5km (9 miles) north of Tavistock at
SX 510848.
Description: Across the promontory that houses the
town is a Saxon earthwork, up to 4.9m (16ft) high in
places. Much of the original Saxon grid plan has
survived in the modern street pattern. Near the church
is the castle, a thirteenth-century tower.

292 Lydney (Gloucestershire)
Roman temple.
Location: 1.6km (1 mile) west of the town itself in
Lydney Park at SO 615026.
Description: Within the ramparts of a hillfort are the
foundations of the fourth-century temple of Nodens. A
native Celtic god who was highly regarded for his
power to heal. Permission to visit should be sought
from the Estate Office at Lydney Park.

293 Lyles Hill (Co. Antrim)
Neolithic enclosure.
Location: 13km (8 miles) north-west of Belfast at
J 248829.
Description: A low bank and palisade, without a ditch,
outlined this Irish version of a causewayed camp.

294 Lympne (Kent)
Roman fort.
Location: 4.8km (3 miles) west of Hythe at
TR 117342.
Description: A few short sections of the walls of the
Saxon Shore fort of *Portus Lemanis* have survived the
later landslides.

295 Maes Howe (Orkney)
Megalithic tomb.
Location: On Mainland, Orkney 8km (5 miles) east of
Stromness at HY 318128.
Description: One of the finest megalithic tombs in
Britain. The mound of this passage grave is 3.4m
(24ft) high and 36m (110ft) in diameter. A passage
11m (36ft) long leads into the mound, designed so
that the light from the midwinter sunrise could
penetrate through to the burial chamber. Look out for
runic graffiti scratched by Viking treasure-hunters.

296 Maiden Castle (Dorset)
Hillfort.
Location: 2.4km (1½ miles) south of Dorchester at
SY 670885.
Description: One of the largest and most impressive of
all hillforts. Within the multiple rings of defences
there are also the foundations of a small 'Romano-
Celtic' temple. Finds are in Dorchester Museum.

297 The Maiden Stone (Grampian)
Pictish stone.
Location: 9.7km (6 miles) north-west of Inverurie at
NJ 703247.
Description: A fine example of a cross slab.

298 Mam Tor (Derbyshire)
Hillfort.
Location: 2.4km (1½ miles) east of Castleton at
SK 128838.
Description: Within the well-preserved ramparts are
the remains of numerous hut platforms.

299 Man, Isle of
See: Andreas, Balladoole, Braaid, Cashtal-yn-Ard, Cronk
Sumark, Kirk Michael, Maughold, Peel and Tynwald.

300 Margam (Glamorgan)
Early Christian memorial stones.
Location: 6.4km (4 miles) south-east of Port Talbot at
SS 802864.
Description: A small museum displays inscribed stones
from the site of the former monastery.

301 Maryport (Cumbria)
Roman inscriptions.
Location: 37km (23 miles) south-west of Carlisle at
NY 030360.
Description: An important collection of inscriptions
gathered from the Roman fort of *Alauna* can be seen
displayed in a private museum. The finds include a
series of eleven altars found buried in pits near the
parade ground.

302 Maughold (Isle of Man)
Viking sculptures.
Location: 4.8km (3 miles) south-east of Ramsay at
SC 493916.
Description: In the churchyard is displayed a small
collection of sculptures from a former Celtic
monastery. There are also the foundations of three
simple chapels.

303 Maumbury Rings (Dorset)
Henge.
Location: On the southern outskirts of Dorchester at
SY 690899.
Description: This site has had a varied history. First
serving as a typical henge, it was later adapted as an
amphitheatre for the town of *Durnovaria* and was
finally fortified with gun emplacements in the Civil
War.

304 Meigle (Tayside)
Pictish stone.
Location: 9.7km (6 miles) north-east of Coupar Angus
at NN 287446.
Description: In the museum is a small collection of
Pictish stones.

305 Mellifont (Co. Louth)
Medieval monastery.
Location: 8km (5 miles) west of Drogheda at
O 010780.
Description: One of the first of the reformed Roman
monasteries to be founded in Ireland. Surviving
remains include parts of the church, gatehouse,
cloister, chapter house and the unusual thirteenth-
century octagonal lavabo (washing place).

306 Merrivale (Devon)
Stone rows.
Location: On Dartmoor 6.4km (4 miles) east of
Tavistock at SX 553746.
Description: Among the many monuments in the area
is a series of three stone rows, the largest, 264m
(866ft) long, is made up of over 200 stones. A small
stone circle and many burial cairns can also be seen. A
similar grouping of stone rows, circles and cairns that

is well worth visiting can be found at Shovel Down south-west of Chagford at SX 655506.

307 The Merry Maidens (Cornwall)
Stone circle.
Location: 6.5km (4 miles) south-west of Penzance at SW 433245.
Description: A medium-sized circle supposedly the remains of petrified dancers caught profaning the Sabbath. In a nearby field are two standing stones that were supposed to be the pipers (SW 435240). A megalithic burial chamber can also be seen nearby at Tregiffian (SW 430244).

308 Mersea Island (Essex)
Roman barrow.
Location: 2.4km (1½ miles) north of West Mersea at TM 022143.
Description: One of the best examples of a Roman barrow, the burial chamber accessible via a modern passage (ask at the farmhouse for key). Finds are in Colchester Museum.

309 Middleham (North Yorkshire)
Castle.
Location: 27.3km (17 miles) south-west of Ripon at SE 128877.
Description: There are two castles – the stone castle that was a favourite residence of Richard III and to the south-west the earthworks of a Norman motte and bailey castle.

310 Mid Gleniron (Dumfries and Galloway)
Megalithic tomb.
Location: 4km (2½ miles) north of Glenluce at NX 187610.
Description: A good pair of chambered cairns.

311 Middleton (North Yorkshire)
Anglo-Scandinavian sculpture.
Location: 3.2km (2 miles) north-west of Pickering at SE 782855.
Description: In the parish church is a small collection of sculptured stones of which the most interesting depicts a Viking warrior.

312 Midhowe (Orkney)
Megalithic tomb.
Location: On the island of Rousay at HY 371306.
Description: A good example of a stalled cairn, typical of Orkney, in which the the burial chamber is divided into separate stalls with the use of large stone slabs.

313 Mitchell's Fold (Shropshire)
Stone circle.
Location: 32km (20 miles) from Wroxeter at SO 304983.
Description: A good example of a slightly flattened circle composed of 16 stones. The 'Altar Stone' is 70m (230ft) to the south-west. A similar circle can be seen nearby at Hemford (SO 324999).

314 Monasterboice (Co. Louth)
Celtic monastery.
Location: 8km (5 miles) north-west of Drogheda at O 043821.
Description: Muiredach's Cross, 5m (16.4ft) high, commemorates a tenth-century abbot and is one of the masterpieces of Early Christian art. There are also two small stone churches and a round-tower.

315 Moneygashel (Co. Cavan)
Cashels.
Location: 4.8km (3 miles) south-west of Blacklim at H 060340.
Description: A series of three stone cashels. The walls of the best preserved survive to a height of 3m (9ft).

316 Monkwearmouth (Tyne and Wear)
Saxon monastery.
Location: 3.2km (2 miles) north of Sunderland town centre at NZ 402577.
Description: Of the original monastery buildings founded in AD 674 the lower part of the parish church's tower, once the west porch, survives. The upper part of the tower, together with the west wall of the nave, is of late Saxon date.

317 Mooghaun (Co. Clare)
Hillfort.
Location: 9.7km (6 miles) from Shannon Airport at R 407706
Description: In the grounds of Drumlohan Castle is the largest Irish hillfort.

318 Moone (Co. Kildare)
High cross.
Location: 8km (5 miles) north of Castledermot at S 789927.
Description: Two finely-carved crosses mark the site of a Celtic monastery.

319 Motte of Mark (Dumfries and Galloway)
Iron Age hillfort.
Location: 1.6km (1 mile) west of Rockliffe at NX 845540.
Description: An important Iron Age and Dark Age centre, defended by a vitrified rampart.

320 Mount Grace (North Yorkshire)
Medieval monastery.
Location: 9.65km (6 miles) north-east of Northallerton at SE 445985.
Description: This priory was founded in 1398 for the Carthusians. The members of this strict and austere order differ from other monks by spending most of their time as hermits in individual cells, one of which has been reconstructed.

321 Mousa (Shetland)
Broch.
Location: On a small island off Sandwich, 11km (7 miles) south of Lerwick at HU 457237.
Description: It is well worth the effort of reaching this remote spot for the broch of Mousa is one of the finest of all prehistoric monuments in the British Isles. Its walls still stand to a height of 13.3m (43ft).

322 Navan (Co. Armagh)
Iron Age assembly place.
Location: 2.4km (1½ miles) west of Armagh at
H 847452.
Description: Navan was once Emain Macha, the
legendary seat of the Kings of Ulster. It consists of an
enclosure measuring 7.3ha (18 acres), surrounded by a
bank 3m (10ft) high and 12m (40ft) wide with an
internal ditch. The interior is empty apart from two
large mounds.

323 Nendrum (Co. Down)
Celtic monastery.
Location: On Mahee Island 8km (5 miles) south-east of
Comber at J 524636.
Description: Foundations of three concentric cashel-
type walls which surrounded the monastery are visible
together with the stump of a round-tower, foundations
of the church and beehive cells.

324 Neroche (Somerset)
Castle.
Location: 21km (13 miles) south-east of Taunton at
ST 272158.
Description: A Norman ringwork castle later converted
to a motte and bailey type.

325 Netley Abbey (Hampshire)
Medieval monastery.
Location: 4.8km (3 miles) south-east of Southampton
at SU 455085.
Description: The church, detached Abbot's House and
eastern range of the claustral buildings, including
sacristy, chapter house and dorter are well preserved.

326 Nevern (Dyfed)
High cross.
Location: 11.27km (7 miles) south-west of Cardigan at
SN 083481
Description: The High Cross, 4m (13ft) high, in the
churchyard is a fine example of late tenth-century
Welsh sculpture. In the church there are also two
Early Christian memorial stones bearing bilingual
inscriptions in Latin and Ogham commemorating
Maglicuncus son of Clutorius, and Vilalianus Emeretos.

327 Newgrange (Co. Meath)
Megalithic tomb.
Location: 4.8km (3 miles) south-east of Slane at
O 007724.
Description: Newgrange is possibly the finest
megalithic monument in the entire British Isles. The
mound, the largest in an extensive cemetery, is 91.4m
(300ft) in diameter and 13.7m (45ft) high. A low
retaining wall, recently restored, runs around the
mound. A total of 97 large kerbstones are embedded
in this wall, some decorated. At the entrance is a
magnificent example of passage grave art, the threshold
stone carved with triple spirals and concentric circles.
Many of the slabs lining the passage to the burial
chamber are also carved. In the stone-vaulted cruciform
burial chamber are two of the stone bowls designed to
hold cremations.

328 Newton (Grampian)
Pictish stone.
Location: 16km (10 mile) north-west of Inverurie at
NJ 662298.
Description: Two Pictish stones can be seen in the
grounds of Newton House. One bears two inscriptions,
in Ogham and an undeciphered script.

329 Normanton Down (Wiltshire)
Round barrows.
Location: 0.8km (½ mile) south of Stonehenge at
SU 118413.
Description: Bush Barrow, the site of the richest burial
in Bronze Age Britain, is part of this group. The
barrows are on private land but a public right-of-way
allows limited access. The grave goods are displayed in
Devizes Museum. Another group of interesting
barrows, Winterbourne Stoke (SU 101417), is situated
3.2km (2 miles) south-west of Stonehenge.

330 North Elmham (Norfolk)
Saxon cathedral.
Location: 9.65km (6 miles) north of East Dereham at
TF 988216.
Description: Foundations of a tenth-century cathedral
that served the local see before it was transferred to
Norwich.

331 North Leigh (Oxfordshire)
Roman villa.
Location: 4.8km (3 miles) north-east of Whitney at
SP 397155.
Description: Of the large fourth-century courtyard villa
on the site, the foundations of the north-west and
south-west wings, featuring mosaics, together with the
bath suite have been preserved under modern cover.

332 Norton (Cheshire)
Medieval monastery.
Location: 9.7km (6 miles) south-east of Liverpool at
SJ 548830.
Description: Surviving remains are slight, but the
monastery has been the focus of an intensive campaign
of excavations. The results are displayed in the
excellent site museum.

333 Notgrove (Gloucestershire)
Megalithic tomb.
Location: 17.7km (11 miles) east of Cheltenham at
SP 096212.
Description: One of the Severn–Cotswold group of
chambered long barrows.

334 Nunney (Somerset)
Castle.
Location: 4.8km (3 miles) south-west of Frome at
ST 736457.
Description: A small moated keep of the fourteenth
century that was probably a reduced copy of the
infamous Bastille.

335 Nympsfield (Gloucestershire)
Megalithic tomb.
Location: 7.24km (4½ miles) south-west of Stroud at SO 794013.
Description: Yet another of the Severn–Cotswold group of long barrows.

336 Oakham (Leicestershire)
Medieval hall.
Location: 48km (30 miles) east of Leicester at SK 882089.
Description: An impressive stone Great Hall of late twelfth-century date survives from a castle.

337 Oakley Down (Dorset)
Barrow cemetery.
Location: Near the junction of the A354 and the B3081 at SU 018173.
Description: A cemetery of 23 round barrows.

338 Offa's Dyke
Saxon earthwork.
Location: Along the border between England and Wales.
Description: Much of the Dyke can be walked today along the Offa's Dyke Path, which starts near Prestatyn and runs south to the Severn at Welshpool. At Knighton in Powys, 24km (15 miles) south-west of Ludlow, there is an information centre. Among the better preserved stretches is the central section, from Battington (OS 249084) to Knighton (SO 284727).

339 Okehampton (Devon)
Castle.
Location: 32km (20 miles) west of Exeter at SX 584943.
Description: The motte is crowned by a tower keep and in the bailey are the hall, solar and kitchens.

340 Old Oswestry (Shropshire)
Hillfort.
Location: 1.6km (1 mile) north of Oswestry at SJ 296310
Description: A fine example of a hillfort defended by six concentric ramparts.

341 Old Sarum (Wiltshire)
Deserted medieval town and castle.
Location: 3.2km (2 miles) north of Salisbury at SU 138327.
Description: Site of a hillfort, Saxon burh and medieval town that was abandoned in the thirteenth century in favour of modern Salisbury. The outer defences, castle and cathedral foundations survive.

342 Old Soar (Kent)
Medieval manor.
Location: 11km (7 miles) south-east of Sevenoaks at TQ 619541.
Description: A late thirteenth-century solar block belonging to a medieval manor house. It consists of a large living-room, with bedroom and chapel *en suite*, over a vaulted undercroft.

343 Orford (Suffolk)
Castle.
Location: 19.3km (12 miles) east of Woodbridge at TM 419499.
Description: An impressive twelfth-century keep standing 27m (90ft) high.

344 Orkney
See: Brough of Birsay, Deerness, the Dwarfie Stane, Maes Howe, Midhowe, Rennibister, the Ring of Brodgar, Skara Brae Taversoe Tuack and Unstan.

345 Overton Hill (Wiltshire)
Neolithic ritual site.
Location: 6.4km (4 miles) west of Marlborough at SU 118679.
Description: The Sanctuary on Overton Hill was destroyed in the eighteenth century, but the position of its stones have been marked with concrete posts. There is also a small group of six round barrows.

346 Parc Cwm (Glamorgan)
Megalithic tomb.
Location: 4km (2½ miles) west of Pennard on the Gower Peninsula at SS 537898.
Description: A fine example of a Severn–Cotswold chambered tomb. Nearby at SS 491905 is Arthur's Stone, a cromlech with a huge boulder as capstone.

347 Peel (Isle of Man)
Round-tower.
Location: 16km (10 miles) west of Douglas at SC 241846.
Description: A typical round-tower, one of only three outside Ireland.

348 Pembroke (Dyfed)
Castle.
Location: In the centre of Pembroke at SM 982016.
Description: A fine stone castle dominated by the great four-storey keep, 24m (78ft) high.

349 Penmachno (Gwynedd)
Early Christian memorial stones.
Location: 2.4km (1½ miles) south of Betws-y-coed at SH 790506.
Description: In the parish church are five important Early Christian memorial stones. The Carausius stone reads CARASIVS HIC JACIT IN HOC CONGERIES LAPIVM— 'Caruasius lies here in this heap of stones'. The Cantiorix stone reads CANTIORI(X) HIC JACIT (V) ENEDOTIS CIVE(S) FUIT (C)ONSOBRINOSI MA(G)LI MAGISTRAT — 'Cantiorix, citizen of Venedow, cousin of Maglos the magistrate'. The Avitorrius stone reads FILI AVITORI IN TE(M)PO(RE) IVSTI(NI) CON(SVLIS) – 'The son of Avitorius, set up when Justinian [the Byzantine emperor] was consul [AD 540]'.

350 Pennymuir (Borders)
Roman forts.
Location: 14km (9 miles) from Jedburgh at NT 755138.
Description: A well-preserved group of three temporary forts The defensive rampart of the largest survives to a

height of 1.2m (4ft) along parts of the north and west sides. Nestling within the south-east quarter are the remains of a second fort. The third, a mile to the north-east, is less well preserved. The bank of the Roman road known as Dere Street can also be clearly traced between NT 772122 and 770128.

351 Pentre Ifan (Dyfed)
Megalithic tomb.
Location: 14km (9 miles) east of Fishguard at SN 099370.
Description: A fine cromlech. (There is another tomb chamber, 1.6km (1 mile) to the south-east, at SN 113346, the Bedd yr Afranc 'Dwarfs Grave'.

352 Pevensey (East Sussex)
Roman fort.
Location: 6.4km (4 miles) north-east of Eastbourne at TQ 644048.
Description: From the Saxon Shore fort of *Anderida* almost the entire circuit of walls has survived, up to 7.6m (28ft) high. As a bonus there is also a small Norman castle in one corner.

353 Pickering (North Yorkshire)
Castle.
Location: 27km (17 miles) west of Scarborough at SE 800845.
Description: A good example of a Norman earthwork castle later rebuilt in stone. The ruins consist of a motte crowned by a shell keep and two baileys, one on either side, surrounded by a curtain wall.

354 Piercebridge (Durham)
Roman fort and bridge.
Location: 1.6km (1 mile) west of Darlington at NZ 211156.
Description: Outside the eastern line of the slight remains of the rampart is a series of 'lillia', camouflaged pits that once contained sharp pointed stakes. On the nearby riverbed the remains of the stone piers and flagstones that once supported a bridge across the Tees can be seen.

355 Pitchford (Shropshire)
Roman road.
Location: 8km (5 miles) south-east of Shrewsbury at SJ 525025.
Description: The agger, or bank, of a road that ran south-west from Wroxeter can be traced for some distance. There is also part of a stone bridge abutment.

356 Pleshey (Essex)
Castle.
Location: 11.2km (7 miles) north of Chelmsford at TL 666144.
Description: Although the stonework has been entirely demolished, the earthworks, including a motte, 18m (60ft) high, are impressive.

357 Poltross Burn (Cumbria)
Hadrian's Wall.
Location: 13km (8 miles) north-east of Brampton at NY 634662.
Description: In the village of Gilsland is one of the best preserved milecastles on Hadrian's Wall.

358 Porlock (Somerset)
Stone circle.
Location: On Porlock Common at SS 845447.
Description: A good example of the smaller type of stone circle.

359 Portchester (Hampshire)
Roman fort.
Location: On Portsmouth Harbour at SU 625046.
Description: *Portus Adurni* is perhaps the finest of all the Saxon Shore Forts. Most of the defensive wall, with medieval restorations, stands to 5.5m (18ft) and 15 out of the original 20 turrets survive. There are also a medieval keep and priory church.

360 Proleek (Co. Louth)
Megalithic tomb.
Location: 5.6km (3½ miles) north-east of Dundalk at J 086119.
Description: In the grounds of Ballymascalon House Hotel is a fine dolmen formed by three uprights and a capstone.

361 Priddy (Somerset)
Henges.
Location: 8km (5 miles) east of Cheddar at ST 540350.
Description: At Priddy is a group of four henge monuments with ditches external to the banks. At nearby Ashen Hill Barrows (ST 538521) is a linear cemetery of eight mounds, 0.4km (¼ mile) south of the henges. To the south also are the Priddy Nine Barrows (ST 538518). A Bronze Age cist can also be seen at Pool Farm (ST 537541). One of the slabs (original in the Bristol Museum), had carvings of ten cup marks and six feet, a concrete cast has been placed on site.

362 Punchestown (Co. Kildare)
Standing stone.
Location: 3.6km (2 miles) from Naas at N 920160.
Description: At 6m (20ft) high the Punchestown Stone is the tallest standing stone in the British Isles. A second, slightly smaller example, 5m (16½ft) high can be seen nearby at Forenaghts (N 940210).

363 Ravenglass (Cumbria)
Roman bath.
Location: 1.3km (*c.*1 mile) south of Whitehaven at SD 087961.
Description: Part of the walls from the bath-house of the fort of *Glannoventa* stand to a height of 4m (12ft).

364 Raedykes (Grampian)
Roman fort.
Location: 5.6km (3½ miles) north-west of Stonehaven at NO 840900.

Description: The defensive bank and ditch of the fort are best preserved along the northern and eastern sides of the perimeter.

365 Raglan (Gwent)
Castle.
Location: 11.26km (7 miles) south-west of Monmouth at SO 415083.
Description: A fine stone castle, whose surviving defences mostly date to the fifteenth century. In the bailey is a good example of a stone hall.

366 Reculver (Kent)
Roman fort.
Location: 4.8km (3 miles) east of Herne Bay at TK 228694.
Description: Most of the Saxon Shore fort of *Regulbium* has been destroyed by the sea. There remains the foundations of a seventh-century church from an early Saxon monastery.

367 Rennibister (Orkney)
Souterrain.
Location: On Mainland, Orkney at HY 397127.
Description: A trapdoor in a farmyard gives access to this fine example of a prehistoric underground passage. Another can be visited at Grainbank, near Kirkwall (HY 442117).

368 Repton (Derbyshire)
Saxon crypt.
Location: 11.3km (7 miles) south of Derby at SK 303272.
Description: A fine stone structure survives from a monastery associated with the royal house of Mercia. The chancel is later Saxon work.

369 Restenneth (Tayside)
Church tower.
Location: 2.4km ($1\frac{1}{2}$ miles) east of Forfar at NO 480511.
Description: The lower part of the church tower at Restenneth was probably the porch belonging to an eighth-century Pictish monastery.

370 Restormel Castle (Cornwall)
Castle.
Location: 3.2km (2 miles) north of Losthwithiel at SX 104614.
Description: A typical example of a motte crowned by a shell keep.

371 Richmond (North Yorkshire)
Castle.
Location: 16km (10 miles) north-west of Northallerton at NZ 17300.
Description: In the south-east corner is a late eleventh-century stone hall. The tower keep, a century younger, is also notable among the ruins.

372 Rievaulx (North Yorkshire)
Medieval monastery.
Location: 4km ($2\frac{1}{2}$ miles) west of Helmsley at SE 570845.

Description: The ruins of this Cistercian monastery, founded in 1132, are second only to those of Fountains Abbey. The eastern part of the church, chapter house and refectory are especially impressive.

373 The Ring of Brodgar (Orkney)
Henge with stone circle.
Location: On Mainland, Orkney, 6.4km (4 miles) north-east of Stromness at HY 294134.
Description: One of the finest examples of a henge enclosing a stone circle. The Stones of Stenness, four survivors from a similar monument are 0.8km ($\frac{1}{2}$ mile) to the south-east at HY 306125.

374 Ripon (North Yorkshire)
Saxon crypt.
Location: 21km (13 miles) north of Harrogate at SE 313711.
Description: Underneath the medieval cathedral is the original crypt of a church founded by St Wilfrid and consecrated in AD 672.

375 Rochester (Kent)
Castle.
Location: 24km (15 miles) south-east of London.
Description: A fine example of a tower keep.

376 Rockbourne (Hampshire)
Roman villa.
Location: 6.5km (4 miles) west of Fordingbridge at SU 120170.
Description: Foundations from a fourth-century courtyard villa. The bath-house is particularly well preserved. The site museum houses some good mosaics.

377 The Rollright Stones (Oxfordshire)
Stone circle.
Location: 4.8km (3 miles) north-west of Chipping Norton at SP 296308.
Description: A good example of a stone circle; 73m (240ft) to the north-east is a standing stone; 360m (1181ft) to the south-east are the four uprights and fallen capstone of a chambered tomb.

378 Rough Castle (Central)
Roman fort.
Location: 1.6km (1 mile) east of Bonnybridge at NS 843799.
Description: On three sides of the fort an earthen rampart and ditch can be traced. The fourth is made up of the Antonine Wall itself. Beyond the wall there are rows of lillia.

379 Roughting Linn (Northumberland)
Cup-and-ring marks.
Location: 15km (9 miles) south of Berwick at NT 984367.
Description: Beneath a small hillfort (NT 984367), is a large, sloping slab of rock covered with over sixty carvings.

380 Rudston (Humberside)
Standing stone.
Location: 8km (5 miles) west of Bridlington at
TA 097677.
Description: A monolith 8m (26ft) high, standing in
the churchyard.

381 The Rumps (Cornwall)
Promontory fort.
Location: 6.5km (4 miles) north of Padstow at
SW 934810.
Description: Three ramparts guard access to two
headlands.

382 Ruthwell (Dumfries and Galloway)
High Cross.
Location: 8km (5 miles) west of Annan at
NY 101682.
Description: The Ruthwell Cross, one of the finest
surviving examples of Saxon sculpture, stands in a
modern annex to the church just north of the modern
town. It is inscribed with the runic text of a Christian
poem.

383 St Albans (Hertfordshire)
Roman town
Location: 9.6km (6 miles) north of London.
Description: Much of the site covered by the Roman
town *Verulamium* is now a public park in which part
of the city wall and a bath-house with fine mosaics
can be seen. More mosaics, brightly painted wall
plaster and numerous other finds are displayed in the
museum. At TL 134074 is a unique Roman theatre.
Nearby, at Prae Wood, the defences of the tribal
oppidum of the Catuvellauni can be seen. The most
impressive section of these earthworks is the Beech
Bottom Dyke at TL 155093, where the ditch that
runs between two banks is still is 27m (90ft) wide
and 9m (30ft) deep.

384 St Andrew's (Fife)
Monastery.
Location: 56km (35 miles) east of Perth.
Description: The eleventh-century tower of St Regulus
and a collection of Early Christian stones in the
medieval dormitory undercroft survive from the
original Celtic monastery. In the late medieval castle a
mine and counter-mine are accessible, from the siege
of 1548.

385 St Lythans (Glamorgan)
Megalithic tomb.
Location: 1.2km ($\frac{3}{4}$ mile) south-west of St Lythans at
ST 101723.
Description: A fine example of a cromlech.

386 St Mary's Isle (Scilly Isles)
Megalithic tombs.
Location: 56km (35 mile) from Penzance.
Description: Bant's Cairn on the north-west tip of St
Mary's Isle at SU 911124 is a fine example of the
local tombs known as entrance graves. Nearby are the
stone foundations of an Iron Age village made up of

circular houses rather like those of Chysauster on the
mainland. Two similar tombs can be seen at
Innisidgen (SU 921127) on the north-east tip of the
island. On the eastern side of the island at Porth
Hellick Down (SU 929108) is a group of five
Neolithic chambered tombs.

387 St Vigeans (Tayside)
Pictish stones.
Location: 1.6km (1 mile) north of Arbroath at
NO 640352.
Description: In the museum is an important collection
of 32 stones. The most interesting is a cross-slab
inscribed with one of only two known Pictish
inscriptions in the Latin alphabet. It reads *Drosten
ipeuoret ettfor cus*. What this means we can only guess,
but Drosten, Uoret and Forcus are personal names.

388 Sandal (West Yorkshire)
Castle.
Location: Near Wakefield at SE 337182.
Description: The earthworks and the ruins of the later
stone castle are well displayed after recent excavations.

389 Scarborough (North Yorkshire)
Castle.
Location: 64km (40 miles) north-east of York at
TA 048892.
Description: An impressive twelfth-century keep
dominates the town. The foundations of a Roman
signal station can also be seen.

390 Scattery Island (Co. Clare)
Celtic monastery.
Location: 3.2km (2 miles) south-west of Kilrush at
Q 970520.
Description: Within the monastery precinct on this
small island in the Shannon Estuary are several small
medieval churches, cross-slabs and a fine round-tower.

391 Sheep Hill (Strathclyde)
Hillfort.
Location: 13km (8 miles) north-west of Glasgow at
NS 435746.
Description: The lines of two circuits of defences, one
vitrified, can be traced around the summit of the hill.
At Greenland Farm (NS 435746) 200m (656ft) north
of the forts are several large groups of cup-and-ring
marks.

392 The Shetland Islands
See: Clickhimin, Jarlshof, Mousa and Stanydale.

393 Silbury Hill (Wiltshire)
Prehistoric mound.
Location: 1.6km (1 mile) east of Avebury at
SU 100685.
Description: The largest prehistoric man-made mound
in the British Isles. Its base covers an area of 2.1ha
($5\frac{1}{4}$ acres) and rises to a height of 39m (130ft).
Excavations have failed to find any trace of a burial.

394 Silchester (Hampshire)
Roman town.
Location: 16km (10 miles) south-west of Reading at SU 640620.
Description: *Calleva* was founded to act as the tribal capital of the Atrebates on the site of an earlier *oppidum*. The town wall, parts of which still stand to 4.5m (15ft), can be traced for much of its length, but the town site is mostly farmland. Just outside the north-east corner of the defences are the remains of the banks of the amphitheatre. There is a small site museum near the Rectory but most finds are on display in Reading Museum.

395 Singleton (West Sussex)
Weald and Downland Open Air Museum
Location: 9.7km (6 miles) north of Chichester SU 870130.
Description: A fifteenth-century yeoman's farmhouse has been re-erected on this site. There is also a reconstruction of a thirteenth-century peasant house, and a less convincing Saxon SFB.

396 Skara Brae (Orkney)
Neolithic village.
Location: On the Bay of Skaill 13km (8 miles) north of Stromness at HY 231188.
Description: A unique Neolithic village, see Chapter 3 for details.

397 Skellig Michael (Co. Kerry)
Celtic monastery.
Location: 13km (8 miles) west of Boles Head at V 248606.
Description: Six intact beehive cells, two oratories, a small medieval church, two crude crosses and 31 grave markers in the associated cemetery make up this remote hermitage.

398 The Somerset Levels (Somerset)
Neolithic tracks.
Location: 8km (5 miles) west of Glastonbury.
Description: A section of the Abbots Way has been reconstructed behind the EJ Godwin Peat factory at Burtle. The Somerset Levels Project Museum and Information Centre, at the Willows Peat Company and Garden Centre in Shapwick Road, Westhay, houses displays on the archaeology of the Levels.

399 Sompting (Sussex)
Saxon tower.
Location: 1.6km (1 mile) north-west of Worthing at TQ 161056.
Description: An eleventh-century tower, featuring typical Saxon stonework, with a unique boat-shaped roof.

400 South Cadbury (Somerset)
Hillfort.
Location: 6.5km (4 miles) west of Wincanton at SY 628252.
Description: According to tradition this hillfort was the site of Camelot, although nothing can be seen

today within the ramparts dating from the Dark Age reoccupation. Finds are in Taunton Museum.

401 South Shields (Tyne and Wear)
Roman fort.
Location: 17.7km (11 miles) east of Newcastle at NZ 366678.
Description: The fort at *Arbeia* guarded the mouth of the Tyne. In the early third century it was converted into a supply depot for the Scottish campaigns of the emperor Septimius Severus. The foundations of granaries that held the supplies can be seen on site, together with the *principia*. The west gate of the fort was reconstructed on the original site in 1986.

402 Southampton (Hampshire)
Medieval town.
Location: 120km (75 miles) south-east of London.
Description: Remains of two substantial Norman stone houses can be seen. Canute's Palace (SU 420110), just off the High Street, consisted of a first-floor hall above a vaulted undercroft at the west end and a warehouse with counting house above at the eastern end. Only the western part of King John's house has survived behind the Tudor House Museum at SU418133. Parts of the twelfth-century town wall have also survived. English Heritage has recently restored and furnished a thirteenth-century merchant's house at 58 French Street.

403 Stafford (Staffordshire)
Castle.
Location: In the southern outskirts of the town at SJ 902222.
Description: The earthworks of the motte and bailey castle of *c*.1070 are well preserved. There are also some fragments of the later rebuildings in stone.

404 Staigue (Co. Kerry)
Cashel.
Location: 11.2km (7 miles) east of Watervile at V 611633.
Description: One of the finest cashels in Ireland, the restored walls stand to a height of 5.4m (20ft). Ten flights of stairs, arranged in pairs, give access to the fighting platform from the interior.

405 Stanton Drew (Avon)
Stone circles.
Location: 9.6km (6 miles) south of Bristol at ST 601634.
Description: The remains of three stone circles, two with avenues, a cove and their outlying stones, can be seen. The best preserved is the central stone circle. Of the two smaller circles the south-west is inaccessible on private land.

406 Stanton Moor (Derbyshire)
Bronze Age ritual monuments.
Location: 24km (15 miles) south-west of Sheffield.
Description: A total of 70 cairns, standing stones and stone circles are scattered over Stanton Moor north-

west of Birchover, including the Nine Ladies, a small stone circle at SK 249634 and another circle together with burial cairns at Doll Tor (SK 238628).

407 Stanwick (North Yorkshire)
Hillfort.
Location: 4.8km (3 miles) south-west of Piercebridge at NZ 179112.
Description: Extensive earthworks have survived from this major hillfort, one of the tribal centres of the Brigantes. Finds from the classic excavations directed by Sir Mortimer Wheeler are on display in York.

408 Stanydale (Shetland)
Neolithic house or shrine.
Location: On mainland Shetland at HU 285503.
Description: An interesting building, 12m (39ft) long, that may have served as a shrine or chief's house.

409 Stokesay (Shropshire)
Defended manor.
Location: 13km (8 miles) north-west of Ludlow at SO 436818.
Description: A good example of a fortified manor house consisting of a late thirteenth-century hall and solar block enclosed by a curtain wall and moat.

410 Stone-by-Faversham (Kent)
Roman mausoleum.
Location: 2km (1¼ miles) west of Faversham at TQ 909610.
Description: This rather undistinguished medieval church incorporates a Roman mausoleum in its chancel. The early work can be easily distinguished from that of the medieval masons by the characteristic Roman use of tile courses.

411 Stonehenge (Wiltshire)
Henge with stone circle.
Location: 3.2km (2 miles) west of Amesbury at SU 123422.
Description: For details see Chapter 4.

412 Stoney Littleton (Avon)
Megalithic tomb.
Location: 8km (5 miles) south of Bath at ST 735572.
Description: A well-restored example of a chambered long barrow featuring a passage with seven small burial chambers.

413 Sueno's Stone (Grampian)
Pictish stone.
Location: On the outskirts of Forres at NJ 047595.
Description: One of the finest of all 'Dark Age' sculptured stones in the British Isles. The front of the stone, 6m (20ft) high, is carved with a cross, on the reverse is a battle scene.

414 Sutton Hoo (Suffolk)
Saxon barrow cemetery.
Location: 4.8km (3 miles) south-west of Woodbridge at TM 288487.
Description: The 11 mounds that make up the royal cemetery of the kings of East Anglia are on private property but can be seen from a public right-of-way that crosses the northern part of the site.

415 Swanscombe (Kent)
Fossil find spot.
Location: 4.8km (3 miles) east of Dartford at TQ 596746.
Description: Barnsfield Pit, site of the discovery of the Swanscombe Skull, is managed as a site of special scientific importance by the Nature Conservancy Council.

416 Taplow (Buckinghamshire)
Saxon barrow.
Location: 1.6km (1 mile) east of Maidenhead at SU 903822.
Description: In the old churchyard within the grounds of Taplow Court is a large barrow that on excavation was found to contain a rich seventh-century burial. The finds are displayed in the British Museum.

417 Tara (Co. Meath)
Royal assembly place.
Location: 44km (27 miles) north-west of Dublin at N 920595.
Description: A series of small raths is scattered over the ridge. There is also a standing stone, identified as the Lin Fail, the inauguration stone that was said to roar when the true king approached it to claim his throne.

418 Taversoe Tuack (Orkney)
Megalithic tomb.
Location: On the island of Rousay at HY 426276.
Description: A unique 'two-storeyed' stalled cairn.

419 Tealing (Tayside)
Souterrain.
Location: On the outskirts of Dundee at NO 413382.
Description: A fine example, apart from the roofing slabs almost intact.

420 Thetford (Norfolk)
Castle.
Location: 17.7km (11 miles) north of Bury St Edmunds at TL 875828.
Description: At 24m (80ft) high, the motte that stands within the ramparts of a hillfort is among the largest in Britain. In the town there are also the remains of the church and claustral buildings of a medieval priory.

421 Thornborough (Yorkshire)
Henges.
Location: 10.5km (6½ miles) north of Ripon at SE 280800.
Description: A group of three typical henges, of which the northern most, protected by trees, is the best preserved.

422 Tievebulliagh (Co. Antrim)
Axe factory.
Location: 4.8km (3 miles) west of Cushendall at D 193268.

Description: A small outcrop of a hard blue stone high on the south-east slopes of the hill was quarried to provide material for axes. Waste flakes and broken rejects litter the scree slopes in this area just beneath the summit.

423 Tinkinswood (Glamorgan)
Megalithic tomb.
Location: 8km (5 miles) south-west of Cardiff at ST 092733.
Description: A good example of a chambered cairn of the Severn–Cotswold group. The tomb chamber was formed from five uprights that support a huge capstone, one of the largest in Britain.

424 Tintagel (Cornwall)
Dark Age site.
Location: 6.45km (4 miles) south-west of Boscastle at SX 045895.
Description: According to tradition Tintagel was the birthplace of King Arthur and there are the poorly preserved ruins of a Medieval castle on the site. Stone foundations belonging to an earlier occupation excavated on the terraces of the promontory were once widely believed to be those of a Celtic monastery.

425 Tintern (Gwent)
Medieval monastery.
Location: 8km (5 miles) north of Chepstow at SO 530000.
Description: The thirteenth-century church of this Cistercian foundation is almost complete up to the roof. There are also parts of the claustral buildings.

426 Tomen-y-Mur (Gwynedd)
Roman fort.
Location: 4.8km (3 miles) north of Trawsfynydd at SH 707387.
Description: A small auxiliary fort of the first-century AD, later rebuilt in stone. A short walk to the north-east of the defences are the earthworks of a small amphitheatre. The Normans constructed a small motte and bailey castle on the site of the earlier fort.

427 Toorwoodlee (Central)
Broch.
Location: 10km (6.2 miles) west of Melrose at NT 466384.
Description: One of the few examples in south-west Scotland.

428 Torhousekie (Dumfries and Galloway)
Stone circle.
Location: 4.8km (3 miles) west of Wigtown at NX 383565.
Description: An example of a small, flattenned circle.

429 Totnes (Cornwall)
Castle.
Location: 6.5km (4 miles) west of Torbay at SX 800605.
Description: The town street plan follows that of the Saxon burh. In the centre is a Norman motte crowned with later stone buildings.

430 Traprain Law (Lothian)
Hillfort.
Location: 8km (5 miles) west of Dunbar at NT 581747.
Description: One of the largest hillforts in Scotland, probably the tribal centre of the Votadini. Site of the discovery of a famous late Roman treasure now in the National Museum of Antiquities in Edinburgh.

431 Tre'r Ceiri (Gwynedd)
Hillfort.
Location: 2km ($1\frac{1}{4}$ miles) west of Llanaelbaearn at SH 374447.
Description: The rough stone walls that surround the summit of the hill survive to a height of 4m (12ft) in places. Within the foundations many huts are clearly visible.

432 Trethevy Quoit (Cornwall)
Megalithic tomb.
Location: 4.8km (3 miles) north of Liskeard at SX 259608.
Description: A fine example of a dolmen.

433 Tretower (Powys)
Castle.
Location: 13km (8 miles) north-west of Abergavenny at SH 186214.
Description: The castle consists of a wide range of defensive and domestic buildings that span the medieval period.

434 Trevelgue Head (Cornwall)
Promontory fort.
Location: Near Newquay at SX 827630.
Description: One of the finest of all the promontory forts, cut off from the mainland by multiple ramparts.

435 Treyford (West Sussex)
Barrow cemetery.
Location: 1.6km (1 mile) south of Treyford at TQ 486058.
Description: Six round barrows are arranged in a line on Treyford Hill.

436 Trim (Co. Meath)
Castle.
Location: 45km (28 miles) north-west of Dublin.
Description: One of the best examples of a medieval stone castle in Ireland, featuring a twelfth-century tower keep.

437 The Turoe Stone (Co. Galway)
Iron Age ritual stone.
Location: 6km ($3\frac{3}{4}$ miles) north-east of Loughrea at M 630223.
Description: The upper part of this small pillar is carved with the curvilinear designs typical of the La Tène style.

438 Ty Isaf (Powys)
Megalithic tomb.
Location: 7km ($4\frac{1}{2}$ miles) south-east of Talgarth at SO 182291.

Description: A wedge-shaped cairn in which there is a forecourt with a false entrance on the north side. The real burial site is located half way down the cairn, where there is a pair of small chambers.

439 Tynwald (Isle of Man)
Viking assembly place.
Location: 4.8km (3 miles) south-east of Peel at SC 277819.
Description: A mound marks the site of the Viking assembly that governed Man. Legislation enacted by its direct successor, the House of Keys, is still read out at the mound once a year on 5 July, first in the ancient Manx form of Gaelic, then in English.

440 Uffington (Oxfordshire)
Chalk figure.
Location: 17.7km (11 miles) east of Swindon at SU 302866.
Description: The White Horse is traditionally attributed to Hengist or King Alfred, but on stylistic grounds resembles those on Iron Age coins. Above it is Uffington Castle, a small hillfort.

441 Unstan (Orkney)
Megalithic tomb.
Location: 3.2km (2 miles) north-east of Stromness at HY 283117.
Description: Inside the cairn the burial chamber is divided into five pairs of stalls using large stone slabs.

442 Valle Crucis (Clwyd)
Cross shaft.
Location: 16km (10 miles) south-west of Wrexham at SJ 203445.
Description: The Pillar of Eliseg was set up to commemorate an eighth-century King of Powys and was inscribed with a, now illegible, record of his genealogy going back to the fourth century. In the village there are also some medieval monastic ruins.

443 Vindolanda (Chesterholm) (Northumberland)
Roman fort and vicus.
Location: 4.8km (3 miles) west of Housesteads at NY 7764.
Description: In addition to the walls of the fort and its *principia*, the foundations of much of the settlement that grew up outside its gate are exposed. These include a bath-house, *mansio* (inn) and houses. A short stretch of the turf wall, the stone wall and a turret have been reconstructed. A possible 'palace' has recently been discovered. Nearby, good stretches of the Wall can be walked at Winshields (NY 7467) and Peel Crag (NY 7567).

444 Wall (Staffordshire)
Roman town.
Location: 22.5km (14 miles) north of Birmingham at SK 098066.
Description: A *mansio* (inn) and a bath-house survive from the town of *Letocetum*.

445 Wallingford (Berkshire)
Saxon burh.
Location: 33.2km (20 miles) north-west of Reading at SU 610890.
Description: The modern street plan follows that of the Saxon burh. The burghal defences, consisting of bank and ditch, are best preserved on the east and south-west sides of the town. In the grounds of Castle House, at SU 610897, is a Norman motte.

446 Walltown Crag (Northumberland)
Hadrian's Wall.
Location: 30.5km (19 miles) east of Carlisle at NY 674664.
Description: One of the best-preserved sections of the Wall, standing up to 2–2.4m (7–8ft) high, incorporating a turret.

447 Wansdyke (Wiltshire)
Dark Age earthwork.
Location: The dyke stretches in two sections from Dundry Hill, near Bristol, to Great Bedwyn in Wiltshire.
Description: Wansdyke may have been built by the British to hold off the Saxon settlement of the West Country. Alternatively the Saxons may have intended it to mark the frontier between the kingdoms of Wessex and Mercia. Two of the best sections can be seen between SU 030670 and SU 195665 and ST 601655–624651 and ST 66041–672639.

448 Wareham (Dorset)
Saxon burh.
Location: 9.6km (6 miles) north of Swanage at SY 923877.
Description: The defences of the burh are best preserved on the western side of the town, where the bank still survives to 2.74m (9ft) in places. Next to the site of the north gate is the Saxon church of St Martin. Four Early Christian memorial stones can be seen in the church of Lady St Mary. The modern street plan closely follows that of the burh.

449 Wayland's Smithy (Oxfordshire)
Megalithic tomb.
Location: 16km (10 miles) east of Swindon at SU 281854.
Description: A fine example of a chambered long barrow, featuring an impressive facade, an entrance passage and four small burial chambers.

450 Wharram Percy (North Yorkshire)
Deserted medieval village
Location: SE 858642, 9.6km (6 miles) south-west of Norton.
Description: See Chapter 10 for details.

451 White Caterthun (Tayside)
Hillfort
Location: 8km (5 miles) north-west of Brechin at NO 547660.

Description: A series of six concentric ramparts form the defences of this impressive site. A mile to the north-east, at NO 555668, is the similar fort of Brown Caterthun.

452 White Island (Co. Fermanagh)
Sculptured stones.
Location: 4km (2½ miles) south of Kesh in Loch Erne at H 1760.
Description: Seven curious figures and a stone head are displayed against the north wall of the church. They probably represent biblical figures and date to between the ninth and twelfth centuries.

453 Wilmington (East Sussex)
Chalk figure.
Location: 4.8km (3 miles) north-west of Eastbourne at TQ 543095.
Description: Just south of the village, on Windover Hill, is the chalk figure known as the Wilmington Long Man. Although last recut in 1870 stylistic grounds suggest he was originally laid out by the pagan Saxons.

454 Windmill Hill (Wiltshire)
Causewayed camp.
Location: 2.4km (1½ miles) north-west of Avebury at SU 087714.
Description: Three concentric rings of banks, together with their interrupted ditches, once surrounded the summit of the hill. But only a few sections of the outer ditch have been left open. Finds are in Avebury Museum.

455 Wing (Buckinghamshire)
Saxon church.
Location: 4.8km (3 miles) south-west of Leighton Buzzard at SP 800025.
Description: The chancel of the parish church is tenth-century Saxon work constructed over even earlier remains.

456 Woden Law (Borders)
Hillfort.
Location: 14km (9 miles) south-east of Jedburgh at NT 768125.
Description: Surrounding the hillfort on three sides are the banks, ditches and artillery platforms that make up a unique series of Roman siegeworks. That nearest the hillfort is the best preserved, it consists of two linear banks and three ditches. The three other siege lines differ slightly in orientation and may all have been constructed independently. None was ever finished and it seems likely that they were constructed for practice after the hillfort was deserted.

457 Woodhenge (Wiltshire)
Henge.
Location: 1.6km (1 mile) north of Amesbury at SU 151434.
Description: Concrete posts mark the positions of six concentric circles of post-holes from a large Neolithic timber ritual building.

458 Wookey (Somerset)
Cave.
Location: 3.2km (2 miles) north-west of Wells at ST 532480.
Description: Excavations uncovered Palaeolithic artefacts in the Hyaena's Den, a rock shelter on the slope below the show cave. A selection of finds is displayed on site.

459 Worlebury Camp (Avon)
Hillfort.
Location: On the northern outskirts of of Weston-super-Mare at ST 315625.
Description: The defences are preserved in places to a height of 3m (10ft), but the most interesting feature of the site is a series of rock-cut storage pits. Finds are in the Woodspring Museum, Weston-super-Mare.

460 The Wrekin (Shropshire)
Hillfort.
Location: 6.5km (4 miles) east of Wroxeter, at SJ 630082.
Description: Possibly the tribal centre of the Cornovii before the foundation of Wroxeter.

461 Wroxeter (Shropshire)
Roman town.
Location: 8km (5 miles) east of Shrewsbury at SJ 565087.
Description: *Viroconium* was founded as the tribal capital of the Cornovii. The main ruins at Wroxeter are those of the late second-century public baths. Part of the south wall of the *palaestra*, the exercise hall, still stands to a considerable height. In the site museum is an Ogham stone of the late fifth century inscribed 'Cunorix son of Maqqos-colini'. Other finds are in Shrewsbury at the Rowley's House Museum.

462 Yarnbury (Wiltshire)
Hillfort.
Location: 3.2km (2 miles) west of Winterbourne Stoke at SU 035403.
Description: An impressive fort defended by a triple set of earthworks.

463 Yeavering Bell (Northumberland)
Hillfort.
Location: 26km (16 miles) south-west of Berwick-on-Tweed at NT 928293.
Description: A stone rampart surrounds the summit of the hill. Within can be traced the remains of 130 round hut platforms. On the plain below was an important early Saxon administrative centre of which nothing is now visible.

464 Yelden (Bedfordshire)
Castle.
Location: 7km (4½ miles) east of Rushden at TL 013670.
Description: Good earthworks from a motte and bailey castle, with a few fragments from the later rebuilding in stone.

465 York (North Yorkshire)
Historic town.
Description: A fine stretch of the defences of *Eboracum*
4m (13ft) high. It includes the well preserved
'Multangular Tower' and the Anglian Tower that was
added in the eighth century. Also in the museum
grounds is Clifford's Tower, a motte crowned by a
shell keep. Recent excavations underneath the Minster
revealed the foundations of the *principia* (headquarters)
of the fort, some of the walls and columns of which,
together with those of the Norman church, can be
seen *in situ*. Visitors who feel that they might like to
trek through the impressive stone sewer system that
served Roman York should write in advance to the
Museum. The York Viking Centre beneath the
redeveloped Coppergate provides a unique experience.
A 'time capsule' takes the visitor through the typical
sights, smells and sounds of the Viking Age, ending
in a reconstruction of the excavation and the museum
hall where a selection of the artefacts discovered is on
display.

466 Y Pigwn (Powys)
Roman fort.
Location: 8km (5 miles) south-east of Llandovey at
SN 828313.
Description: Two Roman marching camps, one inside
the other, can be traced, the earthworks being best
preserved on the north-west side.

467 Ysbyty Cynfyn (Dyfed)
Stone circle.
Location: 16km (10 miles) south-east of Aberystwyth
at SN 752791.
Description: The parish church stands on the site of a
embanked stone circle. Only one of the stones,
however, remains in its original position. Two more
are used as gateposts and the rest have been built into
the wall around the cemetery.

468 Zennor (Cornwall)
Megalithic tomb.
Location: 8km (5 miles) north of Penzance at
SW 469380.
Description: A picturesque dolmen, consisting of four
uprights and a slipped capstone.

FURTHER READING

General

DARVILL, T., *Prehistoric Britain*, Batsford 1987.
DYER, J., *Ancient Britain*, Batsford, 1990.
HARBISON, P., *Pre-Christian Ireland*, Thames and Hudson, 1988.
LONGWORTH, I. H.. and CHERRY, J., *Archaeology in Britain since 1945*, British Museum Publications, 1986.
MEGAW, J. and SIMPSON, P., *Introduction to British Prehistory*, Leicester University Press, 1979.
RENFREW, C., (Ed.) *British Prehistory, a new outline*, Duckworth, 1974.
RITCHIE, A. and RITCHIE, R., *Prehistoric Scotland*, Thames and Hudson, 1981.

Chapter 1

BARKER, P., *Techniques of Archaeological Excavation*, Batsford, 1977.
RENFREW, C. and BAHN, P., *Archaeology. Theory, Methods, Practices*, Thames and Hudson, 1991.
MACKINTOSH, C., *The Archaeologist's Handbook*, Bell and Hyman, 1986.
THOMPSON, M., *General Pitt Rivers*, Moonraker Press, 1977.

Chapter 2

MORRISON, A., *Early Man in Britain and Ireland*, Croom Helm, 1980.

Chapter 3

COLES, B. and COLES, J., *Sweet Track to Glastonbury*, Thames and Hudson, 1986.
CRAWFORD, H. (Ed.) *Subterranean Britain*, John Baker, 1979.

Chapter 4

BURGESS, C., *The Age of Stonehenge*, Dent, 1980.
HADINGHAM, E., *Circles and Standing Stones*, Heinemann, 1975.
MALONE, C., *The English Heritage Book of Avebury*, Batsford, 1989.
MERCER, R., *Hambledon Hill, A Neolithic Landscape*, Edinburgh University Press, 1981.

RENFREW, C., *Before Civilisation*, Pelican Books Harmondsworth, 1973.
RICHARDS, J., *The English Heritage Book of Stonehenge*, Batsford, 1991.
WAINWRIGHT, G., *The Henge Monuments*, Thames and Hudson, 1989.

Chapter 5

FLEMING, A., *The Dartmoor Reaves*, Batsford 1988.
HARRISON, R., *The Beaker People*, Thames and Hudson, 1980.
PRYOR, F., *The English Heritage Book of Flag Fen*, Batsford, 1991.

Chapter 6

BROTHWELL, D., *The Body in the Bog*, British Museum Publications, 1988.
CUNLIFFE, B., *Iron Age Communities in Britain*, Routledge and Kegan Paul, third revised edition, 1992.
—— *Hengistbury Head*, Elek, 1978.
—— *The English Heritage Book of Danebury*, Batsford, 1993.
PERCIVAL, J., *Living in the Past*, BBC Publications, 1980.
PIGGOTT, S., *The Druids*, Thames and Hudson revised edition, 1985.
REYNOLDS, P., *Iron Age Farm*, Colonnade Books, 1979.
SHARPLES, N., *The English Heritage Book of Maiden Castle*, Batsford, 1991.

Chapter 7

BIRLEY, A., *The People of Roman Britain*, Batsford, 1979.
BIRLEY, R., *Vindolanda*, Thames and Hudson, 1977.
BREEZE, D. J., *The Northern Frontiers of Britain*, Batsford, 1982.
EMBLETON, R. and GRAHAM, F., *Hadrian's Wall in the Days of the Romans*, Frank Graham Newcastle, 1984.
JOHHSON, S., *The Roman Forts of the Saxon Shore*, Elek Second Edition, 1979
—— *The English Heritage Book of Hadrian's Wall*, Batsford, 1989.
MARGARY, I. D., *Roman Roads in Britain*, Revised edition Baker, 1973.

MILLET, M., *The Romanization of Britain*, Cambridge University Press, 1990
PERCIVAL, J., *The Roman Villa*, Batsford, 1976.
SCULLARD, H. H., *Roman Britain, Outpost of Empire*, Thames and Hudson, 1979.
WACHER, J., *Roman Britain*, Dent 1978.
WEBSTER, G., *The Roman Invasion of Britain*, Batsford, revised edition, 1993.
—— *Rome against Caratacus*, Batsford, revised edition, 1993.
—— *Boudica*, Batsford, revised edition 1993.

Chapter 8

ARNOLD, C. J., *Roman Britain to Saxon England*, Croom Helm, 1984.
—— *An Archaeology of the Early Anglo-Saxon Kingdoms*, Routledge, 1988.
BRUCE-MITFORD, R., *The Sutton Hoo Ship Burial: a Handbook*. British Museum Publications, third edition, 1979.
HALL, R., *The Viking Dig*, The Bodley Head, 1984.

RICHARDS, J. D., *The English Heritage Book of Viking Age England*, Batsford, 1992.
WELCH, M., *The English Heritage Book of Anglo-Saxon England*, Batsford, 1992.

Chapter 9

ALCOCK, L., *By South Cadbury that is Camelot*, Thames and Hudson, 1972.
EDWARDS, N., *The Archaeology of Early Medieval Ireland*, Batsford, 1990.
THOMAS, C., *Celtic Britain*, Thames and Hudson, 1986.

Chapter 10

BERESFORD, M., and HURST, J., *The English Heritage Book of Wharram Percy*, Batsford, 1990.
CLARKE, H., *The Archaeology of Medieval England*, Basil Blackwell, 1986.
RODWELL, W., *The English Heritage Book of Church Archaeology*, Batsford, 1989.
STEANE, J., *The Archaeology of Medieval England and Wales*, Croom Helm, 1986.

INDEX